LITERARY STRUCTURE, EVOLUTION, AND VALUE

Harvard Studies in Comparative Literature
Founded by William Henry Schofield

38

Literary Structure, Evolution, and Value

*Russian Formalism
and Czech Structuralism
Reconsidered*

Jurij Striedter

Harvard University Press
*Cambridge, Massachusetts
London, England
1989*

Parts I–III of this book were translated from the German
by Matthew Gurewitsch.

This book is printed on acid-free paper, and its binding materials
have been chosen for strength and durability.

Library of Congress Cataloging-in-Publication Data

Striedter, Jurij.
    Literary structure, evolution, and value / Jurij Striedter; parts
    I–III translated by Matthew Gurewitsch.
        p.   cm.
    Portions of the text previously appeared in Texte der russischen
    Formalisten and Die Struktur der literarischen Entwicklung.
    Bibliography: p.
    Includes index.
    ISBN 0-674-53653-3
    1. Russian literature—20th century—History and criticism.
    2. Formalism (Literary analysis)—Soviet Union. 3. Czech
    literature—20th century—History and criticism. 4. Structuralism
    (Literary analysis) I. Title.
    PG3026.F6S69 1989
    801'.95'0947—dc19   88-11036

It is equally fatal for the mind to have a system or to have none. Therefore, it will have to decide to combine both.

Friedrich Schlegel,
Athenaeum Fragments, 53

Contents

Introduction

Is it meaningful in the United States today to write—or to read—a book about the beginnings of Formalism and Structuralism? The story is a familiar one by now, thanks to the mediation by initiators or members of these schools who emigrated to this country, such as Roman Jakobson and René Wellek, as well as to studies such as Victor Erlich's *Russian Formalism.*[1] Recent literary criticism might seem to have moved "Beyond Formalism" and past Structuralism; some of its practitioners have even begun to deconstruct Poststructuralism. A closer look, however, suggests that the very rapidity of this development left the rediscovery of the two early schools—Russian Formalism and Czech Structuralism—partial and insufficient and so underestimated their ground-breaking contributions to modern literary criticism. The debate with Structuralism (mainly with the French variety) appears even to have reactivated some old prejudices about Formalism and Structuralism in general, which a more careful scrutiny of the two Slavic schools would have obviated.

One such still-virulent bias holds that Formalism deals only with forms, neglecting the content of literature, the role of the individual author and his worldview, and the relation between literature and society. Another prejudice, related to the first, is that Structuralism, interested mainly in abstract structures, neglects the historical dimension of literature (literary history as well as the relation of literature to general history). Actually, Russian Formalists did not neglect the role of the author. Boris Eikhenbaum's fundamental studies on Tolstoy, Roman Jakobson's essay on the suicide of Mayakovsky, and Yury Tynyanov's novels about nineteenth-century Russian poets persuasively demonstrate their concern with the work and the life of individual writers. Nevertheless, Russian Formalism was explicitly a reaction against the one-sided focus on the author as a person that had dominated literary criticism from Romanticism onward, whether as the aesthetics of "genius," as biography, or more recently as psychological analysis. This reaction strengthened the Formalists' interest in those realms of verbal art where the person of the author is not dominant—for example, folklore (particularly folktales and fairy tales), the structure of verse and narrative prose, and the theory and history of literary genres. This interest enabled them to correct the lopsided stress on literary production (the author) by focusing on the product (the work) together with its perception (by the reader). These shifts of emphasis were significant in the development of literary criticism down to the present.

In some of their earliest studies the Formalists combined the question of how an author "made" a work (see, for example, Eikhenbaum's essay "How Gogol's 'Overcoat' Is Made")[2] with the question of how literary devices affect the reader (Shklovsky's concept of "Art as Device," particularly as a device of making things unfamiliar).[3] Joining these questions allowed each device and each literary work to be seen against the background of literary tradition and innovation. That in turn led to a focus on literary evolution, which became one of the main topics of Russian Formalism. The charge that this school and its method are ahistorical, therefore, is groundless.

There are better grounds for objecting that the Formalists isolated literature and its evolution from social and political history. Indeed, Formalism stressed from start to finish the "immanent laws" of literature and its evolution. In so doing it was reacting against an overwhelmingly strong and one-sided Russian tradition. The tendency to consider literature primarily as a mirror, medium, or polemical tool of social and ideological conflicts had dominated nineteenth-century Russian literary criticism; it was resanctified when Marxism became official doctrine in the newly established Soviet Union. Russian Formalism, which flourished between 1916 and 1928, must be understood in this context. At the same time, however, the ideological pressure that produced the Formalists' emphasis on "literariness" led to their increasing awareness of the interaction between literature and society, between literary evolution and the larger process of social and political change. In what is regarded as the concluding statement of Russian Formalism, published in 1928 as "Problems in the Study of Literature and Language," Jakobson and Tynyanov characterize the development of the Formalist method as having moved from stressing synchrony to combining the synchronic and diachronic aspects of literature (and language) as a system in evolution. They acknowledge that "the tempo of evolution" and "a specific choice of path" can be explained only by investigating the "correlation between the literary series and other historical series," conceived as a dynamic "system of systems." But even at this final stage they warn that it would be "methodologically fatal to consider the correlation of systems without taking into account the immanent laws of each system"—in the case of literature, without respecting the unique peculiarities of its structures, functions, and intrinsic evolution.[4]

The debate between Formalism and Marxism raged throughout the 1920s. It involved many independent critics and scholars who learned from Formalism, or rejected it and used its polemics to articulate and to promote their own theoretical concepts. The most significant and today best-known example of this kind was the group around Mikhail Bakhtin. In 1928, with Pavel Medvedev's book *The Formal Method in Literary Scholarship,* the group launched a harsh attack against Formalism for its neglect of the ideological and social aspects of language and literature. Bakhtin himself simultaneously put forth his theory of literature and the novel as a polyphonic dialogue of controversial voices, thus introducing his own voice into the ongoing controversial dialogue about literature and its response to social discourse.[5]

The most direct continuation of Russian Formalism was Prague Structuralism—chronologically (it dates from 1926), biographically (Jakobson and other Russian Formalists became leading members of the Prague Circle), and methodologically. Combining its own Czech traditions with tenets of Russian Formalism, Prague literary Structuralism created a unifying semiotic basis for its theory and criticism, which was put forward mainly in Jan Mukařovský's writings of the mid-thirties. This semiotic Structuralism conceives of the literary work as a "sign made up of signs" in "aesthetic function." Literature as verbal art can create and communicate meaning only by referring to linguistic and aesthetic codes and norms, which are handed down and shared by social collectives. In this respect the individual author depends on given sociocultural conditions, their traditions and their change; but he can assent, reject, or modify such established norms and the expectations derived from them. Also he has to organize the elements and aspects used or referred to in his work with regard to their particular function in this work's structure, which is itself dominated by its aesthetic function. So the structure becomes crucial for the work's message. At the same time, its particular selection and aesthetic coordination of the elements it deploys deprives them of the functions they may have in ordinary, nonaesthetic contexts and challenges the established worldview of the collective in question, opening it up to pluralism and change. Literature, perceived this way, fulfills central social and anthropological functions by insisting on the autonomy of its own aesthetic function and structure.

As in Russian Formalism, the emphasis of the Prague Structuralists is on the particular structures, functions, and qualities of literature and their continuous evolutionary change. But Prague Structuralism goes far beyond Formalism by stressing as well the interaction of literature with society; of aesthetic functions, norms, and values with other human values, norms, and functions; of literary evolution with historic changes in social conditions; of collectively shared norms and views with the individual author's transforming challenge to them.

Prague Structuralism was the first school to elaborate a comprehensive theory and methodology of literary reception

4

based on a semiotic concept of literature. It may be seen principally in the theoretical reflections and historical studies of Felix Vodička, one of the leading scholars of the so-called second generation of Czech Structuralists. The literary work as a construct of verbal signs depends on the perception of a responsive, imaginative reader; it becomes an aesthetic object only in such a "concretization." This perception results from the way the reader processes the text through the codes available to him. Hence each new concretization of a text, as it is made public and acknowledged by a given society, tests or modifies earlier perceptions of the work in question, as well as the traditional norms and expectations underlying those perceptions.

What is generally known today as reader-response criticism, or as the aesthetics of reception (*Rezeptionsästhetik*) of the so-called Konstanz school, was preceded and in some respects directly initiated by Prague Structuralism (or even by the Russian Formalists' stress on the role of literary perception with regard to devices, works, and the evolution of literature). At the same time Prague Structuralists consistently emphasized the interaction of all three basic factors—author, text, and reader—correlating them with the temporal and local variability of historical contexts. They also stressed the role of the literary critic as mediator between author, work, and audience, between collective norms and individual reading, and between tradition and innovation—at the same time reminding the critic of his own dependence on inherited historical conditions and social functions. The critic's task, in their view, was to reveal in a systematically and historically verifiable way the aesthetic potential and significance of a given work under changing historical conditions, rather than to use the text as a springboard for the critic's own impressions or speculations.

—————

Clearly, then, in a period that has gone beyond Formalism and past Poststructuralism, it is still useful to examine the ostensibly superseded ancestors. To open and to advance a critical dialogue between their scholarly debates and our own is the main task of this book, whose form may be understood (and, I trust, justified) by an account of its genesis. I started my research on Formalism and Structuralism in the early 1960s as a professor of Slavic Literatures at the Free University in West Berlin and continued it as a member of the group Poetik und Hermeneutik (founded in 1963)[6] and as a visiting professor at Harvard in 1964. These studies, which went on after my move to the newly founded University of Konstanz, resulted in a bilingual (Russian-German) edition of *Texts of the Russian Formalists,* published in two volumes. The first (1969), which I edited and introduced, was dedicated to "Texts on the General Theory of Literature and on the Theory of Prose"; the second (1972), edited and introduced by the linguist Wolf-Dieter Stempel, included "Texts on the Theory of Verse and the Poetic Language."[7]

My prefatory essay for the first volume has become Part I of the present book. Owing to its original function as an introduction both to the edition as a whole and to the contents of the first volume, it seeks to serve as a general discussion of Russian Formalism, as well as to analyze the Formalists' overall theory of literature, along with their theories of prose and of literary evolution. Commenting on the texts included in the German edition—most of which are now available in English translation (see the Selected Bibliography)—it is not confined to them, for it was conceived as an independent essay. It does not pretend, however, to deal comprehensively and systematically with Formalist doctrine as a whole, or with its history, sources, and contemporary ramifications; that has already been done by Victor Erlich. The task of my introduction was, and is, to present the essentials of Formalism in the light of their significance and topicality for today's literary scholars, students, and readers—for all those interested in literature and literary criticism. Following the Formalists themselves in regarding their school and method as an open dialogue, I have tried to correlate this dialogue with our own debate about the tasks, problems, and methods of literary criticism.

In so doing, I have had chiefly German criticism in view—because the essay first appeared in Germany and also because of the strong correlations between the Russian and the German avant-garde. It has not been my intention to claim any direct correlation between, for example, the method of the

Formalists and the German debate about the methodology of natural, social, and historical sciences in the 1960s. Instead, the essay attempts to show how Formalists, working half a century ago, handled problems that are still topical and controversial today. The remarks on parallels between Russian Formalism and German theories of the same period do not claim any direct impact of the former on the latter, even where there may be reason to suppose it, as in comparing Shklovsky's concept of the "device of estrangement" or "defamiliarization" (1916) with Bertolt Brecht's *Verfremdungs-Effekt* (elaborated later, after Brecht's direct contacts with the Russian avant-garde); or Eikhenbaum's theory of *skaz* and narration, exemplified in Leskov (1918, 1925), with Walter Benjamin's famous essay "The Storyteller," written after his visit to the Soviet Union and in connection with the German edition of Leskov's stories.[8]

Information of this kind may have more value for the German reader. This is probably why a part of the essay, comparing Eikhenbaum's theory of narration with that of Benjamin and other contemporary German concepts, was omitted in an English translation.[9] But what may seem a needless digression can, I believe, turn out to be an enrichment by providing information about two different, related cultures, and by providing English-language readers with an opportunity to relate *two* foreign cultures to the terms of their own ongoing discourse.

Readers who are uncomfortable with such intercultural complexities should feel free to begin by reading Part II, which presents the essentials of Russian Formalism and the development of its system in a far more concise way. Its original purpose was to link our edition of Formalist texts with an ensuing collection of texts by Czech Structuralists, translated and edited by our Research Group for Structuralist Methods in the Study of Language and Literature at the University of Konstanz. This edition was prepared in cooperation with Czech Structuralists during the bloom of European Structuralism and the so-called Prague Spring of 1968. Interest in the early Czech versions of Structuralism was growing; the writings of Jakobson, along with Mukařovský's studies on structuralist aesthetics and poetics, were translated and discussed. But the crucial additions and achievements of the second and third generations of Czech Structuralism were almost unknown outside of their homeland. Accordingly, we decided to focus on this group and to start our series with a volume of writings by Felix Vodička, Mukařovský's successor as director of the Prague Institute for Literature, a leading representative of the second generation and a scholar who proved most innovative in his theory and analysis of literary history, particularly the history of reception. Parts II and III of this book originally were prefatory essays to this volume of translations of Vodička's writings.[10]

Once again I had to introduce a new school and a particular volume; in addition, my introduction had to explore the relation between two schools and methods. The first essay (Part II of this book) tries to show how two different schools, growing out of two different national traditions and settings, nevertheless form part of a single and coherent method which evolved in clearly distinguished stages: from the concept of art as device in early Formalism, to literature as a synchronically and diachronically functioning system (a concept shared by late Formalism and early Prague Structuralism), to the semiotic concept elaborated by the Prague Structuralists in the mid-thirties. I attempt to show how each of these stages had its own conception of the individual work, of literature as a whole, and of literary evolution.

The second essay (Part III) deals with the theory and analysis of literary evolution in Czech Structuralism, particularly with Vodička's theory of literary reception and concretization as part of a Structuralist history of literature. The first three parts of the book, taken as a whole, analyze the methodological development from Russian Formalism to Prague Structuralism, as well as the development within the latter. Part III, however, unlike the second and more like the first, intentionally actualizes the problems and their presentation. Mukařovský's and Vodička's focus on the ways in which works of literature have to be concretized by readers under changing historical conditions, together with Vodička's investigations in the theory and history of literary reception, dovetailed with our attempts in Konstanz to elaborate different versions of the aesthetics of reception and the history of reception. It was only fair to ac-

8

knowledge the ground-breaking work undertaken in Prague decades earlier, which was interrupted by political developments and remained scarcely known abroad because of the language barrier. Moreover, it was helpful and challenging to compare that early semiotic approach with our own approaches, which were rooted in the German tradition of historical hermeneutics or based on phenomenology (which also had played an important role in the discussions of the Prague Circle and in the formation of Russian Formalism).

Unlike the preceding three parts, the fourth grew out of the American context. Anxious to respond to this new context in an appropriate way, and knowing that one's thinking and treatment of issues changes according to the language employed, I decided to write this part in English. By no means assuming that this would be an easy task or that I was sufficiently prepared for it, I nevertheless severely underestimated the difficulties. To speak a new language is an enjoyable learning process. An open dialogue allows immediate self-corrections and qualifications through mutual response. To write, however—and to write for publication—in a language not genuinely one's own is a painful process in which one continuously feels that this language must have far better means of expression than what one can muster. The subtleties which the issues require, the shared commitment implied even as one criticizes others, the indispensable notes of irony and self-irony get lost. And if it is painful to have this experience trying to convey one's own thoughts, it is even more so when one is trying to report sympathetically the ideas of others—especially when these others have used a language that is neither one's own nor the language of the prospective readership.

There are problems of purview as well that should be addressed. The selection clearly privileges Slavic, German, and Anglo-American examples while almost totally omitting the crucial French contribution to the development of Structuralism and to the present scholarly debate. Such an omission might be taken to reflect my biographical background and my scholarly training; it must not, however, be taken to indicate any personal bias. On the contrary, I fully acknowledge the importance of the French contribution to the international development and promotion of Structuralism as well as to the ensuing polemics against Structuralism and to the turn toward Post-structuralism and Deconstructionism. But it is precisely because of this dominance of the French version of Structuralism that the earlier and in many respects different Czech version has remained unknown or underestimated. Therefore the achievements of the Czech Structuralists have to be rediscovered and reevaluated beside this well-known mainstream and to be compared with other approaches to the same issues.

Being thus admittedly one-sided in my own selection, I may sometimes create the impression of criticizing other scholars for ignoring Czech proposals when writing on related topics. This is not at all my intention. The language barrier and the scarcity of available translations explain sufficiently such a neglect (unless, of course, the omission is deliberate and polemically motivated). If I occasionally criticize scholars who *have* acknowledged the importance of Czech Structuralism and have even fostered awareness of its significance and topicality, my remarks do not question this achievement but seek merely to clarify misunderstandings or to indicate differences in interpretation. My purpose is not to prove the priority—far less the superiority—of the Czech Structuralists but to reactualize their insufficiently known insights and investigations so that they may take their rightful place in a dialogue that could be stimulating and challenging for both sides.

I have thus tried to keep open the dialogical form of scholarship which they themselves, like the Russian Formalists, cherished and which for both schools was silenced by external forces. To initiate, develop, and apply new critical methods and innovative theories while keeping them open for a contentious environment is a difficult task. Under a rigorous ideological and political system it becomes an admirable, often fatal adventure. By choosing Friedrich Schlegel's fragment as an epigraph (for my introduction to the Vodička volume and now for this book), I wanted to thank the late Felix Vodička and those Czech Structuralists and Russian Formalists who believed in the necessity and possibility of this adventure and pursued it with scholarly and human dignity.

PART I

The Formalist Theory of Prose and Literary Evolution

Russian Formalism, which emerged in 1915, flourished in the 1920s, and was cut short around 1930, has been enjoying increased attention and appreciation in the past three decades. The publication of Victor Erlich's excellent monograph *Russian Formalism: History—Doctrine* in 1955 introduced the history, methods, and theory of the Formalist school to wider circles, especially in the West.[1] In the East (including the Soviet Union), a gradual rehabilitation of the Formalists has been taking place since the end of the 1950s. Selected works have appeared in new editions, and contemporary critics have been harking back, directly and indirectly, to the approaches and insights of the Formalist school. The rise of Structuralism in the West in the 1960s greatly contributed to this renewed interest. During its entire existence Russian Formalism was closely allied with the budding discipline of structural linguistics, which spurred decisive steps in Structuralism as it applies to the most varied fields of science. The example of Roman Jakobson—cofounder and chief exponent of Russian Formalism; charter member of the Cercle linguistique de Prague (and thus a leading representative of so-called Prague Structuralism); and, in the United States during the final stages of his career, the champion whose advocacy brought modern structural linguistics to general recognition—illustrates the closeness of the personal and methodological ties.

Although the more recent vitality of Structuralism may have strengthened the Formalist revival, associating the movements too closely can lead to a historically and methodologically biased view of the Russian Formalists. One must avoid emphasizing only those Formalist inquiries, approaches, and findings that from the start overlapped with those of linguistics and were later elaborated systematically by structural linguistics and poetics: theory and analysis of poetic language and of verse structure. In linguistic Structuralist accounts, areas such as theory of narrative prose, of literary genre, and of literary evolution, which played no less a role in Russian Formalism and were regarded by many Formalists as their truly trailblazing accomplishments, receive scant attention or are dismissed as insignificant.[2]

To highlight the characteristics of Structuralism as it is understood today, on the other hand, diametrically opposed efforts have been made to draw as distinct a line as possible between Structuralism and Formalism. Such attempts usually begin with nomenclature, defining the difference between the schools as the difference between form and structure.[3] This poses problems. The name Formalism, coined by hostile critics and originally used in polemics attacking the Formalist school, leads to misunderstandings. The Formalists themselves frequently cautioned against the misunderstandings that result when their method is tied to the concept of form. Furthermore, the transition from a somewhat static concept of form (the work of art as the sum of artistic devices) to the understanding of the literary work and literary evolution as a functional, structural system was effected within the development of Russian Formalism. This understanding does not represent a later advance made by the Structuralists—let alone an antithetical development. Formalism and Structuralism dovetail not because one succeeds the other, but because direct methodological correspondences and reciprocal interaction between them make a sharp division neither feasible nor necessary. Attempts to sever the connection, to separate a Formalist branch from a Structuralist branch, or an early Formalist phase from a subsequent

Structuralist one, inevitably end with the construction of "pure," "true," "orthodox" Formalism, defined by the features (and only by those) that contradict the later tenets of Structuralism or play no part in it at all. This gives rise to a one-sided and far too static picture of Russian Formalism, which in fact distinguished itself not only by its variety but also by the speedy development and adaptability of its methods and categories, and whose principal methodological demand was constantly to check and correct its own methods and propositions and, when necessary, to replace them with more adequate ones.

The best accounts of Russian Formalism, by members of the movement and later writers, are those that propound the school's theory by reference to its history, revealing the history of Formalism as the logical extension of Formalist literary theory. Already the first comprehensive presentation of Formalism by one of its leading figures, "Theory of the Formal Method" by Boris Eikhenbaum (1925), proceeds in this fashion. After reviewing the first decade of Formalism in light of the development of formal theory in its most important areas of investigation, Eikhenbaum closes with these words, which bear the characteristic stamp of formalistic methodology:

> It is no accident that, although my essay is entitled "Theory of the Formal Method," I have provided a sketch of this method's history. We have no theory that could be presented in a round, tight system. For us, theory and history are fused not only in principle but also in practice. We have learned too richly from history to suppose that history is something we could pass over. The moment when we must confess that we own an all-encompassing theory, sufficient for every individual case, past and future, neither in need of nor capable of further evolution—at that moment, we will have to confess that the formal method has reached its limit, that the spirit of scientific enquiry has abandoned it. We have not reached that point yet.[4]

Similarly, Erlich's book on Russian Formalism devotes the entire first part to the "history" of the school before turning to an investigation of "doctrine." But whereas the exposition of the history of Formalism is a convincing portrayal of the school's theories and methods and their transformations in their various areas of application, the book's second part, which labors at a systematic summary and evaluation of the system, is less successful. The formal method steadfastly resists being systematized as doctrine.

2

The Russian Formalists considered their achievement a theory of literature. Therefore, before asking what they defined as literature, it is useful to ask: What did they mean by theory? Erlich's book and Todorov's introduction to his French anthology of Formalist texts contain much discussion of the extreme positivism or empiricism of the Russian Formalists, regarded in part benignly as the "pathos of scientific positivism"[5] and in part polemically as "positivisme naïve," the methodological naïveté common in the "empiristes."[6] To a degree these observations do describe the facts, especially of early Formalism, but the terms are troublesome. As the word "positivism" is generally used in the arts, and in literary studies in particular, it refers to something else. "Empiricism" is hardly ever used in literary studies in the United States and Western Europe and easily can cause confusion.

From the standpoint of the current German discussion on theories and methodologies in the social and historical sciences, Formalism (especially in its early stages) and its mode of theorizing can best be regarded as a nomological or nomothetical theory.[7] The assumptions, aims, and procedures of theories of this type have been put forth and justified in detail in the work of Karl Popper.[8] But regarding the position and methodology of Formalism, Jürgen Habermas' terse distinction, made in his critical survey of contemporary methodological controversies in the social sciences, is sufficient. He distinguishes between "nomological sciences, which derive and test hypotheses for laws describing empirical uniformity," and "historico-hermeneutic sciences, which take handed-down carriers of meaning for their own and process them analytically."[9] Nomological statements claim neither to interpret meaning nor to define the nature of their object. They are understood to be working hypotheses, which can—and must—be based on observation and proved true or false on the strength of renewed observation. The claim to scientific legitimacy rests precisely *not* on the criterion of absolute truth but on the principle of falsifiability.

How well this notion of science and theorizing conforms to the assumptions of Russian Formalism is evident even in so early a statement as Eikhenbaum's at the beginning of his "Theory of the Formal Method":

> We do not, and never did, have a complete system, an integral doctrine. In our scholarship we value a theory for its use as a working hypothesis by means of which facts are discovered and take on meaning—both through their conformity to general principles and in their own right as data for investigation. For this reason, we do not concern ourselves with definitions, which epigones so thirst for, nor do we erect general theories, which eclectics regard with such tender affection. We set up concrete principles and stick to them as long as they can be verified by the material. If the material requires further refinement or change, we go ahead and refine the principles or change them. In this way we are independent of our own theories, as scientists ought to be; theories and convictions are not the same. No science is ever finished. Science accomplishes its task not in setting up truths, but in conquering errors. (p. 46)

The correspondence is so striking that it raises an issue that to the present day remains central in the methodological controversies between the empirico-nomological and the historico-hermeneutic disciplines. Can the principles and categories that obtain in the natural sciences be transferred to the humanities and to the entire body of social sciences? Does this not presuppose a very uncritical notion of facts and conformity to general principles, proclaiming the observation of such facts as the obvious point of departure without further thought? Are not the facts in the social sciences and humanities usually conditioned by specific intentions, presenting themselves to the investigator mostly in the form of statements that in themselves imply specific interpretations?

As for literary scholarship, one may go further and say that it deals not with statements about facts but with statements as facts. Or, to put it another way: In literary studies the important thing is not just that the object of inquiry is only accessible by means of statements in language. It is crucial that linguistic statements and the form they take are the only object of inquiry. In this respect literary scholarship is the historico-hermeneutic science par excellence. To protect oneself against charges of methodological naïveté, before going ahead and applying empirico-nomological methods in this area one must establish their viability and limitations. In its initial stages Formalism made light of these indispensable preliminaries. To this extent, but only to this extent, the charge against it is justifiable. It was based on positivistic assumptions that were insufficiently thought out and hence "naïve" in their methodology. However, we must recognize the advantages in the choice of such methods and appreciate their potential for self-correction.

At a time when scholarly legitimacy was equated overwhelmingly with or at least measured by the standards of the natural or experimental sciences, literary history and literary criticism could and even had to seem especially jejune, being dominated by untestable speculations and impressions or the mere amassing of biographical, historical, and sociological data of scant literary relevance. Against this background Formalism appeared, despite the frequent biases and supersubtleties of its proponents, as a legitimate attempt to found a form of literary scholarship that might be considered a science (in the sense just outlined), and moreover a science of literature.

Concentration on problems of literary technique and the way it works encouraged close interaction between literary theory, literary criticism, and contemporary literary practice. The close and mutually stimulating connection between the Russian Formalists and the Russian literary avant-garde of the day (especially Mayakovsky and the Futurists) has often been stressed and elaborated by those involved as well as by others.[10] But on occasion so close a connection could compromise the scholarly soundness of Formalist pronunciamentos. Like their friends the Futurists, some of the Formalists had a taste for self-promotion, and liked to *épater le bourgeois*. They enjoyed provocative exaggerations and at times succeeded in presenting sloppiness as bold inspiration and high-handed genius. Shklovsky in particular displays this tendency in many of his writings. It is not surprising that from the start he has been most open to attack, not only by those who opposed Formalism but also by its supporters, even former comrades-in-arms.[11] But as Erlich has warned, we should not blame such overstatements and aberrations on a particular Formalist or on Formalism as a whole; the Formalist school emerged and flourished in revolutionary times, when only those who were willing and able to make a loud noise could make themselves heard.[12]

An important thing to keep in mind—and a necessary one if we are to judge the achievements and limitations of Formalism in the light of its methodological assumptions and procedures— is that a discipline that builds on the understanding that its tenets are neither basic definitions nor immutable truths but working hypotheses to be proved or disproved requires a special position vis-à-vis these tenets. It cannot simply be equated with its initial hypotheses and judged (or found wanting) on the basis of them. The willingness to correct a hypothesis by referring back to the facts and observing them in a new way gave Formalism the supreme chance for self-correction, not only of individual findings but also of its methods and methodological principles. Thus a problem that inevitably arises when empirico-nomological methods are applied in the area of literary scholarship quickly showed up. In the natural sciences and in the experimental branches of the social sciences every proposition is subject to rigorous and almost immediate testing, either by repeated experiments or by a refuted prognosis. But such tests can be applied to literary theory only to a very limited extent or not at all. To thwart the proliferation of arbitrary speculation and untestable constructions—the very evils the Formalists had attacked with their impassioned demand for scientific, positivistic, rigor—it is imperative to secure other means of verification.

In Russian Formalism the chief form of this control function was theorizing in dialogue. The history and theory of the school are a continuous antiphony between the Formalists and their opponents. This is even more notable among the internally divided and mutually critical Formalists themselves, whose diversified interests and methods and highly dissimilar temperaments created a lively framework for debate. The linguists Jakobson and Jakubinsky, the literary historians Eikhenbaum and Tynyanov, the theoretician and publicist Shklovsky, the prosodist Tomashevsky, and Brik, whose major role was as a sounding board and organizer for the others—to name only the most important Formalists from the first decade—all joined, as partners and antagonists, in the fascinating dialogue that advanced the development of the formal method and is indeed its history. Only in this dialogue, in the clash with critical linguists and literary historians, could concretization and correction provide the greatly daring and often no less imprecise hypotheses of Shklovsky with scholarly validity and innovative force. Only collaborative theorizing made Tynyanov, who was always fascinated by poets' lives, a literary theoretician remarkable for his lucidity and precision.[13]

Therefore when Eikhenbaum states in retrospect that "the history of the formal method . . . takes the form of a consistent development arising from theoretical principles, independent of the individual contribution of any one of us," his words must be interpreted critically.[14] True, the history of the formal method took the form of a consistent development arising from theoretical principles. But it was not independent of individual contributions. On the contrary, the consistent methodological development was possible only because at a propitious historical moment the Formalist school gathered together a gifted group of personalities, radically unlike in temperament, training, and interests, in a constellation that favored a constant give-and-take of forward-looking hypotheses and allowed these hypotheses to be tested against the facts of the historico-literary subject matter. The participants did not merely check individual results or propositions; they felt disposed, even compelled, to go further, to question their method itself and its theoretical presuppositions, to examine them, and if necessary to correct them. This allowed them an opportunity to remove an early defect— an empiric methodology that had not been sufficiently examined—in the course of their continuing labors. Formalism made much of this chance, although, in the span of the movement's brief history and in view of its internal and external problems, it was impossible to conclude the discussion of all the questions raised or even to formulate all of them clearly.

In order to understand the history of Formalism we must accept certain consequences of its dialogic character. It is impossible and pointless to isolate single voices from the dialogue and rate them against each other. Nor can a purely historic account of the school capture the character of its dialogue. One must enter into the dialogue and evaluate the questions and answers of the Formalists from the viewpoint of contemporary literary scholarship, for which most of the questions remain valid. Only such an approach gives meaning to historical review. At the same time it establishes the significance and timeliness of the Formalist school for literary scholarship today.

3

The Formalist belief about what constitutes a theory rejected normative poetics just as it did any aesthetics deduced from a philosophical system. Hence the polemic of early Formalism against the aesthetics of Russian Symbolism, which bore the stamp of idealistic philosophy. Hence, too, the later Formalist antagonism toward Marxist literary theory, which meanwhile had climbed to dominance.[15] But a definition of the essence of its subject matter could not serve as the Formalist's point of departure either. Formalism no more answers the question What is Literature? than it does the question What should literature be? This is not to exclude the question of what properties are peculiar to literature. In fact, this last question is both the point of departure and the driving force behind all of Formalist literary theory. But according to Formalist principles, it can be answered only by delimiting the object of study, specifying the investigative approach, and illuminating the historical mutations of the concept of literature itself.

Literature must be set off from other forms and functions of language as one special form of language. Beyond this, it is necessary to show how the line that sets literature apart from other forms of language shifts constantly in the course of literary evolution, thus causing the very concept of literature to change. And the point must be established that literary scholarship can assume full validity as a discipline only when it has defined its specific mode of inquiry (not just its specific object). For, as the Formalists rightly stressed from the beginning, not every study of literature, not even every scholarly study of literature, constitutes literary scholarship. From the perspective of psychology, sociology, history, and other sciences, works of literature can be analyzed by scientific methods and with scientific results as expressions of the personality of an author, as social phenomena, or historic documents. However, such studies do not constitute literary scholarship as such. According to the Formalists, the subject of literary scholarship is, in Jakobson's often cited term, not literature in all its multiple aspects, but what is literary in it, its "literariness."[16]

To restrict inquiry this way sharpens one's sight for literature as a special form of language; at the same time it blurs it for other, not immediately connected problems. Opponents of and apologists for Formalism have often, and not without some good reasons, maintained that its chief failing consists in ruling out all nonformal aspects of literature. There was such a tendency (and danger), and many of the Formalists' supersubtle and one-sided excesses can be traced directly to it. But we must distinguish between what happened in practice, fulfilling dangerous potential implicit in the theory, and what the theory fundamentally prescribed and ruled out. What was fixed in the formal method was merely the line of inquiry, not some checklist of questions. To this extent it certainly allows incorporating social, psychological, philosophical, and other problems—on the condition that the inquiry remain targeted at literature as such, investigating the particular function of these various factors in the system of the work of literature or in literature generally, not simply using literature as raw material for other disciplines and their special concerns. As we shall see, Russian Formalism came to a systematic discussion of this matter quite late. When it did, it left unanswered several important questions. But contrary to a widespread erroneous belief, Formalism never ignored such concerns or evaded them on principle.

The single-minded orientation toward the specifically literary and the polemic rejection of all methods that ask questions not oriented directly toward it has led to the belief, found in practically all disquisitions on Formalism, that one of the school's chief methodological features was concentration on the work of literature itself, and that it corresponded to contemporaneous movements in Western Europe, such as *explication de texte* in France or Oskar Walzel's method in Germany.[17] These analogies are deceptive, especially with regard to German literary scholarship since World War II, where *die werkimmanente Deutung* has played a notable role down through the 1960s. But strict focus on the work and nothing but the work is not part of the theoretical program or of the practice of Russian Formalism. In the body of Formalist writings analyses devoted to single works are remarkably scarce. And even in these scattered cases analysis of the single work is rarely the main point. The aim rather is to illuminate certain literary techniques and procedures by reference to example. If the purpose, use, and effect of these procedures can be clarified by drawing on other literary texts or extraliterary documents (for instance, letters of the author, memoirs by contemporaries, or critical responses), the Formalists willingly used them to good effect. Eikhenbaum's essay on Gogol's *The Overcoat* is a classic example of this approach.[18] But more numerous by far are studies whose focal point is not an individual work but a specific problem, which is examined in light of many works or authors. In his survey Eikhenbaum observed that Formalist writings, especially early ones, characteristically point out a particular literary device in materials selected from widely disparate genres, epochs, and traditions. Thus, between Russian Formalism and the various forms of literary scholarship that set out to contemplate the isolated work of art from as many perspectives as possible there is, despite a common interest in literary form, a difference so basic that it must be stated emphatically.

4

Because formalism understands and examines the literary work as a linguistic form, and literature as a form of language, the question of the relation between poetic and nonpoetic language was at the heart of Formalist debate from the very beginning. At first terminology varied. The linguists

Jakubinsky and Jakobson, for example, distinguished between "poetic" and "practical" language.[19] Shklovsky preferred to contrast poetry and prose, even with regard to linguistic phenomena. Prose in this context clearly contrasts with literature as a whole; it does not mean prose literature as opposed to verse. It soon became apparent, though, that whatever the term employed, each had to be further differentiated. Practical or prosaic language refers to a phenomenon so complex that to do it justice, or even to use it as a methodological point of departure for the investigation of poetic language, further subdivisions or categories are indispensable. Yet it became evident that within literature as verbal art, fundamental differences exist between prose and verse. Thus, in answer to special problems, the branches of inquiry diverged, developing a theory of poetic language and poetry, on the one hand, and a theory of prose, on the other.

The starting point of the theory of prose may be seen in Shklovsky's article "Art as Device," regarded by many, and not without reason, as the virtual manifesto of early Formalism.[20] For when Shklovsky composed it in 1916, the gist of his polemic against the linguistic theory of Potebnya and the Russian Symbolists was to establish a clear distinction between the principles and functions of poetic language and prose (prose in its general meaning). But the article was also to become the cornerstone of Shklovsky's own theory of narrative prose, which in the ensuing years he staked out as his special domain. Fittingly he placed it at the head of his book *On the Theory of Prose* (1925), which already uses "prose" only in the sense of literary prose. In this case, therefore, varying uses of a single term—prose—reflect two distinct and separate meanings that must be taken into account if one wishes to avoid unprofitable terminological confusion and to do justice to Shklovsky's intentions.

The article's title introduces the term "device" (*priem*), which was to become one of the key concepts of Formalism. Its use first brought to light the latent dissimilarity between literary scholarship and the true empirico-nomological sciences. Instead of empiric consistencies, which, observed experimentally, allow the scientist to state and test hypothetical laws, in literature there appear certain devices, which can be observed again and again, from which conclusions are to be drawn concerning literary structures and effects, conclusions which must be tested anew in light of the historic material. It is characteristic of Shklovsky's radicalism—and of early Formalism in general—that he immediately took his ideas a step further. Demonstrating definite techniques in art leads to the thesis that art is nothing but the consistent application and effect of such devices. The title "Art as Device" is in itself a working hypothesis and a polemical program.

Shklovsky singled out the "device of defamiliarization" (*priem ostraneniya*) as the characteristic device of literature. Therewith he invented a term whose importance would extend far beyond Russian Formalism to work its effect on modern art and aesthetics. In Germany and elsewhere it was to become most influential in the late variant of Bertolt Brecht.[21] Whether Shklovsky's notion of defamiliarization adequately sums up the determinant aesthetic feature of literature is a matter open to debate. When Roman Jakobson claimed that Shklovsky's term misses the essence of poetic language and is one of the "platitudes galvaudées" whose significance for Formalism should not be exaggerated,[22] one can understand the feeling of a former champion of the movement, whose later work as a structuralist linguist led him to dissociate himself from an earlier position. Historically speaking, however, one cannot accept Jakobson's judgment as fair. The significance of Shklovsky's notion of defamiliarization for emerging Formalism, for the further development of Formalist theory and practice, and for its later effect and relevance cannot be denied, and such critical historians of Formalism as Erlich have paid it full, due note.

Problems arise in conjunction with the notion of defamiliarization and the examples adduced for illustrative purposes that Shklovsky does not expressly enter into. Nevertheless, they deserve attention because the Formalists' later treatment or neglect of them is in part implicitly predetermined in "Art as Device." Shklovsky's early treatment of the concept points up two distinct purposes of estrangement. First, defamiliarization impedes the kind of perception automatized by linguistic and social conventions, forcing the beholder to see things anew, correcting his relationship to the world around him. Second, in a kind of countermovement, by impeding perception, defamiliarization directs perception to the estranging and impeding form itself. This form and the devices that constitute it become the actual object of aesthetic perception and, finally, the proper object of art. The first aspect of literary defamiliarization—ethical, and directed toward cognition of the world—is unmistakable in the passages from Tolstoy discussed by Shklovsky. This aspect played an important part when Brecht fashioned his new version of the theory of the "defamiliarization effect" (*Verfremdungs-Effekt*). Shklovsky does not deny the importance of this, but he stresses that as a literary scholar only the second aspect of defamiliarization—the aesthetic one—is of interest to him. The way was paved for further developments of the theory by Shklovsky, and thus for crucial aspects of Formalist theory as a whole. The characteristic slighting of the ethical aspects of literature, the relative ignoring of thematic questions, the rather late beginnings of a systematic investigation of the relation between literature and extraliterary reality—all are prefigured in Shklovsky's early article.

Even as we note the flaws in Shklovsky's theory of defamiliarization, it must also be pointed out that the concept of defamiliarization itself contained a necessary corrective. If literature gains and maintains effectiveness only through defamiliarization, once the newly created forms become canonized and thereby automatic, they, too, must be made strange once again. The theory of defamiliarization flows into a theory of literary evolution as a "tradition of breaking with tradition."[23] This mode of thinking does make the change of literature in history appear primarily (if not exclusively) as an evolutionary process within literature alone; but, if we pursue matters to their logical conclusion, stressing the factor of historic evolution raises the question of the relation between literary history as understood here and history generally. This complex of issues also revives the question of the relation between literature and "life,"[24] a question that the concentration on formal elements and strictly intraliterary relationships seemed at first to rule out. And in fact Formalism did take this very route in the decade and a half following the appearance of Shklovsky's article.

24

Shklovsky touches on another theme obliquely, which, unlike the problems just discussed, deserves attention because it was conspicuously neglected in Formalism's later developments: drama. Shklovsky's examples are all from the epic. In one, from *War and Peace*, the description of a performance at the opera is achieved by means of an externalized description of the decor and the action, the observer being unable to follow the words or enter into the dramatic illusion. Instead of simple "deautomatization" of the conventions of literature, defamiliarization here is disillusionment—canceling the dramatic illusion, which is the first principle of the drama of illusion. This captures the very point from which a discussion of the special conditions and possibilities for defamiliarization in drama might have taken off. But Tolstoy—a master of defamiliarization in epic, who could even alienate drama within the epic medium—as a dramatist kept faith with the drama of illusion. Nor does Shklovsky, as his commentator, take up this special problem. Bertolt Brecht was the one who first applied the theory of defamiliarization to the theater and elevated it to a category of modern dramatic practice and theory.

Shklovsky approaches this theme more directly in an essay on *Don Quixote*. He compares the disruption of epic fiction with the dramatic technique of addressing the audience, and this occasions a brief digression on the role of illusion in drama: "As regards the theater, in it the illusion must probably be of a flickering kind, that is, sometimes apparent, sometimes altogether concealed. In his mind, the spectator must experience a change in the way he perceives stage action, partly as something 'intended,' partly as something 'real.'" There are plays whose whole effect depends on the spectator's "consciousness of the flickering illusion": "In these plays stage action is perceived partly as playing, partly as life."[25]

Shklovsky's brief remark goes to the heart of a crucial matter. He recognizes that defamiliarization, by canceling illusion, presupposes the prior creation of illusion, and that the deliberate interplay of generating and destroying illusion can produce special theatrical effects, indeed constitute a special form of drama. This is probably the chief reason why it was in drama that theory and techniques of defamiliarization were to develop most radically. Unlike lyric and epic, in which only language makes reality perceptible, drama has another kind of palpable reality in its scenery and actors. This duality of planes—the contrast between actor and role, stage reality and stage illusion—permits both an interplay of the two and the dissolution of one or the other.

This duality might explain why the theory of defamiliarization in drama was not developed by the Formalists and why they neglected problems of drama in general. There were occasional statements like those of Shklovsky and some short studies of individual plays from a literary-historical point of view,[26] but the only comprehensive studies of drama are those of S. D. Balukhaty, which, since they concentrate wholly on Chekhov, make for a highly specialized perspective.[27] A Formalist theory of drama able to take its place beside the Formalist theories of poetry and narrative prose does not exist. That is not so surprising as it first appears. A theory of literature defining and analyzing literature as a specific form of language can be better established and more consistently applied in the realm of lyric poetry and narrative, which are "purely verbal," than in drama, which, being an art of the stage, also depends on other media of presentation and expression. This reservation did not automatically apply to motion pictures. This pioneering art form, new in the Formalists' time, seemed—particularly in the era of the silent pictures—to have no pretensions at all as an art of language, using instead its own language of images and image sequences. By examining the devices and structures that make up this "language," and comparing them with those of literature considered as an art of words, it might be easier to reach better results than with the complicated literary and theatrical mixed form of drama. This may explain why some leading Formalists served prominently as theoreticians and critics of film, and even as filmmakers.[28]

This shows clearly that the history of the formal method is a "consistent development arising from theoretical principles" and that it would be a mistake to attempt to explain Formalism's mode of inquiry and choice of materials merely by linking it with prevailing movements of the times. The period of Russian Formalism was no more the heyday of experimental avant-garde poetry and of the great Russian silent films than it was the epoch of the famous Russian revolutionary theater and its great directors. This theater and its directors, though, were not moving toward drama of the "pure," poetic word, but toward "unbound," "total" spectacle, in which the word would rank beside—often below—the scenic, choreographic, pantomimic, and even acrobatic potential of the stage arts, which were to be realized to the full.[29]

5

The questions just discussed arise only when one reviews Shklovsky's article from the vantage point of later developments in Russian Formalism. Shklovsky and his theory of prose were confronted by a different, more urgent set of questions. Granted that the work of art is the "sum of devices," what devices besides defamiliarization go into that sum? What devices of summing up are essential for the overall construction? Is there a correspondence between these integrating devices and those of the linguistic forming of the parts? These questions are discussed in Shklovsky's article on "The Connection between the Devices of Plot Construction and General Stylistic Devices."[30]

Again the purpose is to point out general rules in very diverse materials, which range from folktales and romances to Victor Hugo and Maupassant and beyond to chase sequences in the movies. The devices Shklovsky discovers are, correspondingly, very general: repetition, parallelism, sequencing, climax, and so on. They are important both for plot construction and as stylistic devices in general, but such all-encompassing categories say little about the special plot techniques of narrative prose or about the complex interplay of narrative construction and style. In this respect the title promises more than the article can deliver. But Shklovsky's ideas proved pioneering as soon as he or others applied them to particular areas or used them as the point of departure for questions of general literary theory.

The special area in which these ideas were most productive was the study of fairy tales. To some extent this results from the nature of fairy tales. Thanks in part to its anonymous oral transmission, this genre has polished, terse, and distinct principles of style and composition. Moreover, events and characters are completely subordinate to the demands of a linear action, there are no psychological motivations. Fairy tales buttressed Shklovsky's notion of the primacy of plot construction. This, rather than a special interest in folklore, explains why in his early articles Shklovsky frequently drew on folklore, thus opening this area for Formalist narrative theory.

There was, moreover, the special situation of the study of fairy tales at that time. For schools of aesthetics and literary history that paid tribute to a work of art chiefly as the expression of a poet's personality, anonymously transmitted fairy tales were as inadequate a subject of investigation as for schools of literary criticism whose first concerns were with the sociopolitical problems of their own time. As a result, fairy tales were left to the special discipline of folklore studies (sometimes of a more national, sometimes of a more comparatist sort). In Russia at this time the field was dominated by the so-called ethnographic school.[31] This school, however, was concerned almost exclusively with aspects of subject matter, particularly the origin and kinship of motifs. Its prime tenets were that the motif answers fundamental problems of human existence in nature and society; that the far-reaching correspondences among primitive life forms explain parallels in fairy tales from different peoples and different ages when common ancestry or borrowings can be ruled out. Shklovsky attacked these tenets. A fairy tale, he maintained, is not an unmediated reflection of prevailing custom; formal parallels of the type mentioned cannot be explained by cultural analogy or dismissed as coincidences, but result "from the existence of particular laws of plot construction." Hence the usual "analogy of motifs" studied by the folklorists and comparatists must be complemented by or even give way to the "analogy of patterns" of possible plot constructions.[32]

As was often the case, Shklovsky supplied only the polemic program and certain tentative openers. His own "patterns" are, as I have mentioned, too general, and the material too various for any one part to have been investigated systematically. Such an investigation of the special area of the fairy tale did not appear until a decade later, with Vladimir Propp's

Morphology of the Folktale,[33] later acclaimed as "one of the most valuable Formalist contributions to the theory of narrative art."[34] Propp, who continued to deal almost exclusively with fairy tales and folklore and today is among the best-known scholars and theoreticians in his field, developed his method further after the Formalist school was disbanded.[35] He retained a Formalist's eye for the connections that relate general rules for constructing verbal works of art and specifics of genre and transmission (in folklore, anonymous oral transmission especially) to the particular structure of a given work. But he also inquires into the connections between poetic structures and extraliterary reality (in folklore, especially custom in its anthropological, ethnological, and sociological aspects). In this he goes far beyond the position of Shklovsky and early Formalism, but he satisfies the demand of late Formalism to relate the verbal work of art (a specific system with specific structures) to an overarching system of systems and its general laws of structure. This very point makes it possible to link Propp's Formalistic methods and results with other schools, older and newer, and their methods. Such links exist with the previously mentioned ethnographic school and similar movements (such as the so-called Finnish school) that investigate the origins and spreading of fairy-tale motifs. Other links connect Propp with Soviet-Marxist folklore studies, which stress relationships among social conditions, national custom, and themes or forms of folk poetry, and whose proponents value Propp chiefly for contributions in this area.[36] Links could even be established with the morphological method of André Jolles, who explicates fairy tales in terms of "Simple forms."[37] But the most crucial link is the one with present-day Structuralism, or rather with those of its proponents whose chief interest is in a system of systems and its anthropological basis. It is no coincidence that in 1958, when the English edition of Propp's *Morphology of the Folktale* was published in the United States, Claude Lévi-Strauss used the occasion to point out similarities and differences between form and structure, and between Formalism and Structuralism (of Lévi-Strauss's own particular stamp).

Although Shklovsky's discussion of plot construction lacked a specific field of application, it did serve as the basis for further development of his own aesthetic theory. His polemic against the environmental thesis of the ethnographic school led him to the following counterposition: "I would like to add a general rule: A work of art is perceived against the background and through association with other works of art. The form of a work of art is determined by its relationship to other, existing forms . . . *A new form comes into being not to express a new content, but to replace an old form that has lost its artistic character.*"[38]

Thus, indirectly Shklovsky once again takes up his own definition of art as defamiliarization, developing it along the lines discussed in my remarks on "Art as Device." On the one hand, the exclusive focus on the artistic function of defamiliarization (neglecting any extra-artistic reference or implication) now takes the form of a thesis: Changes in art and in artistic forms occur through a process, wholly contained within the realm of art and indispensable to it, whereby automatized forms and devices give way to new ones that defamiliarize them afresh. On the other hand, Shklovsky's limiting his attention to the independent realm of art corresponds to an expansion within this realm, achieved by the generalization of the evolutionary factor. Because a work of art can be perceived properly only as a form, and a form only as a differential quality—a deviation from an established canon—the traditional norms must always be considered.[39] It is no longer enough just to note the presence of certain devices; one must also inquire into their purpose and function within the given work. Since these can be established only within the context of literary evolution, the aspect of literary *history* (in this special meaning) becomes an indispensable feature of formal analysis.

In view of such conclusions we must do more than simply describe and itemize individual plot devices. The techniques of fitting plots together must be considered within the context of literary evolution. Shklovsky draws this conclusion in the third essay of his *Theory of Prose* ("The Construction of the Story and the Novel").[40] Although he discusses particular devices by means of which minor narrative details can be fused together in a story or individual stories can be fused into narrative cycles or novels, he also, in addition to providing the simple catalogue of types, traces the historical development from narrative cycle to the novel of the modern age. His outline begins with collections of tales and novellas of oriental provenance, with their various framing and motivating techniques (storytelling to stall for time, to win a contest, and so on). From immediate contact with this tradition, a distinct "European framing type" emerges, whose particular character and significance are defined by its "motivation of storytelling for the sake of telling stories."[41] The picaresque tradition is closely allied; in it—until *Gil Blas*—the central figure (not yet in any full sense a "person"), seeking his fortune or simply traveling, serves as the thread on which individual episodes are strung. The watershed of this development, where the problem of personal individuality and integrity of the central figure first arises, is *Don Quixote,* the subject of Shklovsky's fourth essay, "How *Don Quixote* Is Made."

Shklovsky asks how the material is fitted into the novel and how it is motivated. He investigates the questions in two areas: Don Quixote's speeches and the interpolated novellas. Going through the novel sequentially, he shows the variety of Cervantes' devices and how again and again they are exposed to make plain "the artifice of construction and motivation." Shklovsky concludes that Cervantes originally conceived of his hero as the carrier of story, not as a full-blown person—not even as the "Don Quixote type" for which modern writers such as Heine and Turgenev have celebrated him.[42] Rather, Shklovsky argues, the type—the figure of Quixote—came into being as the result of the novel's structure. Even as he wrote the novel, Cervantes recognized that burdening its hero with learned disquisitions and similar matter, which could not be adequately motivated by the figure's origins and education, resulted in a peculiar doubleness or split, which he then put in the service of his artistic intents.[43] Moreover, the plight of the Knight of the Woeful Countenance at the Duke's court allowed a new tone of humaneness, which leads, as it were, to a change of masks and a "new and thorough reexperiencing of the old material." Sancho Panza fares similarly in his adventure as governor, in which events and speeches are no longer simply piled on the character as they would be according to the old device, but rather the figure enters into a consciously experienced relationship to them. Here again "a new and thorough reexperiencing of the old material may be seen; this is already a step into the modern novel."[44]

Shklovsky's analysis of *Don Quixote* is a suggestive experiment and anticipates much that had to wait for later students of Cervantes (unfamiliar with Shklovsky's article) to examine systematically and confirm.[45] In view of the widespread inclination (not confined to Russia) to regard Quixote as a type or as a person, Shklovsky's caution against projecting modern concepts of personality on an old narrative tradition is justified. We need not debate here whether his hypothesis that Don Quixote's divided nature can be explained by its genesis remains convincing. More important, because it is characteristic of Shklovsky's method, is his neglect of thematic relationships. True, he points out that it is precisely Don Quixote's speeches on learning that lead to the figure's peculiar splitting. But for Shklovsky, the motivation for these speeches is purely technical. He does not mention, and probably did not see, that Don Quixote's great speech at the beginning of the novel on the ideal of the scholar and the knight introduces one of its major themes, which was also one of the great preoccupations of Cervantes' time. Whether the doubleness of the central figure corresponds to this double theme and how is not asked. Nor does Shklovsky examine the other major theme—the conflict between reality and the ideal—or its significance for the novel's composition. Here his neglect of thematics on principle, and his inclination to dismiss as insignificant all the ideas that are given voice within a work, or at best to admit them as motivations, prove deleterious.

This one-sidedness is a weakness of Shklovsky's literary theory in general, but even more of his practical criticism. Shklovsky himself recognized the problem. His essay on the Russian Symbolist Andrey Bely and so-called ornamental prose is basically a study of the relation between an author's ideology and artistic technique as exemplified in a particular work.[46]

Shklovsky asks how Bely's late conversion to anthroposophy influenced his strongly autobiographical novel of childhood, *Kotik Letaev*.[47] Bely, Shklovsky says, undoubtedly meant to propagate the ideas of Rudolf Steiner, with whom he was already deeply involved, and meant especially to spread the anthroposophic "doctrine of the layering of phenomena," which presents every object with, as it were, multiple shadows from different light sources.[48] In art this anthroposophic view corresponds to the predilection for presenting phenomena on several levels and for shuttling constantly from level to level. The characteristic representational mode of Bely's novel—to show the world first in the particular refraction of a child's consciousness, as a "swarm" of images, only gradually suggesting an "order"[49] in or behind the symbols—corresponds, according to Shklovsky, as much to the anthroposophical doctrine as it does to the fundamental principle of art that comes into play in modern ornamental prose and its literary technique. But what is important for the reader (as well as for the critic) are the technique and its effect, regardless of the anthroposophical purpose, which the reader need not know: "In the battle between anthroposophy and the artistic device it brought into being, the device consumed anthroposophy. And Andrey Bely's ornamental prose flowed in easy confluence with other currents of ornamental prose (Leskov, Remizov) called into being by other causes."[50]

What Shklovsky demonstrates here with reference to Bely's novel is by no means unusual in Russian literature. Its pronounced sociopolitical commitment often led to expressly polemical and ideological conceptions. This was true even among the most important writers, though either they achieved a convincing integration of the ideological purpose in the structure of the work, or the autonomy of the structure and its needs prevailed over the original conception and the author's ideology. (The evolution of Dostoevsky's *Devils* is one striking example.) Shklovsky is correct in stressing the role of the autonomy of the work's structure and of artistic devices, and their ability to withstand the ideological position or thematic conception of the author (which are primary only in terms of the genesis of the work). This does not necessarily argue against the importance of an ideological purpose in a work's genesis or against the importance of thematics (including its structural functions). Ideology and an author's thematic conceptions, however, no longer figure as objects of inquiry or judgment criteria appropriate for literary scholarship. What counts is the degree and manner in which they are artistically integrated into the work itself. With this understanding, one can concur with Shklovsky when, alluding to the Marxist tenet of the primacy of being over consciousness, he writes: "A philosophical Weltanschauung is for an author merely his working hypothesis. Or, to put it more precisely, the consciousness of a writer is determined by the being of the literary form . . . If an extraliterary ideology, unsupported by the required technical mastery, intrudes on the literary domain, the work of art will not succeed."[51]

Shklovsky is not attacking a particular ideology or ideology in general, as is proved by his simultaneous polemic against biographical or psychoanalytic interpretation.[52] Whether the fact that in Bely's novel the world is seen from the viewpoint of a child given to dreaming and often sick can be motivated biographically or psychoanalytically, he argues, both aspects simply motivate the artistic necessity to present the world in an estranged manner, thus intensifying the artistic perception and, by means of shifting perspectives and modes of presentation, offering the reader shifting perspectives on the world and the work. Bely achieves this by the particular techniques of his ornamental prose, whose development had been strongly influenced by anthroposophy. Tolstoy achieves something similar in *War and Peace* by juxtaposing dissimilar perspectives, though here the estranging technique is rooted in a moral stance and purpose. However dissimilar the personal motives and the literary devices, Shklovsky concludes, "what is important for the author to create within his work is multiple interpretability."[53]

Unfortunately Shklovsky did not elaborate this thought, which bears indirectly on one of the most important and difficult problems in the contemporary debate on literary and aesthetic theory, in which the aesthetics of perception are crowding to the fore.[54] If a verbal work of art is considered excellent because it maintains its appeal to ever new readers and generations of readers, giving new answers when asked novel questions, "multiple interpretability" must be prefigured in the work itself. Because social conditions and ideological concepts (and thus pronouncements on the so-called eternal themes) obsolesce fairly quickly, in the long run a work can meet this requirement only if the capacity dwells within its structure. On the one hand, the structure's degree of layering and its "multiple interpretability" must be great enough that, despite being fixed in the text, they allow a constantly renewing, even continuing dialogue between the work and its readers. On the other hand, the structure must, for all its openness, have enough force and justness in its own right to make the questions and answers point back to the work itself, thus preserving the character of the conversation as genuine dialogue and preventing its random proliferation. The various artistic devices and their interplay in the functional system of the work must create and fix this structural capacity to be understood in many ways. The layering of images and symbols in Bely and the plurality of perspectives in Tolstoy play an important role in achieving this.

In the course of literary evolution this role can be filled by the dominance of one principle over the other, but also as an interplay between the two. To recast, in the spirit of Formalist practice, a theoretical tenet as a question for literary history, one might ask if the dismantling of metaphor and symbol (which were distinguishing features of the Classic and Romantic period) by Realism would not have led, in realistic literature itself, to an impoverishment of layering and of multiple interpretability if the new school had not begun to develop and perfect techniques for the multiplication of psychological and narrative perspectives. One might ask further whether at the turn of the century, when these possibilities were exhausted and the repertoire of devices had grown automatic, modern narrative prose did not for that very reason return to the traditions of metaphor and symbol, striving for a combination of symbolism and perspectivism. Subtly differentiated both in its psychology and use of multiple perspectives, rich in its imagery, the ornamental prose of the Symbolist Bely is a typical and telling illustration of these tendencies.

6

As Shklovsky's essay on Bely proves, early Formalism in general and Shklovsky in particular did not on principle deny the significance of ideological intent and the role of thematics in the work of verbal art, but only emphasized the primacy of the structure of the work and its formal devices—sometimes launching very biased polemics and programs. Consequently the theory worked and still works best when applied to works and genres in which the thematic and ideological features recede, even to vanishing, behind marked formal structures and devices.

Two basic types can be distinguished. The first includes genres that, in accordance with the special circumstances or purpose of their creation, demand particular forms of plot construction and subordinate all the material they incorporate (including ideological content, psychological problems, and descriptions of social milieu, if any) to this one supreme demand. A paradigm for this category, and one Shklovsky studied, is the detective story. The second type, almost diametrically opposed, includes works or genres in which the plot has almost no weight of its own, and reflections on the principles or devices of construction become the plot (*syuzhet*) or theme, as in the parodic novel or in certain instances of so-called plotless prose. Shklovsky made special studies in this area as well.

While still formulating his theory of defamiliarization, Shklovsky analyzed the riddle, whose purpose is to impede perception artificially. It is not surprising that he became interested in the figure of the detective as a "professional unraveler of mysteries," and in the stories built around this figure—the mystery story or the mystery novel.[55] Working from the example of Conan Doyle's detective stories, he identified certain shared structural patterns, which are also common to crime stories generally, and demonstrated how the need to create suspense by posing riddles and to heighten suspense by delaying the right answer determines the entire composition, even to the point of assigning special characters to functions dictated by the construction (for example, Dr. Watson and the State Investigator who, as "perpetual dimwits," suggest "false solutions"). Incidentally, the problem of ideological conception also comes up briefly in this context, when Shklovsky mocks the pseudo-sociological thesis that Conan Doyle's fiction—which makes Sherlock Holmes a *private* detective and the *state* investigator an idiot—mirrors the individualistic, private-enterprise social structure and ideology of bourgeois England. Even in sociological terms, he writes, this is not accurate, since the British government itself was tailored precisely to the private and individualistic interests of the bourgeoisie. And even assuming that a Soviet writer would make the state detective his hero and the private eye the dummy or, alternatively, have Sherlock Holmes enter state service, "the structure of the story (the question now under investigation) would not change."[56]

Put into later, structural terminology, this would read: What is fixed are the structure of the system and the structure's determining "functions" (in the sense Propp uses this term), which are filled according to social conditions, ideological conceptions, and so on, and remain variable. But if one regards the work of art as such a functional system (and not simply as a sum of devices), the general rule must be perceived in its concrete manifestation, and every device must be examined for its specific function within the system. Shklovsky acknowledged this. "Chekhov said that if a story tells us there is a gun on the wall, later it will certainly fire. When emphasized, this motif edges into what is called 'fatality' (Ibsen). This rule in its usual form does indeed correspond to a general rule governing artistic means, but in the mystery novel the gun on the wall does not fire. A different one does."[57]

Again a "general rule governing artistic means" is assumed—in this case the aesthetic norm demanding that every detail within a work of art fulfill its purpose. Chekhov's remark makes this assumption. But the transition to fatality à la Ibsen is not in fact brought about by simple emphasis. There is a prior translation of the purely aesthetic rule into a rule of personal behavior. For the persons involved this translation alone gives the objects surrounding them the character of necessity, which, aesthetic distance being abandoned, is felt as threatening inevitability. When such behavior and feelings are turned to use as aesthetic themes in their own right (emphasized as motifs), what comes into being is a poetry of fatality, which is so characteristic of Ibsen (and is not unknown in Chekhov). In a mystery novel, on the other hand, the supposedly inevitable serves only to mislead. This specific demand of the genre is the supreme determinant and apparently prevails over the general rule, the general validity of which thus seems questionable. But the function that determines the genre (the suggestion of a false solution) can only be fulfilled because (or if) the reader, believing the general rule, expects that it will be observed and by this expectation is put on a false scent. Besides, the reader is not relying on the "general rule governing artistic means," but only on the customary form in which it is applied, connecting it with extra-aesthetic rules of his or her life experience. (The purpose of a gun is to fire; in a work of art every detail must serve its purpose; ergo, this gun will fire in this work.) This interprets the work as a mere report of events, not as a concatenation of effects. For the gun that in the chain of events does not fire, does in the complex of effects fulfill its purpose, which, however, is specifically aesthetic and which, in this specific genre, consists in misleading rather than in firing. The supposed infraction of the rule only confirms the general rule as one that specifically governs artistic means, and thus illuminates how it works. But it is indispensable, on the one hand, to search beyond the customary form in which the rule is applied, and, on the other, to discover in any given case the characteristic variant of the ground rule and its specific function in the system.

Leading the reader astray need not be limited to thrusting a wrong solution ahead of the true one. More radically, it can raise a protest against the aesthetic norm itself, against the general propensity for seeking meanings behind every detail of a work of art (whether in points of the plot, features of the social setting, or symbolic references). The purpose and rationale of such protest can take many forms. A quasi-realistic conception might be paraphrased like this: Not everything in life is significant, and that is precisely what this meaningless detail in the work is meant formally to reflect. A more artistic conception could be: Art does not need to justify everything in terms of meaning, not even in an intrinsically artistic sense. A kind of combination of both conceptions, which might be styled hermetic, could be stated thus: By denying the recipient the association of meanings he seeks, it provokes him critically to reconsider the premises, first, of his own grasp of what art is, and thereby, of what he is, and what the world is.

Even in these conceptions the detail is meaningful in that it functions as part of the overall effect; its functions are different, less direct, and more available for the reader's own participation than those (disappointing or fulfilling) expectations mentioned earlier. This is especially true in the hermetic conception, which in this particular sense moved to the center of discussions of aesthetic theory later and played no part in the theory of Russian Formalism.[58] The Formalists were most interested in the various artistic possibilities of parody, understood in its broadest sense.

Shklovsky's premise that art is defamiliarization and operates by exposing its own devices squared with few areas of art so well as with the phenomenon of parody. In the field of plot theory, parody (particularly in the form of the parodic novel) once again takes a kind of central position. It lies, as it were, midway between the extremes of plot-bound narrative prose of the fairy-tale or detective-story variety and literature beyond plot, which abandons plot construction altogether. On the one hand, it is not tied to any particular devices of plot construction and is characterized by its free play with them. On the other hand, declassing the conventional devices and using them as raw material, the parodic novel plays its game *through* the material, estranges it, and thus creates its real plot (*syuzhet*). This goes far toward explaining why Shklovsky liked to support his discussion of plot with evidence from parodic novels (*Don Quixote, Tristram Shandy*), and it is the reason why he regarded Sterne's as the paradigm of this type of novel, if not indeed of the genre of the novel itself.

In this case the affinity between the object being discussed and the investigator's theory or method was particularly strong, and of Shklovsky's interpretations of individual works, the one on *Tristram Shandy* is most faithful to its subject.[59] The article, therefore, does not call for explication or comment; however, a brief remark about scholarship concerned with the work is in order. In discussions of the novel and narrative prose *Tristram Shandy* plays an important role; a favorite example for illustration, it is often interpreted in a manner close to Shklovsky's in many ways. A reader more familiar with such discussion than with the history of *Shandy* scholarship and Russian criticism in the twenties might receive the impression that Shklovsky's statements are fairly self-evident, but his claim to have discovered *Shandy* for Russia is well founded. Sterne was an important influence on the Russian Sentimentalists of the late eighteenth and early nineteenth centuries, but this influence resulted primarily from his *Sentimental Journey*. *Tristram Shandy* was not translated in its entirety until much later, and it was Shklovsky's analysis of the novel that triggered the Russian craze of "Shandyism."[60] In Western *Shandy* scholarship Shklovsky's views did not begin to circulate—independent of his article, which had not been translated—until about three decades later. As far as I know, it was K. E. Harter, writing in 1954, who first made direct reference to the piece by the Russian Formalist.[61]

Shklovsky's article ends with the claim that "Tristram Shandy is the most typical novel in world literature." Erlich charges that this is a strong assertion, that it is false, and that it betrays "the modern bias of the Formalist in favor of non-objective art, his tendency to mistake the extreme for the representative."[62] The bias cannot be denied, nor can the provocativeness of Shklovsky's closing statement. Yet it is not enough simply to explain his thesis by referring to an orientation to nonobjective art or to dismiss it as wrong; one must inquire into the role of the parodic novel within the genre of the novel more generally.

The connection between these problems becomes clearer in light of another essay dating from the same time—"Literature beyond Plot" (1921)—which at first seems to have nothing to do with the parodic novel or Sterne's work.[63] Here Shklovsky investigates the prose of the essayist Vasily Rozanov as an example of plotless literature. He shows that the dissolution of traditional plot constructions enables literature to take up new themes and devices (or such as were hitherto deemed unliterary), thus becoming an important factor in literary evolution. This raises the urgent question whether novels that are deficient in plot or violate the traditional novel's device of plot construction are not the ones with special importance for the genre and its evolution. "Leo Tolstoy's *War and Peace*, Sterne's *Tristram Shandy*, with their almost complete lack of a frame tale, can only be classified as novels because they specifically transgress against the rules of the novel. The purity of a genre is itself . . . only to be understood as opposition to a genre that cannot entirely find itself a canon. But the canon of the novel as a genre is, perhaps more often than any other, capable of being thoroughly parodied and changed from its very foundation" (p. 230).

What in this article remains a short digression points to a particular notion of genre, one characteristic of Formalism. A genre is not simply a firm canon, the rules of which are or are not purely realized. It is a constantly shifting, evolving system of references, in which the profoundest offenses against currently valid models or rules go at least as far in shaping the genre as do reinforcements. This is especially true of a genre like the novel, which reached full development, a position of dominance, and a theoretic basis only after the primacy of normative poetics had ended. This may in part account for the fact that, at different times and for the most varied reasons, this genre frequently has given rise (and still does) to talk of being in a crisis. These crises have always proved to be creative, demonstrating the genre's capacity constantly to be "changed from its very foundation." Such changes occur whenever the genre is thoroughly parodied. That is why *Don Quixote, Tristram Shandy,* and *Dead Souls* are as much parodies or antinovels as they are self-confirmations, self-regenerations, and reference points of the novel. To this extent the parodic novel in general and Sterne's novel in particular are not normal representatives of their genre, though they *are* especially typical.

But if one stretches the notion of parody so far and assigns it so vital a function, one must at the same time provide a comprehensive and precise definition of the function and application of the concept. Shklovsky does not meet this requirement. In accordance with his own polemical temper and his thesis of art as defamiliarization, he sees parody almost exclusively as the mocking or joking exposure of devices that have become automatic—thus primarily as a form of destruction. But a parodistic work of art is itself always a "constructed deconstruction," and only by constructing through destructing can it have a constructive effect, can it fundamentally change the tradition it thoroughly parodies.

Tynyanov saw and formulated all this far more clearly

than Shklovsky. His article "Dostoevsky and Gogol: Toward a Theory of Parody"[64] appeared the same year as Shklovsky's piece. Although one of its author's earliest publications, this essay clearly exhibits the hallmark of his approach: the combination of richly documented literary-historical studies with general literary theory. As in many of his early writings, Tynyanov compares two authors. For the study of the special phenomenon of parody, this has the advantage of allowing a greater degree of precision in showing *how* and *what* is being parodied. Thus, for example, the author advances a persuasive case for the parodic character, which all previous scholarship had let pass unnoticed, of Dostoevsky's tale *The Village of Stepanchikovo*. Looking at the parody and the model side by side, one may establish the different functions of identical devices in each system and thus the dissimilar purposes of both systems, and moreover establish not only the relatedness of the parody but also its independence. Only thereby does it become clear why such a parody can retain its effectiveness even when the parodic reference is missed or forgotten. The constructive aspect of parody is stressed no less than the destructive aspect. For Tynyanov "parody fulfills a dual task: (1) it mechanizes a particular device; and (2) it organizes new material, in which is included the old, now mechanized, device." And only its duality makes parody a driving force behind literary evolution generally. For "every literary succession is above all a struggle, destruction of an old entity and new construction out of old elements"; it is not "a straight line . . . connecting the younger representative of a given literary branch with an older one."[65]

The similarities to Shklovsky's positions are as plain as the differences in emphasis and orientation. Both Formalists work with the pair of terms "device" and "material"; both regard parody as a laying bare of conventional devices, which thereby become the material of devices of a higher power; both recognize in this an analogy between parody and literary evolution in general. But whereas Shklovsky stresses destruction, Tynyanov accords the central role to a new construction; whereas for Shklovsky parody serves principally to probe into and reconfirm his previously formulated premise of art as defamiliarization, for Tynyanov the literary-historical analysis of parodic texts and the outline of a theory of parody he derived from it are the starting points for a theory of literary evolution (which he went on to develop and test further).

7

Before discussing the Formalist theory of literary evolution we must investigate one more aspect of prose theory, which despite its general significance is hardly considered in Shklovsky's *Theory of Prose:* narrative style. Formalist principles and interpretive categories for the analysis of style and verbal construction were more intensively and systematically worked out and tested in the area of poetry than in prose. The poem, being smaller and hence easier to see whole, is verbally more tightly structured by various organizing principles (line, stanza, rhyme and sound patterns, meter and rhythm, and so on). As such the poem allows specifically verbal and stylistic aspects of literature and the character of the literary work as a complex system bearing the stamp of particular stylistic dominants to be grasped more readily. Jakobson (and later Tynyanov) had taken this direction early on successfully. Shklovsky, the declared theoretician of prose, borrowed from their ideas. Within his *Theory of Prose* there is a marked shift from the demonstration of general devices in dissimilar materials to the analysis of individual works or genres, as well as a change from a more additive conception (the work as a sum of devices, the genre as a canon of rules) to a more constructive and evolutionary one (the work as a functional system, the genre as an evolving one). But even in his most successful analyses of individual works, he was more at home tracking down fundamental possibilities of poetic construction than carefully weighing different kinds of factors within a system, and working out the system's specific stylistic features.

Eikhenbaum, on the other hand, combined from the start a distinct bent for monographic studies on individual authors with general theoretical and literary-historical interests. Almost from the start in his monographs he began to study not only pure lyric poets, like Anna Akhmatova, but also authors who alternated between lyric poetry and prose, like Lermontov, as well as writers who worked only in prose, like Gogol, Tolstoy, and Leskov.[66] In the area of prose he was at first most interested in phenomena that stand at the point where general prose theory and specific stylistics intersect, and especially in the so-called *skaz,* a richly developed narrative technique in nineteenth- and twentieth-century Russian prose, which, lexically and syntactically, in metaphor, theme, and point of view, is patterned on the narrative manner of an oral narrator from the simple folk, or rather stylized according to the hypothetical notion of such a narrator. This special topic may serve to illustrate the treatment of problems of narrative style within Formalist prose theory.

To the problems of the *skaz* Eikhenbaum devotes not only his article on Gogol's *Overcoat* (1918), but also "The Illusion of the *Skaz*" (1918) and "Leskov and Modern Prose" (1925). The distribution and the sequence are characteristic. At the start there are, side by side, a detailed analysis of a work and a brief theoretical examination of the phenomenon; this is followed by an investigation of the phenomenon's transformation within literary-historical evolution. In an unmistakable correspondence to Shklovsky's plot theories, which were formulated at roughly the same time, Eikhenbaum begins his article on *The Overcoat* by inquiring into the fundamental significance of plot in narrative literature. He defines plot as the "interweaving of motifs by the aid of their motivations," and distinguishes between primitive narrative, which is sustained by interest in the plot, and narrative in which the plot "ceases to play an organizing role" and is at best required to "interweave individual stylistic devices." But what interests Eikhenbaum in narrative prose of the second kind—and this sets him apart from Shklovsky—is the fact that in it, "the narrator in one way or another thrusts himself to the fore," and that his personal tone can become the organizing principle that determines style. Eikhenbaum tries to identify the specific character of this tone. In *The Overcoat,* he writes, we find the *skaz* in the variant most characteristic of Gogol, with the oral narrator unfolding his presentation as a "system of various pantomimic and articulatory gestures," underscoring and distancing in the manner of an "actor." One must distinguish two essential stylistic levels:

the "purely comic *skaz*," and a pathetic declamation, conceived as an aesthetic contrast to the first.[67]

Eikhenbaum interpreted even the so-called humane passages of *The Overcoat*—passages in which individual figures or the narrator express their compassion for the suffering hero—as purely aesthetic, formal effects. Because, since *The Overcoat* was first published, these passages have been venerated in Russia as a kind of sacrosanct paradigm for socially responsible *littérature engagée* (and are regarded so to this day), his Formalist interpretation touched off impassioned protest. Heated discussions still continue among Gogol scholars.

Eikhenbaum's own reading is typical of early Formalism in that its resolute polemical stance indirectly presupposes a strict division between purposes and interpretations that are strictly formal and those that rest on content—a premise which has maintained itself throughout the ensuing quarrels. But this neglects the question of perception. Especially when interpreting Gogol's story in the manner of Eikhenbaum—as a virtuosic, masterly game played by the comedian narrator—one would have to point out more clearly how the game with words and literary conventions is also a game with the expectations and preconceptions of the reader. The narrator, being ironic, never fully identifies with his hero and repeatedly makes him look ridiculous. On the other hand, he constantly triggers pathetic, humane affects, with the result that he releases the reader's own aesthetic *and* ethical emotions, which may turn against the hero's heartless colleagues and superiors, against the unjust social order, but also against the narrator himself, whom a reader may experience as too distanced. This can happen when the reader, prompted by his own emotions and expectations, makes light of the narrator's ironic distance and assumes a direct satiric position of his own. This happened in Russia, even in Gogol's own time, when his works, deeply rooted in the romantic tradition with all that implies in terms of irony and metaphysics, came up against literary criticism that with dramatically increasing insistence judged literature by the standards of social criticism and realistic expectations and demands.[68] The same thing can happen, independent of this particular situation in literary history, if a later reader, distanced and emotionalized by the narrative style, takes sides with the tormented creature, in spite of the narrator's ironic distance, which he is aware of. Thus the reader may, in his own eyes, appear more humane than the narrator, who all too easily is erroneously equated with the author. Seen in this way, the ironic distance of the narrative and the aesthetic effect need not preclude a humane impulse but may even heighten it by mobilizing the humane powers of the reader himself, instead of using the narrator's clear partisanship to shepherd the reader along.

Such a reading, canceling the false alternative as either purely aesthetic or ethical, would conform to Eikhenbaum's own summary, in which he characterizes *The Overcoat* as a "grotesque"—which agrees with the tendency of later scholarship to honor Gogol as one of the great masters of the grotesque.[69] One of the chief features that sets the grotesque apart from ordinary satire is that the grotesque, depicting a closed world of distorted proportions, cannot directly incorporate a moral counterposition in the portrayal, and yet is only fully effective if the reader does grasp the unexpressed contrast. This caused a basic conflict that marks Gogol's work, its effect, and indeed, even his biography. The moralistic and religious Gogol was deeply alarmed at the recurrent accusations that the author of *The Inspector General, The Overcoat,* and *Dead Souls,* works of an admitted master of exposure and negation, was incapable of portraying the positive. Any attempt to refute this charge directly in his literary works would necessarily have imperiled the basis of his grotesque art. This contradiction, which proved insoluble for Gogol, led ultimately to the destruction of his artistic work and then his own life.[70]

This critical digression is not intended to detract from the significance of Eikhenbaum's analysis of *The Overcoat.* His article remains one of the most stimulating and important contributions to Gogol scholarship, and it is rightly considered a classic of Formalist interpretation. If Eikhenbaum's study neglects the role of shifting perspectives as the condition for the interplay of aesthetic and ethical impulses, concentrating instead on the purely stylistic features of Gogol's *skaz,* it does so not only because early Formalism had a general aversion to interpretations predicated on a worldview but also because what fascinated Eikhenbaum most about the *skaz* were its verbal and stylistic aspects rather than questions of perspective, which only later came to play a central part in his study of narrative. This point is even clearer in light of the article "The Illusion of the *Skaz*." In it the Russian avant-garde philologist wholeheartedly concurs with German philological avant-gardists like Sievers or Saran, who demanded that the single-minded concentration on the history of motifs and ideas finally be supplemented by an investigation of specifically linguistic matter (sound patterns, rhythm, and so on), and that the traditional "philology of the eye" be countered with a "philology of the ear" (*Ohrenphilologie*).[71] The *skaz*, considered as a transposition of the idiosyncrasies of oral speech into written literature, is the ideal object for such inquiry. It has the further advantage of cracking the virtual monopoly of verse on sound analysis and similar approaches, thereby allowing for a kind of prose philology of the ear, which does greater justice to certain narrative forms and stylistic traditions of prose (Eikhenbaum would say to its articulatory aspects). That the aim can be achieved only if the methods and mode of inquiry of literary studies are combined with those of general linguistics and linguistic stylistics merely confirms one of Formalism's chief postulates, which was emphasized in this early phase.

For an entrenched literary historian like Eikhenbaum, however, this combination harbors a danger, for it inevitably lures him to a region where a linguist may justly complain that his treatment of linguistic facts is inadequate, and his command of linguistic categories insufficient. Vinogradov—though no Formalist, a leading expert on the Formalist school, with which especially in its early phases he engaged in constant lively debate—took issue with Eikhenbaum's essays on the *skaz* in just this way, objecting not only to specific inaccuracies but also to the fundamental linguistic inadequacy of Eikhenbaum's definition of and distinctions within the term *skaz*.[72] His own attempt to define the term more precisely, to distinguish it more clearly from oral speech on the one hand and different types of written speech on the other, and to set up a kind of catalogue of types

47

of *skaz* is a well-justified correction and supplement to Eikhen-baum's analyses and hypotheses.

Such amendments run the risk of making definitions and distinctions that from the standpoint of a specialized discipline (in this case, linguistic stylistics) are sharper and more systematic at the price of the exclusion or neglect of other aspects of the phenomenon that played a part in the original, less precise, but more multifarious, characterization or description. The fact that the complexity of the *skaz* makes it equally illuminating for investigating problems of linguistics, stylistics, point of view, plot construction, and general narrative technique, and that its nature can be illuminated only by the combined effect of all these aspects, is the methodologically decisive one, and it is easily lost from view in purely stylistic systemizations. In investigating the *skaz* the Formalist and literary scholar Eikhenbaum is as much in need of the corrections of Vinogradov, a linguist, as Vinogradov is on the challenge and complementary view in the Formalist's theory and analysis of the *skaz* as narrative.

Similar words may be said regarding the study of point of view. How powerfully (and how early) the Russian Formalists pointed the interests of scholarship in this direction may be gauged by examples already mentioned in other contexts: the function of the defamiliarizing point of view of an outsider (in Tolstoy's descriptions of war or of the theater) or of an animal (in examples from folklore and from Tolstoy's horse story "The Strider," which Shklovsky discusses in "Art as Device"); the refracted point of view of a child (in Bely's *Kotik Letaev*) or of the folk narrator of the *skaz;* the misleading points of view in the mystery novel, and so on. But in the decades since Formalism was outlawed, progress in this area has been so remarkable as to make it practically a whole new field of study compared to whose best results the efforts of the Formalists may seem crude. Moreover, the Formalists, who were averse to inquiry along the lines of the history of ideas and initially concentrated on intra-literary matters, almost ignored the question of how the development of particular techniques of perspective relates to general changes in views of the world or reality. But in more recent literature, literary criticism, and literary scholarship these questions came to dominate attention—questions, for example, of the way the mediation of reality is made objective, subjective, or relative by stressing or downplaying the authorial or personal point of view, by dispensing with an epically authenticated interpretation of mediated reality in favor of divergent views of different individuals, or general questions about the representation of reality in literature and the literary relationship of reality and illusion.[73]

It is important to elucidate these important matters, but here, too, there is danger that intense, more systematic progress in one narrowly defined direction is bought at the price of neglecting others, no less important, that were considered more fully before. For example, German research in this area tends to interpret the special verbal structures that determine narrative point of view chiefly as the expression of transformations in conceptions of the world and the self, underestimating the reverse aspect, that is, distinctions in point of view as linguistic or stylistic effects. But one of the main advantages of Eikhenbaum's analysis of *The Overcoat* is that it addresses this point. Eikhenbaum was sophisticated enough in questions of perspective to recognize that, on the one hand, the narrator of *The Overcoat* characteristically keeps his distance from the hero, but that, on the other hand, the distinction between them is not consistently sustained (the alogical trains of thought, certain peculiarities of speech, and so on constantly play over from the level of the hero onto the level of the narrator). According to a strict reading in terms only of point of view, this last point might easily be misconstrued as a flaw. But Eikhenbaum's analysis, based on style, could show that Gogol's purpose was precisely not to maintain a consistent contrast of points of view between narrator and character but to establish the contrast of particular levels of style, thus blurring the levels of perspective and creating the ambivalence that gives rise to the specifically grotesque effect (including the misunderstandings and quarrels in the critical history of the work). Categorizing Gogol's style strictly in terms of point of view (thus making everything depend on the ironic refraction by a distancing narrator) fails to account for the fact that this style is fully developed not only in Gogol's narrative prose but also in his plays, in which the level of narrator does not exist; however, a characterization of Gogol's style based on contrasting stylistic levels (each using stylistic devices of contrast) is valid for the interpretation of Gogol's complete works.[74]

Just as it was characteristic for Eikhenbaum, unlike Shklovsky, to start from the interpretation of an individual work as a poetic system and to inquire into the dominant features of a particular author's style, so it was typical of Formalist working methods in general subsequently to investigate, on the one hand, the phenomenon of the *skaz* in its historic development and its role in contemporary literature, and, on the other, to use the previous investigations as the basis for inquiry into the fundamental tasks and possibilities of a theory of prose. From Gogol, for whose style the *skaz* is only one of the shaping factors, Eikhenbaum turned to Leskov, who more than any other writer owed his fame to his penchant for the *skaz* and his masterly command of its technique. To be sure, he also owed his fame to Eikhenbaum, who called attention to this aspect of Leskov's work, revealing him as a great storyteller, while previous critics had dealt chiefly with political, social, and religious problems in Leskov's work, measuring him against great Russian novelists like Tolstoy and Dostoevsky and failing to appreciate his individuality and importance. That old and new *skaz* techniques played an important part in Russian narrative prose just before and after the Revolution (in Remizov in particular, though in many other writers as well, especially those of so-called ornamental prose) certainly aided the revaluation of Leskov. This connection became evident in terms of literary history and significant for literary theory thanks in large part to the investigations of Eikhenbaum and other Formalists.

The essay on Leskov appeared in 1925, the same year as Shklovsky's book on the theory of prose and Eikhenbaum's own survey of the development of the "Theory of the Formal Method" in the first decade of its existence.[75] In this retrospective summary he singles out the Formalist theory of prose for particular praise as an original and innovative achievement, relying wholly on Shklovsky's contributions (other than these, he discusses only his own article on *The Overcoat*), thus stressing plot construction and motivation as the linchpins of Formalist narrative theory.[76] In the essay on Leskov, however, he subjects this conception to brief but thorough criticism. It is appropriate, he claims, for this criticism to be formulated here, in this new study of the *skaz,* since investigations of the *skaz* and the narrative style of individual prose writers had convinced Eikhenbaum that a Formalist theory of prose, too, would have to begin with categories expressly related to language that determine the various levels of the verbal work of art. The plot, which in general determines only the highest level of the total construction, is not such a category. Yet such an effort had been undertaken, for instance, in Tynyanov's recently published programmatic volume *The Problem of Poetic Language* (1924), which attempts to erect a Formalist theory of poetry on the basis of verbal rhythm and the overlap of rhythmic and semantic structures.[77] Something analogous had to be found for prose in order to correct Shklovsky's one-sidedness and place Formalist narrative theory on a more solid basis, more directly related to language.

> The theory of prose is still in its beginning stages, for the very reason that the basic formative elements of prose have not been investigated. The theory of verse forms and genres, taking rhythm as its point of departure, has a solid basis in principles in a way the theory of prose does not. The plot is not so closely linked to the word that it could serve as the starting point for the analysis of all aspects of narrative prose. It seems to me, therefore, that the inquiry into *narrative form* can serve as a starting point for constructing a theory of prose.[78]

In the few years remaining to Formalism after 1925, neither Eikhenbaum nor the other Formalists had a chance systematically to develop this new, revised conception of Formalist narrative theory. Eikhenbaum himself was above all a literary historian and analyst, not a systematic theoretician. Having recognized and articulated the possibility, indeed necessity, of such a theoretical conception, he was concerned primarily in discussing it with friends, colleagues, and students, and testing its validity in special monographs and literary-historical studies. This he did in his own work; moreover, he did it as the instigator of Formalist workshops and seminars.[79] The most graphic illustration of the latter aspect of his activity is the volume *Russian Prose* (1926) edited by Eikhenbaum in collaboration with Tynyanov, which includes individual studies, mostly by younger Formalists, who had been inspired by these workshops.[80] It is an attempt to demonstrate, by reference to a particular phenomenon within a specific historic phase (Russian narrative prose, mostly of the Sentimentalist and Romantic schools), the synchronic interplay and the diachronic transformation of various genres, narrative forms, and stylistic traits. The focus is as much on what is historically unique as it is on the fundamental problems of literary theory and history that it exemplifies. The 1926 volume shows how Formalist theory in its final years increasingly merged with literary history, elevating literary evolution to its favorite theoretical topic. This also accounts in part for the fact that Eikhenbaum's conception of a theory of prose based on narrative form failed to develop as a full-fledged theoretical system, though it acted all the more potently as a theoretical stimulus for the literary-historical study of such forms and their interrelations.

8

How justified Eikhenbaum's call for a theory and investigation of narrative forms was and how timely it remains does not have to be established from the vantage point of the present. Few areas of literary scholarship since that time have been dealt with so intensively and deployed so fully as the theory, analysis, and historical investigation of narrative forms. But it is sufficient to survey the example of some German contributions in this area to notice, besides the parallels that exist, extensive and fundamental differences. Both concentrate on form. But quite apart from the fact that the term is usually employed in very dissimilar significations, this resemblance, if it is the sole essential one, is exceedingly general. The difference may be grasped most readily in terms of two criteria: language and evolution. To be sure, in both cases literature is conceived of as verbal art. But for Russian Formalism the linguistic material, the devices whereby it is manipulated, its structure, and the points that distinguish all these from extraliterary linguistic systems are always at the basis of inquiry. For the German morphological schools and similar movements this is true in certain cases only and never to so great a degree. In accordance with the different weight they ascribe to the purely verbal factors, the Russian Formalists and the Germans make different basic distinctions in matter and method. The Russian Formalists separate poetry (verse) and prose; the Germans almost without exception divide literature into the categories of lyric poetry, epic, and drama, sometimes in the sense of the traditional genres, sometimes with the help of variously derived categories of "the" lyric, "the" epic, and "the" dramatic.[81] Often the threefold division hearkens back, more or less explicitly, to Goethe's notion of the natural forms of lyric, epic, and dramatic poetry, which are almost invariably associated with conceptions of the organic growth of literature and its forms. Any such organic conceptions, however—even used in the metaphoric sense to describe development—were as alien to the specific Formalist conception of evolution as were pure typologies that deny or pass over the evolutionary factor.

Even admitting that the two schools share the focus on formal aspects, the similarity between the formal and the morphological approaches should not be overestimated. This is true even in the matter of citing forerunners (which, methodologically speaking, is of doubtful value). From among German literary scholars, Oskar Walzel has been cited as such a forerunner again and again.[82] Unquestionably the Formalists knew Walzel's work, which accorded far better with their notions than did the more familiar German literary history of the time; and in many respects it was an important stimulus. With him they shared a common interest in the "artistic *form* of poetic works."[83] But the fact that Walzel works with the dichotomy of *Content and Form in the Poet's Work of Art*[84] limits the similarity. Walzel's prime interest in his theory and analysis of literature is less in its specific structure as a verbal art, as opposed to other devices and structures of language that are not literary, than in the "mutual illumination of the arts."[85] It is no accident that Viktor Zhirmunsky—who was closely associated with Formalism at its inception but quickly came to regard it as too purely formal and too one-sided in restricting itself to intraliterary phenomena—chose to justify his rejection of the Formal school in an introduction to a Russian translation of one of Walzel's works. But his criticism is leveled principally at biases of early Formalism and does not do full justice either to the linguistic or to the evolutionary aspects of the Formalist conception of form. And this was precisely the point where the crucial differences lay between the notions of the Formalists and those of Walzel.[86]

Of other related movements in more contemporary German literary studies, the morphological method of André Jolles deserves, in my view, special attention. In his case, agreement with Russian Formalism is not limited to the supremacy of form. He conceives of form, or rather of "Simple Forms," specifically as forms of language. This is why Jolles investigates—rather than works of art, which bear a stronger individual stamp—simple forms, such as riddles, fairy tales, and the like, "which occur within language itself, without the agency of a poet, so to speak, creating themselves from language itself."[87] If one recalls what Shklovsky, for instance, had to say about the autarchy of verbal devices and principles of construction in the riddle and the fairy tale, the similarity of the approach (and of many results) is remarkable. At first one may formulate as a mere nuance what, in the light of a more extensive comparison, turns out to be a far-reaching distinction. For Jolles, language is at work; for the Formalists, one works with language. Jolles starts with certain "mental activities," which correspond with certain "pure simple forms," which realize themselves in language as "simple forms made conscious" and finally as "referred forms."[88] The Formalists start with basic devices, some of which might be understood as correspondences to certain attitudes of mind (for instance, the device of defamiliarization), and which in any given work of art are made conscious as referred ones. But in Jolles's metaphysics of language, language is a being (*Wesen*); for the Formalists it is an array of instruments or a functional system. And, above all, the simple forms of Jolles are conceived of as a kind of primal forms that develop organically, and he directly cites Goethe's morphology as the model for his morphological method. This is something fundamentally different from applying the same devices to dissimilar systems and in dissimilar functions. It is different, too, from a conception of evolution characterized by the defamiliarizing break with tradition and the continual reconstruction from elements of the old system that has been destroyed.

The various typological systems proposed in German literary studies of more recent decades also seemed in many respects to satisfy Eikhenbaum's demand for a theory of prose based on narrative form. The claim might at least be made for those attempts that do not set out to interpret the essential nature of storytelling or start off from primal forms, but rather try to inventory and systematize typical narrative forms and techniques, as, for example, in Lämmert's *Forms of Narrative Construction.*[89] He sketches out the situation he is departing from, which is in many ways comparable with that which faced the Russian Formalists decades before. In both cases the challenge is to oppose the historicism dominating literary studies by working out empirically and justifying theoretically a theory of general rules and laws governing the construction of narrative prose. The Formalists, too, taking their polemical stance, incurred the basic danger of such typological systems, which abstract their general principles and raise them to absolutes at the expense of the individual, concrete artistic system and of literary evolution. But their method had the advantage, first, that the very term device presupposed an application and an effect, and thus tended less toward isolation and stasis than the term type, and, second, that the terms defamiliarization or differential quality, which were basic to the entire system, inevitably incorporated the evolutionary factor. For the Formalists, therefore, despite their explicit turning away from historicism and as a consequence of their method itself, the necessity arose to combine synchrony and diachrony and to present the theory of narrative literature as the contiguity and continuity of such systems. This made it difficult to bring the presentation to a systematic conclusion, but it also kept the system open to the evolutionary facts of literature.

In contrast to the ahistorical typologies of narration, Walter Benjamin attempted, shortly after Eikhenbaum issued his call, to use the historical conditions and transformations of narrative as the very basis of a narrative theory; he even chose the same point of departure: Leskov. Benjamin's essay "The Storyteller: Reflections on the Work of Nikolai Leskov" appeared in 1936, about a decade after Eikhenbaum's article on Leskov.[90] The parallels are so numerous that one might at first suspect that Benjamin's piece derives directly from Eikhenbaum's, especially because Benjamin's direct contact with Russia (via the Muscovite stage director Asja Lacis) and his collaboration on the Soviet Encyclopedia occurred in the very years when Eikhenbaum was working on his article on Leskov. Shortly after that article appeared, Benjamin visited the Soviet Union (winter 1926–27). Apparently he did not begin to read Leskov intensively until just after that journey, although the occasion of his study was primarily the appearance of a German edition of Leskov's work.[91] I have not, however, been able to establish any direct connection between Benjamin and Eikhenbaum, or any direct knowledge on the former's part of the pertinent Formalist writings. Rather, there is much to suggest that two kindred spirits recognized Leskov's exemplary significance for the problem of narrative—and particularly for the relation between oral and written narrative—and made him the subject of an essay.

For Benjamin, genuine narration presupposes that "wisdom" can be communicated on the basis of shared "experience." This prerequisite, however, was lost through the mutation of the "secular historical forces of production" and of social conditions. The very rise of the novel, a form of loneliness and frustration or, as Lukács terms it, of "transcendental homelessness,"[92] heralded the "decline of narrative." The new phenomenon of the press, which substituted "information" (as quickly forgotten as absorbed) for narrative (which "reminds"), hastened the process along, leading at the same time to a crisis of the novel. Leskov's place as one of the last great storytellers is possible because of his rich hoard of experience, which draws directly from the wisdom of the people.

At first it is notable and illuminating that Benjamin, whose interests are in the interrelations of cultural and social history, reaches results or formulations of problems similar to those of the Formalists, despite his completely dissimilar purpose and method. Like them, he recognizes the fundamental differences between oral narration and explicitly literary narrative forms. Like them, he does not take such forms for ahistoric alternatives, but rather as possibilities within a historical evolution of narrative itself. For him as for the Formalists, therefore, the influence of more recent bookish forms such as the novel on oral narrative, and of even more recent forms of publication on the story and the novel, assumes great importance. But Benjamin is more concerned with the macrostructures, Eikhenbaum with the microstructures of the evolutionary process. Benjamin draws his arc so wide—over centuries, even millennia—as to give the impression that after the primal age of genuine narrative a decline sets in, almost linear in its effect (though Benjamin meant it to have dialectic significance), whereas the Formalists were interested precisely in the continual, often rather short-term way orientations change: individual phases of bookish narrative literature are followed, as soon as their systems have grown automatic and exhausted themselves, by the reorientation to forms and devices of oral narrative, which, when they in turn become exhausted, give way to more bookish ones again.

Seen in this way, Leskov no longer appears as a late example of a genuine storyteller but rather as one of the great representatives of the *skaz* tradition, which is patterned on oral narrative and which had achieved dominance before him in Gogol and would achieve it again after him (notwithstanding the constantly increasing importance of the press) in postrevolutionary narrative prose. The revival of the tradition and its purpose at various dissimilar points in literary history cannot be understood as a simple return or a linear continuation, but as a "new construction from elements of the old." This fuller consideration of the microstructure of the evolutionary process and especially the factors of style and point of view that the term *skaz* includes prevents us from projecting Leskov the storyteller onto some ideal of unadulterated, primal oral narration. Unlike the Formalists, who were interested in the *skaz* more generally, Benjamin fails to consider that, by interposing the *skaz* narrator, Leskov identifies the shared experience and the manner in which it is shared as belonging specifically to that narrator. The special structure and effect of Leskov's storytelling rest precisely *not* on a "naïve relationship of the hearer to the teller,"[93] which according to Benjamin is fundamental to genuine oral storytelling, but on a non-naïve, refracted relationship of a reader (or auditor) to a narrator who, by the aid of particular techniques of style and point of view, is stylized to appear naïve.

We see again how easily insufficient attention to linguistic and stylistic aspects can lead to the failure to recognize or rightly to characterize literary-historical qualities, even in the case of a critic so interested in history, so well versed, and so aware of questions of narrative structure as Benjamin. But in this case, too—especially in this case—it would be wrong to pit the advantages of one method against the disadvantages of the other rather than to see how in both approaches advantages and disadvantages are mutually conditioned. By concentrating on the *skaz* in Leskov, the Formalists underrated fundamental traits of his tales that Benjamin, with his special approach, did discover, whether directly or by pointing up characteristic features of the tradition of oral narrative. Examples of such features are the importance of workmen and traveling folk as carriers of oral narrative[94] (it is no coincidence that Leskov has a particular fondness for them as *skaz* narrators), and the kinship of oral narration and the chronicle[95] (which, aside from the *skaz*, is Leskov's characteristic genre).[96] These two examples show that it is not simply a question of pointing out traits that have more to do with content or more to do with form, but of discovering the social and historical prerequisites for particular narrative structures. And in this point Benjamin's view has a distinct advantage, even if one has good grounds to criticize, in part or *in toto,* his way of attributing individual well-characterized cultural phenomena to particular changes in the conditions of production.[97]

9

The Formalist theory of literary evolution was not the application to literature of a general philosophy of history or of preconceived historical concepts. It developed out of the Formalists' basic hypotheses and their continuing discussions, was formulated with reference to individual problems, step by step, and was systematized only toward the end of the Formalist period. Tynyanov's article "On Literary Evolution" (1927), as the first explicit treatment of the theme, is a kind of summation of the discussions of the foregoing decade. To gain an understanding, therefore, of the significance of the Formalist conception of historic change in literature, it is best to reenact the process of gradual expansion and theorizing in various areas of application. The beginnings of the process are evident in what has already been discussed. Both in Shklovsky's premise of art as defamiliarization, and in the fundamental notion of the semantic shift, the factor of deviation and change prefigures the evolutionary aspect, at first not excluding extraliterary changes in habits and norms, then, increasingly, as a strictly intraliterary event. In the example of parody we have seen how Tynyanov's investigation of a work of art as a system showed the dependence of this system on the context of literary evolution, and how he stressed the constructive character of the evolutionary process, unlike Shklovsky, who presented it as more destructive.

In the following period Tynyanov, who along with Jakobson contributed most to articulating the Formalist theory of evolution, systematically developed what he had begun in his article on parody. If the work of art is understood to be not a sum of devices but a system of devices with functions specific to that system, it becomes necessary to refer each individual device to a synchronic system and to a diachronic one. For the specific function of each individual factor can be perceived and determined only if one views it, on the one hand, in relation to the other factors of the same system (the element's "synfunction"), and, on the other hand, grasps the specific application in the system as a deviation from the traditional applications of the same factor (the element's "autofunction").[98]

In this connection, the term *ustanovka* becomes central to Tynyanov's thinking. Jakobson had introduced it as a Russian equivalent to the German term *Einstellung*.[99] Like this German word, the Russian one can mean at once the orientation of one thing to something else, and the arrangement of all the parts within a system (corresponding to its external orientation). As the Formalists applied *ustanovka* to literature, it can designate both the intention of a work and the organization of its structure in accordance with this intention. It can also mean a general orientation as, for example, in Jakobson's definition of poetry as "nothing but an utterance organized with an intention toward expression."[100] It can also mean the attitude of a producer or perceiver of literature. Thus the usual translations— intention, orientation, set—render only part of what is meant. That Tynyanov associates *ustanovka* with intention is clear from his remark that what is often understood by the term is the intention an author pursues in his work. But he adds at once that the teleological aspect is something he wants to avoid.[101]

For Tynyanov, it is only through *ustanovka* that the work as a functional system also becomes a system with an intentional reference, and that the historical or evolutionary aspect becomes a cardinal point of his general theory. He distinguishes three levels of the intentional relation: (1) Every factor of a work of literary art has an intentional relation to the complete work of art as a system. (2) This system has an intentional relation to the system of literature and literary evolution. (3) Literature and literary evolution have, through language, which is both the medium of literary creation and the medium of social communication, an intentional relation to the entire human environment in its historical and social transformations.[102]

On all three levels, but especially on the second one, the reference from the part to the whole is often made indirectly, through the mediation of style and genre. The author, who produces the work, and the reader, who receives it, relate the individual work, its elements, and their organization to definite, familiar traditions of style and conventions of genre, either because the work at hand confirms them or because it violates or defamiliarizes them. Only against this backdrop—or by this process of mediation—can the specific construction of the work, the synfunction of the elements that depends on it, and its effect on the autofunction be properly perceived. By such a confirmation or violation of generic norms, the individual work and its reception alter the canon of the genre and become a factor in the evolution of the genre itself and its relation to other genres. For Formalism the phenomenon of genre becomes an indispensable aspect of the analysis both of individual works and of literary evolution. It thus moves to the center of Formalist evolutionary theory and the Formalists' literary-historical investigations, both of which are largely devoted to questions of function and tradition of genres, of the relation of genre structure to stylistic intention, and of the changing hierarchy of genres and its connection with the change of stylistic traditions.

The characteristic Formalist conception of genre has been discussed in connection with Shklovsky's essay on *Tristram Shandy* and in view of the genre of the novel. What Shklovsky outlined, Tynyanov formulated explicitly, incorporating it into a system. For him the genre, like the individual work of art, is a system of definite, functionally coordinated devices; it is marked by distinctive dominants and a particular intention or *ustanovka*. Unlike the individual work of art, which always represents the individual concretization of such a system, the genre exists and is effective only as a reference system, whether because on the basis of correspondences between several representative works certain organizational principles are regarded as intrinsic to it, or because the laws of its organization have already been defined in descriptive or normative poetics.[103]

In "The Ode as Oratorical Genre" (1922) Tynyanov used the history of this genre in Russia to demonstrate the close, but constantly shifting, reciprocal effect between generic structures and stylistic intentions.[104] For Lomonosov, he wrote, what determined the organization of the genre was the linguistic orientation to solemn, emotive delivery—the oratorical stylistic intention. This stylistic intention, being a linguistic intention, on the one hand pointed beyond the realm of the purely literary. (The orientation to delivery in a large hall still exerted a noticeable effect in Lomonosov's work.) On the other hand, as a principle of construction, it determined the poetic organization of the genre and the specific functions of individual devices within the system. But once the genre has been organized in this fashion, there is danger lest it become automatic, so the structure of the system must be reorganized and the functions of devices redistributed, in order to achieve the same intention (emotional uplift via direct address). Or, the linguistic and stylistic intention of the genre can alter. The younger classicist Sumarokov, for example, aimed not at pathetic emotionalizing but rational *clarté;* in the service of this new intention he opposed Lomonosov's conception of the ode with his own. In the ensuing period the scale of variations ranged from further regrouping and functional revamping to satiric defamiliarization and direct parody. Thus the genre of the ode was able to assume functions earlier exercised by other genres, and, conversely, the oratorical stylistic intention of the ode as Lomonosov practiced it could later pass over to other genres. Similarly, a completely forgotten genre could be rediscovered by later generations and brought to new eminence, either because the intention that was dominant before has gained new significance in the later historic context or because a formerly secondary feature of the genre has, by reason of a new timeliness, become the real dominant.

The intentions and criteria that originally determined the formation of a genre can recede or even disappear in the course of its development. Therefore, a "logical classification of a genre by one criterion" is, Tomashevsky writes, "inappropriate, and must be replaced by a descriptive historical one."[105] This does not rule out the abstraction of a general criteria, but such criteria must be so general that they cannot, in themselves, completely characterize the inherent evolution of a specific genre nor its relation to other genres. It is sufficient to adduce the most difficult example, which is also the most characteristic and the one the Formalists studied most often: the novel.

The classification of the novel as, for example, a story of lovers' adventures is valid for certain types of novels and for certain periods, but totally inadequate for others. As the few examples already discussed show, it is not even possible to base the genre more generally on the central role of the hero or the dominance of plot (*syuzhet*), since notable representatives of the genre and pivotal moments in its evolution are marked by the erosion of the hero or the plot. If we wish to reduce all conceptions of the novel to a single common denominator, we are left with E. M. Forster's famous remark, extending the definition of Abel Chevalley, that a novel is "any fictitious prose work over 50,000 words."[106] But that transforms the characterization of a genre into the "seemingly trivial, but extremely important, distinction between short and long forms of the art of narrative."[107] In the Formalist conception of genre as a historical reference system, however, the erosion of plot or hero, being a deviation from genre conventions, can be a genre criterion. Furthermore, the relationship of short and long forms in the historical evolution of the genre can be understood as synchronous rivalry or periodic alternation of different dominants. Eikhenbaum followed this line in his essays on *skaz,* as did Shklovsky in his studies on the relation between plot-oriented and plotless narrative prose. They showed how phases in which the plot-oriented long form of the novel developed and dominated were followed by a turning away from this automatized form to short and plotless forms that permitted greater emphasis on narration as a linguistic process. K. Skipina considered the conspicuous dominance of short forms in the output of Russian Sentimentalism (despite its enthusiasm for the sentimental novel of Western Europe) as the result of the Karamzin school's demands for linguistic and stylistic reform, novelty of style being easier to test and more striking to see in shorter, fully stylized models than in the long form of the novel, whose construction is so complicated and plot-oriented.[108]

The dominance of different forms in successive periods does not exclude their coexistence and reciprocal effect in the same period. This is true both for the synchrony of short and long forms and for the synchrony of genres in general. As in analyzing individual works the Formalists investigated not only the synchronous aspect (the only one to be considered in work-immanent interpretations) but also diachronic interrelations, so in the theory and analysis of genres they give full weight not only to the diachronic process of evolution (which histories of genre tend to concentrate on in order to establish a genre's immanent evolution) but also to the synchronous hierarchy of genres. And as the individual work, diachronically considered, points beyond itself to the overarching system of the genre and its evolution, so the genre, considered synchronically, points beyond itself to the overarching system of the literary epoch or period.

For the Formalists the epoch, too, is a system with a characteristic intention (*ustanovka*) and corresponding dominants. Genres particularly suited to expressing this intention advance to the head of the hierarchy of genres and become the dominant ones of the epoch. These may be brand-new genres, or they may be genres with a rich tradition, now restructured to accord with the new basic intention. In the 1820s, for example, the old genre of the heroic poem becomes, in the version of the Byronic poem, the dominant genre of Russian Romanticism; some twenty years later the *ocherk*, earlier known as a satiric sketch of manners or essay, becomes, in the version of the physiological *ocherk*, the dominant genre of the so-called natural school. These are only two of the examples studied in monographs within the Formalist circle.[109] It is important to note that the very term dominant takes into account the "coexistence of the contemporaneous and the noncontemporaneous."[110] Genres that have been replaced in their dominant position in the hierarchy, or that are not even retained in the new canon supplanting that of the preceding epoch, can continue to exist and remain productive—whether as collateral lines to which the primary movement again and again makes polemical and other reference, or as undercurrents neglected by the representative authors, critics, and reading public, but which can always be taken up anew as soon as the principal line itself begins to run down, losing its effect and its appeal.

This is true both of individual genres and stylistic traditions and of whole literary schools:

> Every new school in literature is a kind of revolution, something like the appearance of a new class. But of course this is only an analogy. The conquered line is not destroyed; it does not cease to exist. It is simply driven from the crest and dives under; it can reemerge at any time, for it remains a constant pretender to the crown. The situation is further complicated by the fact that the new sovereign is usually no pure restorer of the earlier forms, but rather bears traits of other, more recent schools, even traits inherited, though now relegated to a subservient role, from its predecessor on the throne.[111]

All of the Formalists agree with this thesis of Shklovsky, which Eikhenbaum cites in his *Theory of the Formal Method* (1927), even if Tynyanov speaks of sons in opposition to their fathers preferring their grandfathers[112] while Shklovsky regards the succession from uncle to nephew as more characteristic (that is, renewal via recollection of a "collateral line").[113] All such relationship patterns are of course only analogies and, as such, must be handled with care; filiation always being a construction and self-justification by the descendents, the fathers or adopted fathers they track down are not necessarily to be held responsible for them even as illegitimate offspring. What remains crucial is that in every case the changes are seen both as a breaking off and a picking up—that, to quote Tynyanov once again, "literary tradition or succession" is understood not as a "straight line" but as the "destruction of an old entity" and a "new construction from old elements." Thus, in a strict sense the Formalist concept of evolution is as distinct from the notion of organic growth as it is from the notion of revolution.

When Tynyanov speaks of a "new construction from old elements," it does not mean that he sees evolution solely in the constant reshuffling of a fixed stock of devices, forms, and genres. For him the succession of systems and schools is not only a demarcation within literature but also the drawing of new boundaries between literary and extraliterary uses of language. In some periods, because of the attitude (*ustanovka*) of a ruling school, certain linguistic forms, including whole genres, that before (and, often enough, soon thereafter) were regarded as nonliterary, can be incorporated into the school's genre system, and even achieve dominance. Tynyanov explains this with reference to the letter as a vivid and important example, showing how an extraliterary genre becomes a "Literary Fact." Judgment about what is already to be regarded as literature and what is not yet to be so regarded thus depends on the immediate organization of the literary system in its immediate evolutionary phase. The questions, "What is literature? What is genre?" with which Tynyanov starts his article "The Literary Fact"[114]—he answers by pointing out their evolutionary character and the inappropriateness of all ahistoric definitions. Just as every device, every work, every genre, and every literary school can act and be grasped as factors only within an evolutionary process, so too can literature as a whole.

Earlier than Tynyanov and more systematically than Shklovsky, Roman Jakobson explicated the role of schools for literary evolution and the problem of their self-interpretation and interpretation by others, using Realism as his example.[115] The Russian debate on Realism has been hindered by the compounding of Realism as a historical school with Realism as a typological concept, the result then being proclaimed the norm of all true art.[116] Jakobson, conversely, makes a sharp distinction between the literary school of the nineteenth century (Realism C) and the claim, advanced by most authors and schools, of portraying what is in fact real (Realism A). The latter intention, he writes, aims in two directions. As a claim to being true to reality it is oriented toward extraliterary reality. This claim can be made good only through certain literary devices. In the opinion of the young, the devices and construction principles of the old are inadequate, despite the fact that the old in their day made the same claim, which meanwhile has lost its persuasiveness. A new artistic system is needed to meet the constantly reiterated demand for the presentation of what is real. The intention with respect to extraliterary reality must translate into a new orientation within literary tradition, only thereby becoming a factor of intraliterary evolution.

Some years later Boris Tomashevsky indirectly developed these thoughts of Jakobson's and the theses of Shklovsky when he distinguished within literary evolution two dissimilar basic attitudes toward the palpability of literary forms and devices.[117] One strives to lay the device bare so as to accentuate its intrinsic significance. The other, conversely, strives, by motivating devices in particular ways, to minimize or conceal them as far as possible in order to stress the reference to extraliterary reality. When the Formalists speak of motivated art, they mean art of this latter type.

The term motivation, which we have encountered in connection with Shklovsky, thus acquired a new meaning and was further differentiated. Tomashevsky distinguished three kinds (or intentions) of motivation. The first is the "compositional motivation," in which class he also includes, for example, the deliberate misleading of the reader in the mystery novel. The second type, which he called "realistic motivation," serves to make the material introduced into a work seem likely. He stresses that the notion of what is accepted as likely and realistic depends partly on the construction itself and partly on the prevailing literary and extraliterary conventions. Precisely for this reason, he argues, the third type, "aesthetic motivation," is the decisive one, because the particular aesthetic position of authors, schools, and epochs determines what themes and forms are deemed real, or artistic. The quarrel between old and new schools, the actual motivating factor of literary evolution, usually takes off precisely from this last point. Whereas the young reject the canon of the old as being neither real nor artistic, the old deny the aesthetic character of the new.

As in this respect Tomashevsky agrees with Jakobson's conception of literary evolution and of Realism, so Jakobson for his part later investigated varying positions with respect to the palpability of devices, tying them in with the distinction between metaphoric and metonymic kinds of expression.[118] Where semantic shifts, the exposure of devices, or constant interplay of several levels of reality is intended, he says, metaphor dominates; if inconspicuous or flowing transitions are the aim, metonymy does. One should consider, therefore, whether in this respect metaphor is not more suited to lyric poetry, metonymy more suited to prose. This state of affairs makes it clear why Realism as a particularly highly motivated art was to a great extent a school of prose, and of emphatically metonymic prose at that.

Even if the Formalists' reflections of this type remained for the most part hypothetical, and if most exponents of the school were far less interested in motivated art than in defamiliarizing art that deliberately lays bare its devices, by indicating the different attitudes toward palpability and by taking a sharp look at the inner connections between the realistic intention and the motivation of stylistic devices of literary schools, Formalism pointed out new paths of understanding, especially with regard to Realism. Because Realism was soon thereafter elevated to the status of sacrosanct artistic norm in the Soviet

Union, while in the West the contributions of Formalism became known only sporadically or much later, many of the Formalists' suggestions were not paid attention to or elaborated until more recently. *Styles and Periods* (1964), by the Zagreb scholars Aleksandar Flaker and Zdenko Škreb, represents a remarkable attempt to characterize periods as stylistic complexes with distinct motivations and in this way to separate out Romanticism, Realism, and Modernism, is based directly on theories and findings of Russian Formalism, and has a special introductory chapter devoted to "The 'Formal Method' and Its Fate."[119] And in a German monograph on Russian Realism (1967), Dmitri Czizhevsky, too, works with the term motivation in defining Realism, stressing, with a direct reference to Jakobson, the "turning to metonymic stylistic means" and asserting that "Realism is the first emphatically antimetaphorical style in the history of European literature."[120]

One important aspect of Jakobson's article on Realism expands the concept of evolution far beyond what Shklovsky and Tynyanov propose. Jakobson stresses that the changing conception of what is considered real or realistic depends not only on the polemical intentions of authors and schools as they oppose their predecessors but also on the conceptions or expectations with which readers approach the works of different schools and systems. Consequently, in addition to the claim of authors and schools to be realistic (Jakobson's Realism A) the aspect of aesthetic perception emerges, of the readers' or beholders' accepting a work as realistic (Jakobson's Realism B). But what applies to the reader must also apply to every later critic or scholar—with all the concomitant historico-hermeneutic problems this implies. If one says that Tynyanov proceeds from an investigation of literary evolution to the evolution of the concept of literature itself, Jakobson's path leads in the final analysis to an evolutionary, historically relativized conception of literary scholarship. The Formalists never denied this. They were well aware of it and pointed out again and again that the categories and above all the questions with which they approached the works of earlier periods were neither identical to those of the periods themselves nor timeless in their validity, but accorded with their own, historically determined, dissimilar situation.[121] This insight was the premise for the combination of literary history, literary theory, and the practical criticism that was an immediate stimulus to contemporary Russian writing. This combination was deeply characteristic of the Formalist school's purpose and effect.

But what in practice could exert so stimulating an effect, in theory imposed fundamental methodological problems that the Formalists did not pursue. Although Jakobson, in his early article, considered the question of the historic contingency of one's own position in judging the production of others, later studies of the Formalists on the problem of evolution concentrate more and more definitely on the succession of systems and schools and the principles governing that succession, without reflecting on the historical character of their own school and system or presenting it as a part (and the basis) of their theories and analyses.

Formalism's overall attitude toward history and historicity remained vague and contradictory, despite the fact that the historic dimension (in the sense of intraliterary evolution) was a central topic for the school. It is not surprising, therefore, that even judges who hail the contribution of the Formalists as an innovative achievement raise objections on this point. And it is telling that some complain that Formalism is too historical, and others that it is not historical enough.

10

Complaint about excessive historical relativity is voiced chiefly when commentators are attempting to establish a kind of bond between Slavic Formalism or Structuralism and Anglo-American New Criticism. René Wellek, in whose biography the two movements are, as it were, conjoined, advanced, during the 1930s and especially in the *Theory of Literature* (1949) he wrote with Austin Warren, the opinion that, despite all due regard for historical change, it is imperative to maintain the timelessness of certain categories and values.[122] Erlich, sometimes with direct reference to Wellek, seems to take a similar position in the second, systematic and critical part of his book on Formalism. First, however, he presents the historic consciousness of For-

malism as an advantage over New Criticism: "The 'canonization' of change made the Russian Formalists much more
history-minded than was the case with the bulk of their Western
counterparts. Not all the Anglo-American 'New Critics' may
share T. S. Eliot's notion of literature as a simultaneous order.
But most of them are ostensibly less concerned with literary
change than with what remains unchanged. The Slavic Formalists had, if anything, too much historical sense."[123]

What constituted "too much" is not persuasively demonstrated. When Erlich goes on to say that the Formalist theory of
evolution as defamiliarization and deviation can explain the
fact of change but not its direction, the point is valid—in later
work the Formalists made it themselves—but this suggests too
little rather than too much historical consciousness. The criterion that separates the New Critics from the Formalists is far
more likely to be found in the circumstance that for New Criticism the aesthetic norm is paramount, for Formalism, the deviation from the norm; and further, that the Formalists,
because of their critical relativism, take their own norms to be
historically relative, whereas the New Critics who addressed
these matters postulate the necessity and possibility of absolute
standards. But this postulate of New Criticism is a disputed one
and little suited as a basis for criticizing the historic consciousness of the Formalists. Understandable as the effort is to save
the criteria of one's own artistic judgment from the danger of
complete relativity, this aim cannot be reached by drawing a
line between literature, which is historically conditioned, and
the position of the critic or scholar, which is thought to hold
itself aloof from historical conditions. The hermeneutic circle is
not dissolved simply by being treated as the Gordian knot.

In 1967 Hans Robert Jauss attacked this position from
the viewpoint of historical hermeneutics.[124] He discusses Formalism thoroughly, praising its accomplishments (including its
contributions toward understanding the inherent historic
change of literature), but, unlike Erlich, he claims its theory of
evolution is insufficiently historic and cites two objections. The
first concerns the hermeneutic distance of historic mediation
between the work and its later readers, among whom is the
literary scholar. Rather than ignore this distance, he reasons,

one must make it the starting point of a new concept of literary scholarship as literary history oriented toward the aesthetics of reception (*Rezeptionsästhetik*). It should start from the premise that every literary work is conceived with a view to particular, historically determined expectations and is always received under the aspect of ever new expectations and questions, changing throughout history, so that the conception, effect, and study of a literary work can proceed only in the form of a continuing dialogue of "questions and answers" and as an approximation or (in the sense of Gadamer's hermeneutics) as a "merging of horizons" of expectation, an objectifiable "reference system of expectations" being deducible "for every work in the historic moment of its appearance from a previous understanding of its genre, from the form and theme of known works, and from the contrast of poetic and practical language."[125] As his words suggest, Jauss does not intend to set up a direct counterposition to Formalism, but instead to pick up critically and continue systematically at the point where Formalism had been content to confess its own historicity rather than going on to draw the methodological conclusions, one of which is the understanding—which Jürgen Habermas put in general terms and Jauss articulated for literary scholarship—that the empiric or nomological concept of theory and method cannot simply be transferred to the social sciences and humanities, because they are concerned with the historically conditioned interpretation of historic phenomena and therefore require their own historico-hermeneutic methodology.

The second aspect of Jauss's critique—the more specifically historic one that complements the more specifically hermeneutic one—has to do with the Formalists' concentration on purely intraliterary evolution and their neglect of its connection with general history.[126] Here, too, Jauss is chiefly concerned with the factor of receptional aesthetics and its general historic conditions with regard to the relationship of literature and life, of aesthetic perception and moral effect. In contrast, most Marxist critics of Formalism focus on the general historical conditions for literary production, in the sense of the social and political position and intentions of individual authors, schools, and so on. The common thread is the charge that Formalism inappropriately isolates literature and the inherent evolution of its forms from life as it is lived and its historical processes of change. This reproach is well founded and serious, so let us first cite arguments in favor of Formalism, as, in their own time, the Formalists themselves did. Formalism from early on stressed that as a special science of literature it set out to investigate only what is literary about literature, its *literariness*, and not to study it in all its historical implications. Second, the Formalists repeatedly insisted that a distinction be made between literary evolution and the genesis of individual works. They granted that extraliterary causes could be of great importance for the inception and intention of a work (one need only recall Shklovsky's discourse on Bely and anthroposophy), but, they argued, it is not the task of literary scholarship to explain literature from such causes but to set forth the position of a work thus generated or caused within the system of literature and its evolution and to determine the work's function in that system.[127] Third, they distinguished various, partly intersecting levels of action or "series,"[128] and conceived of literature and literary evolution as one of many such series. The connecting medium, according to the Formalists, is the linguistic series, because it belongs both to the literary and extraliterary domains. By differentiating between practical and poetic language, the Formalists made language the point of departure for their theory and analytic practice; for them the linguistically mediated connection between literature and extraliterary life was a given.

The argument that literary scholarship deals only with the specifically literary does not invalidate the fact that, not only in terms of its inception but also of its intention and effect, this literariness itself is organized with a view to extraliterary reality. This interrelation is one of its most substantial features. If we ignore or make light of it, we cannot even grasp literature *as* literature more than partially. The Formalists had seen this (Jakobson, for instance, in his definitions of Realism), but in their theory and study of literature they usually disregarded it, whereas Formalist linguistics developing toward Structuralism systematically inquired into the connection and differentiation of specifically literary and extraliterary phenomena.

Although all references to reality in literature are conveyed through the medium of language, consideration of the series of language alone is not enough to characterize the interaction between literature and the extraliterary reality whence it originates, which it is directed to, which it suggests, and in which it is received and understood and has its effect. True, the Formalists repeatedly assured that the consideration of the series of language, being the "nearest to hand," could and would only be the bridge to the more remote ones; but in the framework of Formalism this remained an unfulfilled promise. However, many often fundamental shifts in literary tradition cannot be explained except as responses to definite extraliterary situations and changes, and not as a simple reaction to the automatization of previous literary forms. The objection that it is not the task of literary scholarship to explain such processes, only to describe them, merely begs the question. For the description of dissimilar contiguous and successive literary systems as an evolutionary concatenation and as the result of defamiliarization contains explanations that call for further justification. Persuasive as it is, the Formalist thesis that literary evolution is not organic development, no straight line from fathers to sons, it remains doubtful whether the moment of shift can always be explained only by the age of the fathers, that is, the system's condition with respect to automatization. And it remains unclear why this particular uncle or grandfather and not some other one becomes a cardinal factor under this particular aspect rather than some other one, why this particular extraliterary phenomenon and not some other one is suddenly elevated to the status of a literary fact, displacing the boundary between literature and extraliterary life in a particular direction.

Let us take as an example Tynyanov's article "The Literary Fact." It takes a polemical stance against the characterization, then widespread in Russia, of Sentimentalism as a school of bathos and weepiness. Tynyanov reinterprets it as a completely linguistic, literary reaction against the poetic system of Classicism, which was already automatized. In this context, he writes, the canonization of the extraliterary form of the letter as a literary fact of increasing dominance played an important role. Although this makes sense, it does not answer the legitimate question why, when writers turned away from the high rhetorical style of classicism, they turned particularly to the letter. (After all, the epistle, too, was part of the Classicists' canon of genres, whereas canonizing other forms Classicism had regarded as unequivocally extraliterary would have made possible a far sharper defamiliarization and opposition.) Negation alone is not enough; the counterposition must be designated as a position, in this case the desire for a personal, individual point of view and way of writing, which the form and style of the private letter especially satisfied. This turns a mere description of the phenomenon into a historical explanation. But it belongs to the explanation for the choice of this particular direction that, during the extraordinarily long dominance of Classicism in the strictly poetic area, a gradual and fundamental change in political, social, and cultural matters had taken place (and continued), moving the individual and his right to individual development to the forefront. Only under these general historic conditions did it become clear how obsolete the Classicist canon had become, which allowed the new concept of Sentimentalism (including its cultivation of the intimate epistolary style) to become the new, dominant system. This accords with the fact that in the writings both of the Western European models for Russian Sentimentalism (such as Rousseau) and of their Russian followers (Radishchev, for example), the new direction is articulated both as the emotional presentation of personal feelings and as a protest against sociopolitical suppression of individual claims.

The point, once again, is not simply to juxtapose cause and effect but to understand the relationship of general historical change and specifically literary shifts as one of mutual interaction. The literature of Sentimentalism did not simply mirror sociopolitical processes, nor was it merely a reaction to them. It was an essential factor in the changing social consciousness that was responsible for evolutionary or revolutionary changes in political and social conditions. That is why political institutions reacted so strongly to the challenge presented by this tendency in Sentimentalist literature—for example, by passing a death sentence against Radishchev and then sending him into exile. This event was but the most striking symptom of a general suppression of the sociopolitical branch of the Sentimentalist school in Russia, so that only the other, emotional and lachrymose, branch could develop, which hastened the automatization and dethronement of the school as a whole. Thus, this example of Russian Sentimentalism shows how inextricably certain literary and general historical developments are bound together and makes it clear that they must be considered in their interconnectedness. This cannot, however, be accomplished by substituting the extreme of a purely form-immanent concept of evolution for the opposite extreme of a direct derivation of literary forms and formal transformations from the sociopolitical conditions and their changes in the course of history.

This problem, which was played out as the confrontation of Formalism and Marxism, sealed the fate of the Formalist school. The facts, relationships, and results of the historic quarrel between the Russian Formalists and the Marxists, who had acceded to power, need not be gone into here. Erlich has described and explained them in a manner that tries to do justice to both sides.[129]

Readers less familiar with the situation may be surprised that in the very place and at the very time that Marxism was becoming the ruling doctrine, a concept of literary scholarship that made light of questions about the connections between literature and society, and actually denied their relevance for literary studies, could develop and even for a short while set the tone. This contradiction can easily lead one to believe mistakenly that the concept and effect of Russian Formalism can be understood as a blank contradiction to Marxism, which was in power, as a mere reaction to it. But the restriction to purely formal aspects was most marked in the early stages of the formal school, thus before the Soviet takeover, and it was directed against all tendencies to treat and interpret literature not as a verbal art but as a medium for conveying extraliterary factors, whether such tendencies were of Marxist or non-Marxist provenance, whether the perspective was sociopolitical or, for example, religious. And the gradual opening to questions concerning the relationship of literature and life occurred initially neither under the pressure of ruling Marxism nor as an accomodation to it, but as the consequence of the Formalists' own methods and the discussions within their school.

To be sure, this changed in the mid-twenties, when Marxist criticism, backed by political power, demanded that the Formalists acknowledge the sociopolitical contingency of literature. Erlich has noted that it was not least as a reaction to this pressure and as a diversionary tactic that in the second half of the decade the Formalists turned increasingly to topics that present a kind of conjunction of literature with the general economic, political, and social conditions. Such topics were the sociohistorical conditions and societal functions of writing as a profession and of particular publishing forms and media (such as magazines and the daily press), and the emergence of new classes of readers and of "literature for the masses," written especially to satisfy their needs. In the last years of Formalism these problems played an important part in many publications, but even more particularly in Formalist seminars and research groups.[130]

However interesting and informative this area is for the literary scholar, the historian, or the sociologist, and however remarkable the material the Formalists produced and the insights they attained presenting and describing the literary environment in this sense, it is not a sufficient answer to the basic question about the relationship of "Literature and 'Life.'"[131] A confrontation between Formalism and Marxism could have contributed enormously to the solution, for the question of the connection between literature and society, and hence of the connection between literary evolution and general history, which the Formalists had as far as possible evaded, was at the center of Marxist literary theory. But the prerequisite for any such rapprochement, or even for an ongoing, mutually stimulating confrontation, would have been the willingness to discuss critically the foundation of both methodologies. Until the mid-twenties, with a handful of Marxist critics, including ranking party officials, still willing and able to justify their criticisms of Formalism objectively and to discuss some of their own positions critically, there seemed at least to be certain tendencies in this direction. In the polemical anti-Formalism campaign at the end of the decade, even that disappeared.[132] By then Russian

Marxists had become so dogmatic in their interpretation of the doctrine of base and superstructure, especially with respect to social and historical inquiry, that serious analysis of these problems was impossible. But without such a discussion of the basics, any combination of Formalist and Marxist methods had to be an unsatisfactory compromise. In fact at the time and later a few Marxist literary scholars took over certain elements of Formalist theory, or at least of its analytic technique, and the growing attention to artistic and formal mastery in Soviet Marxist literary history as it was written in the following years was among other things a reaction to insights or challenges of Formalism, which was officially proscribed.[133] But basically such appendices have as little to do with real Formalism and its crucial insights as the Formalist contributions to the subject of the literary environment have to do with Marxism.

In the past few decades Marxism has been attempting to pursue the critical discussion of the premises of its aesthetic theory that it refused to undertake during its polemical altercation with Formalism. A first step in this direction, which had important ideological repercussions, was Stalin's "Marxism and the Questions of Language Studies."[134] It gave greater independent weight to the superstructure as against the economic and social base, opening the way, even beyond the particular sphere of linguistic and literary studies, for a critical reexamination within Marxism of the relationship between being and consciousness in society. With regard to a rapprochement between Marxism and Formalism, or to the methodological premises of both aesthetic theories, those Marxist contributions deserve special attention that rather than carrying on the immediate quarrel about art as the "mirror of social circumstances" take a step back and inquire into the Marxist conception of reality. The Prague philosopher Karel Kosík, for example, makes the point that the "fundamental social reality," which includes economic circumstances, is "human praxis" itself, in which "human consciousness [acts] both in a registrant and projective capacity," thus altering the circumstances.[135] He argues that the very same is true for art as a specific modality of such praxis as an active "reality within reality" of social circumstances, and not merely as their mirror. Only this explains why

77

a work of art remains effective, both aesthetically and socially, when the historic circumstances that helped determine its genesis have long since changed. The "truth of the work" lies "not in the chronological situation, in the social contingencies, or in the historicity of circumstances," but rests on the "repeatability" of its reception as an ever new "realization of the relation of subject and object" under historically different social circumstances.[136]

Such a conception of Marxist aesthetics signals a clear departure from all Marxist literary theories based on the mirroring thesis, including that of Lukács. Far more than such theories, this one permits inquiry into Formalist tenets and categories, including the Formalist concept of literature as something that is made to produce an effect.[137] But as a Marxist theory, and unlike the evolutionary theory of Formalism, it still links art—because of its nature as socially active praxis—inextricably with social reality in all its historicity.[138] And, going beyond both Formalism *and* traditional Marxist aesthetic theory, it emphasizes that this historicity of art must also be understood precisely as the continuing effect of the work under constantly changing historic circumstances. In this last point Kosík's view approaches that of Jauss, who criticizes both Formalist and Marxist literary theory for insufficient attention to the aesthetics of effect in its special kind of social relatedness and historicity, and takes off from this dimension to develop his own concept of literary scholarship as a history of literature.

Although Jauss confronts Formalism directly, contemporary confrontation and debate usually proceed indirectly, with the later form of Structuralism in its several varieties taking the place of Formalism. Early Prague Structuralists, like Jan Mukařovský, had already evinced a greater interest in the social conditions and intentions of literature than the Russian Formalists had. In Czechoslovakia the tradition of Structuralism again became very lively and productive in the 1960s. A similar situation prevails in other Slavic countries, even the USSR, where there has been increasing reconsideration of Formalism. What is perhaps even more important is that after the Marxist theory of language was challenged (which was made possible in part by the appearance of Stalin's papers on linguistics), structural linguistics established itself rapidly. The discussion of structural methods, once begun in this area, spread to the ideologically more sensitive area of literature, partly as a direct resumption of the native line of Formalism, partly as an outline for a new structural poetics or concept of literary scholarship.[139] Because these revivals of Structuralism are taking place in a sphere of Marxist dominance, the association of Structuralist and Marxist modes of inquiry is given a priori. The chances for a debate not based on crude polemics and vituperation but on an objective inquiry into the methodological similarities and methodological differences and their causes seem far better now than during the original confrontation between Russian Formalism and Marxism or during any part of the Stalinist era.

Clear proof that the conflict between Structuralism and Marxism is not dictated simply by the dominion of Marxism in the Eastern countries, but is suggested by the subject matter itself, is the fact that Western exponents of Structuralism are engaged in a lively discussion of the same problems. The more searchingly Structuralism inquired beyond the specific structures and structural types of individual systems or fields of life into the structural correspondences between them and the conditions that make them possible, the more important the problem of the social function and contingency of such systems became—for instance, the problem of the connection between literary and social structural types and changes. But these questions had long been important for the literary and aesthetic theory of Marxism, which thus could become as interesting for Structuralism as, conversely, Structuralism with such an orientation could become for Marxism. French Structuralism is a particularly illuminating example because of the multiplicity of its roots, tendencies, and methods. On the one hand, non-Marxist Structuralists (like Claude Lévi-Strauss) have endeavored to trace the social correspondences of artistic structures.[140] On the other hand, Marxists (like Lucien Goldmann) have tried to salvage the mirror theory by interpreting art not as the mirror of sociohistorical contents but as the mirror of sociohistorical structures (within the structure of the work of art).[141] Others inquire into the compatibility of both concepts, whether

79

in the context of general methodological definitions of Structuralism, like Roland Barthes',[142] or as a special topic, as in L. Sebag's *Marxism and Structuralism.*[143]

My aim in this introduction to the subject is not to answer the specific question whether and in what way Marxism and Structuralism or Marxism and Formalism are reconcilable. It is to demonstrate that since the time of Formalism, directly or indirectly picking up where the formal method left off, attempts have been undertaken from various positions to supplement critically the findings of the Russian Formalists in an area they paid too little attention to: the connection between literature (as production and reception) and society in its changes through history. The development of the formal method pointed in this direction. And just before the enforced termination of the Formalist school, in their jointly written theses of 1928, Jakobson and Tynyanov, looking back into the past and forward toward the future, very clearly marked out this path for the Formalist program.[144]

One might disagree over whether to regard these theses as a late summation of Russian Formalism or as an early program of European Structuralism, both because of the program itself and because at the time they were written Jakobson had been living in Czechoslovakia for years, and had been one of the cofounders of the Prague Structuralist Circle. But for reasons noted at the beginning of this part, it seems neither possible nor appropriate to draw a sharp boundary. From the early writings of Shklovsky, to Eikhenbaum's "Review and Prospect" of 1925, until Jakobson and Tynyanov's program of 1928, the inclination and ability retrospectively to summarize past findings and critically to revise them, thus formulating a new program, was characteristic of the method and history of Russian Formalism. However, this program, as a last critical self- and reappraisal, does indicate most clearly how, in the scant decade and a half of its existence, Russian Formalism had developed toward Structuralism.

In the realm of synchronic study Tynyanov and Jakobson see the decisive progress within Formalist linguistics and literary scholarship in the replacement of a cumulative notion of form ("the mechanical agglomeration of material" or mere "classification of phenomena" that goes along with it) by the "concept of system or structure."[145] In the area of diachronic investigation into the "evolution of literature," the advance is the greater attention paid to the "functional point of view" of the literary devices and of the "literary and extraliterary material used in literature."[146] The most important experience gained, however, and the most important new demand, is the indispensable conjunction of synchrony and diachrony: "The opposition between synchrony and diachrony was an opposition between the concept of system and the concept of evolution; thus in principle it loses its importance as soon as we recognize that every system necessarily exists as an evolution, whereas, on the other hand, evolution is inescapably of a systematic nature."[147]

Thereby they arrive at the impasse, already discussed, of a "scholastic 'formalism,' "[148] strictly limited to intraliterary or intralinguistic phenomena or changes, which, although capable of indicating "the immanent laws of the history of literature and language" as well as determining "the character of each change in literary (linguistic) systems," cannot explain "the tempo of evolution or the chosen path of evolution." Therefore, "the question of a specific choice of path or at least of the dominant, can be solved only by means of an analysis of the correlation between the literary series and other historical series. This correlation (a system of systems) has its own structural laws, which must be submitted to investigation."[149]

But a "system of systems," spreading into the "series of actually existing structural types (types of structural evolution),"[150] is, in different ways, the theme of both Structuralism and of avant-garde Marxism—and of the debate between them. The analysis of the correlation between the literary series and other historical series (and the concomitant hermeneutic problems) is the subject of the more recent brand of historic literary scholarship with its orientation toward the aesthetics of reception. This program points to all of these, yet without anticipating them. What allows it to point ahead is the self-critical realization that the restriction of Russian Formalism, which in view of the historical conditions in which it developed was almost inevitable, to the immanent laws of the system of literature had to be expanded toward the correlation of the literary series with other historical series and an overarching "system of systems." But the program is ahead of many later developments by virtue of the Formalist insight that appears as a caveat in the conclusion of the whole program: "It would be methodologically fatal to consider the correlation of systems without taking into account the immanent laws of each system."[151]

Today, many decades after the writing of these theses and after the violent end of Russian Formalism as a school, neither of these views has lost any of its timeliness. They still strike to the heart of the contemporary debate of literary scholarship, warranting, indeed demanding, that this debate assimilate what Russian Formalism achieved, attempted, or sketched out as a program. It is part of the nature and importance of that movement's achievement that such assimilation can occur neither by mere recollection nor by mere adoption, but presupposes the critical willingness to test the findings, tenets, and questions of the formal method against our own methods and modes of inquiry, and conversely to test them against those of the Russian Formalists.

PART II

From Russian Formalism to Czech Structuralism

In discussing the significance of Czech Structuralism in the history of criticism, the question of its relation to Russian Formalism plays a crucial role.[1] Chronology and biographical data suggest that the Prague school should be regarded as an extension of Russian Formalism. In 1928 Roman Jakobson and Yury Tynyanov, leading Formalists, published in the Russian journal *Novy LEF* their theses on "Problems in the Study of Literature and Language," considered the summarizing and programmatic close of Russian Formalism, which shortly thereafter ceased to exist as an independent school.[2] By then, however, Jakobson had already been living and working in Czechoslovakia for years. Together with the Anglicist Vilém Mathesius, the linguist Bohuslav Havránek, and other scholars, he had founded the Prague Linguistic Circle in 1926.

At the First International Linguistic Congress at The Hague in 1928 theses for linguistic analysis were worked out by members of the Prague Circle (Mathesius, Jakobson, and Trubetskoy) and by representatives of the Geneva school (Séchehaye and Bally). For the First Congress of Slavic Philologists in Prague (1929), the members of the Circle presented a program of their own.[3] And like the breeding grounds of Russian Formalism before it—the Moscow Linguistic Circle, which Jakobson had started, and the Society for Research in Poetic Language (Opojaz) of Petersburg—the Prague Circle did not limit itself to purely linguistic problems. The intent was to interconnect linguistic and literary scholarship closely, to develop a new literary theory and methodology for literary scholarship in association with the findings and demands of modern linguistics. The conjunction was prefigured in Jakobson's writings in both areas.[4] Since the 1930s, however, the development of the Prague school's theory of literature and art, of its own poetics and aesthetics, progressed chiefly in the work of Jan Mukařovský, who elaborated suggestions from Formalism, combined them with other ideas, and modified and expanded them.

Thus Czech literary Structuralism (the only aspect I will consider) also picks up on the mode of inquiry, the tenets, and the findings of Russian Formalism. This connection was never seriously contested either by the Czech Structuralists or by other authors who have investigated these problems. There is disagreement—in some cases, direct opposition—only in judging the intensity, exclusivity, and significance of the connection.

René Wellek, who was a member of the Prague Linguistic Circle before emigrating to the United States, interprets the "literary theory and aesthetic of the Prague school" as an extension of Russian Formalism, denying the importance of native Czech influences.[5] Victor Erlich, too, characterizes Czech Structuralism as a direct continuation and "redefinition of Formalism."[6] The close ties between the schools are similarly stressed (though for different reasons)—indeed, it is claimed that they are almost indistinguishable—in polemics attacking "formalistic" approaches to literature in general.[7]

Accounts by the Czech Structuralists usually accent the importance of the native tradition, pointing out, above all, the parallel progress of two distinct traditions of Czech aesthetics and art criticism.[8] Both go back to the nineteenth century and arose in the debate between the adherents of the aesthetics of Hegel and the aesthetics of Herbart. Herbartism, at home in Prague ever since, led to the development of Czech aesthetics concerned with form-immanent problems (occasionally referred to as the Prague School of Formal Aesthetics[9]), which found expression around the turn of the century in the writings of Josef Durdík and Otokar Hostinský. Otokar Zich, a student of Hostinský and Mukařovský's predecessor in the Prague Chair for Aesthetics, modified this line decisively and extended it even before the founding of the Prague Linguistic Circle (independently of the development of Russian Formalism). Zich, coming not from linguistics and poetics but from music, establishes the idea of the work of art as form by "explicating the artistic form as an ensemble of conceived meanings." This emphasizes, on the one hand, the semantic aspect of the work of art and, on the other, its correlation with the subject who conceives it and his aesthetic experience as a "phenomenon of psychically constituted meanings." To this extent it may be said that Zich combines "formal analysis (gestalt analysis) with the empiric and psychological conception, and, above all, with a conception that at heart is already semantic."[10] If early Russian Formalism sought chiefly to find how a work of art is made,[11] for Czech formal aesthetics since Zich this question was closely linked with the question of its meaning and the (psychic) conditions for perception—notions that Zich's student Mukařovský and Czech Structuralism developed further.

The native form-oriented aesthetics also had an indirect effect. In the criticism of art and literature it encouraged concentration on problems of form and style, as in the outstanding work of such critics as F. X. Šalda, Arne Novák, and O. Fischer. Their activity immediately preceded the development of Czech Structuralism and accompanied it, which, together with the already mentioned tendencies in aesthetics, created a remarkably propitious climate for the reception and critical discussion of individual authors or entire schools whose interest centered on the work as form and aesthetic object. This favored the assimilation of Russian Formalism. It also favored such things as the debate with phenomenology as propounded by Edmund Husserl and Roman Ingarden and attention to the aesthetic philosophy of Broder Christiansen and Ernst Cassirer's *Philosophy of Symbolic Forms*.[12]

On the other hand, there was the tradition of Czech Hegelianism and of Czech Marxism, which arose from it. This tradition fostered interest in questions about the relationship between art and society, between literary history and general cultural or social history. This intellectual tradition, too, was represented by noted critics (such as Teige, Václavek, and Konrad), some of whom also intervened in the Czech reception of Russian Formalism and, especially in the 1930s, engaged in critical debate with Czech Structuralism as it developed.[13] In this context it should be remarked that Czech Marxism in the thirties, unlike Russian Marxism in the twenties (in its altercations with Formalism) and unlike Czech Marxism after 1948, was not yet the binding political philosophy. This facilitated open discussion and made it possible to accept or reject critical arguments by reason of their systematic validity rather than in order to make an outward show of conformity or in self-defense. Thus, this early dialogue with Czech Marxism impelled Mukařovský to broaden the scope of questions concerning the conditions of aesthetic perception beyond the structure of a work and the psychic state of the individual to the social collective; to fix the aesthetic norms and values in the social collective; and to investigate the aesthetic function in its interaction with other social functions.[14] This kind of systematic inquiry—which from Mukařovský's time on has marked the aesthetic theory and literary criticism of Czech Structuralism—into the social function of literature and into the social conditions of literary production and reception constitutes an especially conspicuous difference from the basic concept of Russian Formalism. In recent years especially, this difference has received greater attention and has been emphasized repeatedly in accounts of Czech Structuralism by the Structuralists themselves and by others. In Czechoslovakia in the late 1960s it provided the conditions for a new and fruitful dialogue between Czech Structuralists and Czech Marxists (like Karel Kosík or Robert Kalivoda). Beyond the Czech border, in more current theoretical debate, with its controversies between Structuralism and Marxism and between systems theory and the history of philosophy, the Prague school is of great interest as an early attempt methodologically to relate structural analysis with process description, to extend the investigation of specifically literary structures and processes to an investigation of their social conditions and functions, and to mediate between the two on the level of theory.

If we want to trace the genesis and development of Czech Structuralism in the history of criticism, consideration must be paid to these factors and many others involving the native Czech context; it is not enough just to posit a direct line of descent from Russian Formalism to Czech Structuralism.[15] But whereas those authors who derive Czech Structuralism solely from Russian Formalism, or largely equate the two, underestimate the multitude of factors that contributed to the development of Czech Structuralism as well as the systematic features that distinguish it from Russian Formalism, several accounts by the Czech Structuralists themselves do not escape the danger of buying their proof of the (undeniable) independence of the Prague concept at the price of a definition of Formalism that is excessively narrow. For the purpose of a starker contrast, a pure or typical Formalism is posited, corresponding most nearly to the early, extreme conceptions of certain Russian Formalists (chiefly Viktor Shklovsky). Other approaches and later developments must then be passed over or played down, even to the point of ignoring leading Russian Formalists who were responsible for them (as, for example, Tynyanov).[16] But because the late phase of Formalism was crucial to the initial phase of Prague Structuralism, what results is a one-sided picture not only of Russian Formalism but also of its significance for Czech Structuralism.

In this quarrel over the genesis of Czech Structuralism, which continues to the present day, it is useful to recall that the Formalists and Structuralists themselves distinguished expressly between genesis and evolution, between the reconstruction of genetic series and evolutionary ones. They did not deny that many and diverse historic and biographical conditions and impulses can be identified and are important in the genesis of a work, an oeuvre, or a literary school. But their interest as literary historians was directed primarily to the development of literature as an evolutionary series. Given this perspective, what is crucial is whether and how a work (or an oeuvre, a school, an epoch) as a *system* differs from the earlier system to which it is to be compared, which elements and principles are adopted, what is modified and how, what new features develop. This requires, first, the description of the phenomena in question as systems. If they are systems that undergo constant change (as is the case, notably, with schools), the diachronic process must be divided into individual synchronic systems or sections. These may be compared, and, from the differences that are ascertained in this manner, one can deduce which evolutionary tendencies are inherent in the system itself and in what manner the system reacts to external influences. From this an evolutionary series can be reconstructed in which the individual systems figure as phases of evolution. Naturally an evolutionary series of this kind is an abstraction from the multiplicity of the concrete, a schematic reduction and construction made after the fact for descriptive purposes and from a particular point of view. But as such, it at least gives reliable information about the systems in question, their distinguishing features, and their systematic relations. By contrast, genetic series often (explicitly or implicitly) claim to trace given causal connections to a given basic factor, which (in the selection, concatenation, and hierarchic ranking of factors) merely camouflages the character of a schematic reduction and construction without actually canceling it.

If, applying the distinction between genetic series and evolutionary series to the relation of Czech Structuralism to Russian Formalism, we try to reconstruct particular, distinguishable concepts of theory and methodology from both of them, we find that an evolutionary series with three phases is more appropriate than the usual bipolarity—which is simpler and seems to recommend itself because of the existence of two nationally located schools. Basing the reconstruction of the three systems on their respective notions of the individual work of art (which then defines the notions of literature as a whole and literary evolution), one may label the three concepts or phases of the evolutionary series in this way:

1. The work of art as the sum of devices, which have a defamiliarizing function whose purpose is impeded perception.
2. The work of art as a system of devices in specific synchronic and diachronic functions.
3. The work of art as a sign in an aesthetic function.

88

This classification is a schematic construct (in the sense elaborated above). Not only are the borders blurred, the three concepts themselves resulted from constant processes of modification. Each successive concept adopted individual basic principles from the one preceding; it can to this extent be considered as its continuation or redefinition, the other one, conversely, as its predecessor. But from the point of view of theory and methodology, it is possible and appropriate to identify each of the three concepts as a new system.

2

The notion of the work of art as the sum of devices, with a defamiliarizing function whose purpose is impeded perception, derives from the early articles of Shklovsky, especially from "Art as Device" (1916).[17] The first part of the formula points to the two chief features of Shklovsky's concept: the individual device is the point of departure and chief object of interest; and the linking of devices to a work of art is defined as a sum, thus in terms of simple addition. Even with regard to this initial position, these two points apply only if one deliberately stresses the features that distinguish it from later Formalist and Structuralist theories. In reality this earliest concept already contained hints pointing further. Shklovsky himself linked his definition of art as device to the observation that the fundamental device of art is the device of defamiliarization. Its task, he reasoned, is to break through modes of perception and presentation that frequent use have rendered ineffective and automatic, and thereby, on the one hand, to permit "new seeing"[18] of reality and, on the other, to draw attention to the presentation itself, thus achieving an aesthetic effect. But this (though at this stage only indirectly) already combines the notion of the device with a particular function (within literary tradition and with respect to extraliterary reality or the experience of it). The emphasis on the functional aspect may be seen far more distinctly in the work of the Formalists with linguistic training and orientation, Jakobson and Jakubinsky, even in their earliest Formalist writings. In the discussion about poetic and practical language, which was of central importance to the

Society for Research in Poetic Language (Opojaz) and to early Formalism, the two authors determined that this distinction is at bottom functional, depending on particular language use.[19] As early as 1919 Jakobson stated that "practical language" was language in its "communicative function"; poetry, however, he said to be "language in its aesthetic function," defining the aesthetic function of language more closely as "utterance organized with an intention toward expression . . . by laws that are, as it were, intrinsic."[20] It is significant that what immediately follows this definition is the sentence later cited as the programmatic summation of the early phase of Formalist literary studies: "The subject of literary scholarship is not literature but literariness, that is, what makes a given work a work of literature."[21]

To this degree, W. Stempel's observation that Formalism very early gave a "fundamentally functional definition of practical and poetic language" may be extended to Formalism's overall conception. But one must hasten to add that this "did not mean that [the functional definition] was immediately recognized in all its implications."[22] However, precisely because this functional approach contained a multitude of far-reaching implications, without fully developing them or even formulating all of them as such, later concepts and phases could adopt it, extend it, and make it the central point of their theory and analytic practice.

The notion of the additive principle was supplanted even more fully and rapidly. Shklovsky himself replaced it by positing several levels within the work of art, on which similar devices of construction are applied (see his article "The Connection between the Devices of Plot Construction and Stylistic Devices in General" [1919]).[23] After the multilevel model had succeeded the notion of the purely cumulative sum, further quantitative and qualitative elaboration of the multilevel model followed. Instead of investigating the bipartite division between plot and style, one might turn to the relationship between the phonic and syntactic levels,[24] or to the tension between phonic and metric organization, on the one hand, and the syntactic units of meaning, on the other.[25] The conclusion of this development, which overlapped with phases 2 and 3, was a hierarchic multilevel model, in which one climbs from the lowest level of the smallest elements of language, sounds, up to the most encompassing units of meaning and overall construction. The notion of the relations among various levels, too, underwent changes. In his early article Shklovsky had still been looking into the use of similar principles of construction on various levels. For phases 2 and 3 it is characteristic that each level is seen to have its own specific principles of construction, and precisely by means of them to enter into a relationship of tension with all the others, supporting them, modifying them, contrasting with them. Within the specific individual system (work, genre, and so on), one single level with its principles of construction subordinates the others and, as the dominant, deforms them.

Phase 2 thus distinguishes itself from phase 1 in starting neither with the individual isolated device nor with the general function of defamiliarization, but with the concrete work as a system of diverse elements and principles of construction on various levels in specific functions. The specification works in two directions. Each given element (or device) is distinguishable in its particular function from other elements and functions within the same work-as-system. (This is its specific synchronic function, or, in Tynyanov's terminology, the synfunction or constructive function of an element.) This particular function, however, at the same time represents a selection from the array of various basic possible applications of the same element (its specific diachronic function or, in Tynyanov's term, the autofunction).[26] Whether we diachronize this second aspect directly—that is, experience (and if necessary describe) the chosen use in correlation to a traditional array of different uses of the same element in various previous works-as-systems—or whether we generalize and comprehend the particular use as one selected from the element's general functional potential, we realize the application of an element in the concrete work as a selection and combination for the purpose of a specific function within this system.[27] And because each given synchronic function, specific to a given work, can be realized only as a diachronic function, directly or indirectly related to a handed-down repertoire of possible applications, a tension results between these two dimensions of every element of the work as a whole. This tension makes the work's structure dynamic, as, conversely, every concrete work, by its specific selection and combination of elements and devices, actualizes the tradition and makes it dynamic.

The theoretic elaboration and practical application of a descriptive model corresponding to this conception of work structure were at the heart of phase 2. And the model that had been developed on the basis of the individual work could then be applied to literary systems of a higher order—literary genres, for example, or epochs—by identifying the elements and constructive principles of these systems, too, in their synchronic and diachronic functions in order thus to describe the specific functioning of each system as a whole.

This model is taken up as part of the theory of phase 3 and, above all, as a guideline for its analytic and literary-historical practice. But here it receives a new theoretical and systematic basis: the theory of signs, or semiotics. It remained for phase 3 to take the inquiry back a step and investigate—before looking into the function of individual devices and elements within a work—the peculiar mode of functioning and existence of language systems in general (and verbal works of art more particularly) as signs. The point of departure was Saussure's theory of the linguistic sign and thus the recognition that the elements of a linguistic utterance do not have meaning in themselves. Only as parts of a particular system of signs, with particular rules for construction and for ascribing meaning and with particular codes for encoding and decoding, do they become carriers of meaning. By referring to the conventional codes, the sender (in the case of a work of literature, the author) of the linguistic message (the work) chooses the linguistic signs appropriate to his meaning that are available to him and arranges them. Conversely, on the basis of the codes available to him, the receiver (the reader) ascribes particular meanings to the signs given to him in the text. From these meanings and their interrelations he reconstructs the meaning, the sense, of the message (or, in the case of a work of art, concretizes it anew).

Accordingly, a clear distinction is now made between the work as a series of linguistic signs fixed for the purpose of artistic communication (in the terminology of Czech Structuralism, the work as "artifact") and the work as a fabric of meanings concretized by the receiver on the basis of this artifact and with the aid of conventionalized codes. Only this fabric of meanings is capable of becoming the actual object of aesthetic contemplation and valuation (in Czech Structuralist terminology, the "aesthetic object").

In this process every individual linguistic sign integrated into the work has a dual function. As a potential carrier of meaning it refers the reader to an extraliterary reality, which it signifies. At the same time it acquires meaning for the reader through its specific function in the work as a complex of meanings, as a structured aesthetic object. The second direction of meaning refracts the first, deflecting as it were every individual statement from its orientation to a preexisting reality back to the work itself, only entering back into relationship to external reality via the work's overall structure. In this respect the work as a whole is the genuine carrier of meaning. As verbal material in a particular configuration with a particular meaning potential, concretized in the act of communication by the aid of traditional codes, it can therefore be understood in its entirety as a sign of a higher order, constructed from linguistic signs.

As such the work is a sign in a specific aesthetic function. Whereas in the usual, purely communicative, use of language the conjunction of particular meanings and particular linguistic elements seems obvious, serving only to convey information about a given reality, in the aesthetic sign (because of the directional duality just discussed) the conjunction becomes problematic. It is exposed as tension between verbal material, its meaning, and the concrete reference of the sign, and it is exploited aesthetically, for instance as tension between the phonic and semantic levels of a work of poetry or between the construction of a work as a web of poetic meanings and the experiential meaning of the real world. The incorporation of each linguistic element in the structure of the work tears the element from its purely referential and communicative function, complicates the construction of meaning, alienates the perception of reality in the medium of language, and thus—as a total sign—creates a changed seeing of reality as the "total context of social phenomena."[28] Thus, the aesthetic function does not simply cancel the linguistic symbol's relationship to extra-aesthetic reality, but redirects it via the structure of the work of art in its totality as a sign. In so doing, it also directs attention to the aesthetic sign as a construct with a specific structure and intended meaning. The work as aesthetic sign itself becomes what is actually significant—and what is signified.

The work of art as an aesthetic sign is an autonomous sign. This does not simply cancel the communicative function of the literary work of art, which in literature as a thematic art (and, within literature, especially in prose) remains active. But in the case of a sign of this type the communicative function remains bound to the "autonomous function." And the "dialectic antinomy" between these "two semiological functions" (or the "double semiological meanings") is basic for the individual work as it is for literature as a whole, particularly in its relationship to reality and the constant change in the course of the "development of these (thematic) arts."[29]

Hence the semiotic theory and description of the literary work reach from the smallest structural element to the work's overall structure and its relation to extraliterary reality. Phase 3 sets up a consistently articulated aesthetic—"aesthetic" used here in the sense of a theory of how works of art exist and have effect, as opposed to a corresponding "poetic," a theory of the principles of literary construction. This aesthetic is a specifically semiotic one. And because, according to this theory, the work of art as an aesthetic sign constitutes itself only when it is concretized by a receiver, the theory is most emphatically an aesthetic of reception.[30]

In view of contemporary theoretical debate, especially the part of it dealing with the aesthetics of reception, I must add that in this case aesthetics of reception should not be misconstrued as dealing exclusively with the reader. True, the Czech Structuralists discuss in detail both the general theoretical and the historical problems of reception by readers and critics. But the aesthetic aspects of the work and the aesthetics of production are just as integral to their theory and their investigations. The activity of the reader—with its personal and collective, general anthropological and historical precon-

94

ditions, procedures, and results—is always bound to the work with its structural singularity as artifact and aesthetic object. And, in turn, this is possible only because the producing author—on the basis of his individual intention, with an audience (as a collective of individuals) in mind, and with the help of codes collectively handed down—has created an individual structure, unique to the work, thus constructing a sign that in its aesthetic function initiates a multitude of individual concretizations.

3

Just as we can distinguish three different concepts of the work of literature, each characteristic of a phase in the evolutionary series from Russian Formalism to Czech Structuralism, we can distinguish three corresponding theories and descriptive models of literary evolution. Phase 1 develops its evolutionary concept out of its central notion of defamiliarization. In consequence of the premise that literary scholarship should limit itself to what is specifically literary in literature, both the notion of defamiliarization and the evolutionary concept derived from it are understood as strictly intraliterary phenomena. If not only the literary devices of defamiliarization but also the extraliterary reality that they defamiliarize, which the devices allow to be seen anew, were the object of investigation and theory, we might also conceive of literary evolution as a series of defamiliarizing reactions to the emergence and automatization of extraliterary phenomena and perceptual habits.[31] But a purely intraliterary conception of evolution must derive literary change from the particular nature and function of literary defamiliarization. If literature is characterized as the application of artistic devices whose task is to defamiliarize methods of presentation that have become automatic, then every defamiliarizing device runs the risk of becoming conventional, automatic, and hence ineffectual as soon as it has been accepted and become familiar. It must in turn be defamiliarized by new devices. Constant seesawing between automatization and defamiliarization becomes the principle of literary evolution. Or, to put it more sharply: basing literature on the device of defamiliarization leads to defining literary evolution as a defamiliarization of devices.

Against this early evolutionary concept the objection may be raised (and soon was) that the radical exclusion of all extra-literary factors leads to an untenable isolation of the series of literary development from all other social series and their development, that even within literature the theory accounts only for the aspect of innovation, not for that of continuity, and so on. Although all this is true, it does not diminish the historical importance of this programmatic limitation, imposed with a deliberate polemical bias. Its very extremism directed attention to intraliterary causes and sequences of the replacement of traditional forms by new ones, and these causes were often neglected in literary criticism and literary historiography (especially in Russia). The Formalists themselves soon realized that this schema could at best capture changes of literary forms as such, but could not explain the tempo of evolution, which varies greatly from case to case, nor the particular choice of evolutionary direction.[32] However, this criticism applies not only to the evolutionary concept of phase 1, but to any version of strictly intraliterary evolutionary theory. What related specifically to phase 1 and was crucial for the transition to phase 2 was more likely the fact that even as a purely intraliterary evolutionary scheme this one came into conflict with its own theoretical and methodological notions, forcing a change in the concept overall. For it followed from this evolutionary scheme that particular devices, which had a defamiliarizing effect under particular conditions, under altered circumstances occurred as something now automatic, features that had to be defamiliarized. Thus it was not sufficient to point up general defamiliarizing devices and to erect a theory of literature on them. What also had to be shown was why, under different conditions, the same devices achieve different effects (becoming or not becoming defamiliarizing devices according to the particular effect). The general functional definition of literary devices as deformation had to be extended to the identification of these devices as factors of construction, and thereby to the description of concrete work structures as the organization of elements and devices in specific functions. The concept of phase

1, centered on the device, gave way to that of phase 2, centered on the work as functional system.[33]

Because phase 2 conceives of and describes the literary work as a system of linked elements and constructive devices in specific functions, it must refer to literary tradition and evolution to describe the work. In order to determine whether and how particular elements or devices achieve particular effects and thus can fulfill particular functions in a particular aesthetic system, it is necessary first to establish the manner in which they are predetermined by tradition, whether and how they have already been assigned particular fixed functions, or whether convention has rendered them so thoroughly automatic that they no longer have any artistic effect. Since the relationship between function and formal element is an evolutionary relationship that changes within tradition,[34] the particular assignment of function to formal element and vice versa can be determined only by referring back to literary evolution. The reader and critic or scholar inquiring into the specific systematic functions of particular elements or devices in a work confronts this problem as much as does the author when he or she constructs the work. The author, wishing to achieve a certain intention through his work, requires elements and devices that can fulfill particular functions suited to that intention. In this he is independent of tradition to the extent that he can choose from its array and then decide whether he wants to use the elements and devices he has chosen in the manner that they are used in the prevailing tradition, or whether he wants to deviate from it or oppose and defamiliarize it. But in any case he is dependent on tradition—on the state of literary evolution—to the extent that every element chosen and every manner of use relates back to its traditional use. To this degree the "autofunction, that is, the correlation of any element to the series of analogous elements in other systems and other series . . . [is] the condition for the synfunction, the constructive function of that element" in the given, concrete work.[35]

If even the functioning of individual elements and devices within a work depends on how their autofunction, related to tradition, is integrated as a constructive synfunction of the specific intention of the work, the realization of this intention of

97

the work as a whole depends on which part of the literary tradition, which intraliterary series, the work as a system is coordinated to. The coordination is achieved with the aid of the system of genres, which assigns individual works to a particular series as a reference system on the basis of particular features of structure and particular signals (as, for instance, the generic terms novel and comedy), and also governs the linking of particular formal elements with particular functions within this series. This explains the extraordinary importance of literary genre and generic theory for the entire theoretic concept (and for its descriptive models). It explains, too, why in this concept the term genre is understood neither as a static system of norms nor as a historical entity, but only as a regulatory principle guiding the construction and reception of literary works. As such a reference system it has continuity in itself and establishes continuity for the individual works as representatives of this genre. In its momentary regulation of the "relationship of functions and formal elements,"[36] however, it is itself subject to constant change, even if the respective decisions or regulations often raise claims to validity as timeless, invariable norms. This change also affects the dominant, which a genre as a system of hierarchically arranged elements and functions possess no less than does an individual work as a hierarchic system. Hence a feature that was long distinctive of a genre and may easily come to be regarded as a timeless invariable of that genre can lose its privileged position or even disappear altogether as a generic feature (as, for instance, the romantic adventures of the hero in the novel).

Such recasting and refunctioning within a genre point beyond its limits to the overall system of genres. Within this system particular intra- and extraliterary functions correspond to particular genres, which in turn must be structured accordingly. But if the structuring of a particular genre is so strongly regulated in the poetic of the genre, the pattern begins to grow automatic. The structure must then be altered so that the same intention can be realized and the same function can be fulfilled. If, though the function as such remains timely, the required alteration exceeds the genre's capacity, the function must be transferred to another genre, while the old genre either adopts new functions or vanishes from the prevailing genre canon.[37]

The same model may be applied on the higher levels. Every literary school is understood and described as a system by which, for particular chronological phases of evolution as a whole, particular systems of rules and norms are established and made binding, in which particular functions are assigned to particular forms, and in which the whole obtains a hierarchic structure with one or more dominants. But because a school is only one system, historically effective and dominant in a particular period, its emergence and success do not simply terminate the continued existence of other schools, directions, noncanonized genres, and so on. In the epoch in question, however, they are not dominant, they do not form the contemporary crest of literature,[38] and their valuation is prejudiced by the norms of the crest literature of the day. Nevertheless, as collateral lines or substrata of literature they can be reevaluated and even raised to the crest as soon as the dominant school has lost its privileged position and a newly forming literary system (new schools, new epochs) seeks new points of reference or new series for reference within literary tradition.

As this happens, not only does the border between canonized and noncanonized schools, genres, and so forth shift, the border between the forms and systems of language acknowledged as literature, on the one hand, and extraliterary language use, on the other, shifts as well. Forms and genres that once fulfilled only extraliterary functions can in particular periods be taken up in the literary repertoire of particular schools, be elevated to the status of literary models, and become literary facts (as, for example, the letter in European Sentimentalism). Conversely, such genres and forms, canonized as literature, can themselves serve as models affecting the extraliterary use of language, whether at the time when they are canonized or after they have fallen from the crest.[39]

At this juncture it becomes clear that individual literary series and literature itself as a series interact with other, extraliterary series, and that the mediation takes place principally via the linguistic series, which is common to both the literary and the extraliterary domains.

The limitations of this theoretical model and of all intraliterary theories of evolution become evident. For descriptive purposes the model holds as long as the intent is to describe the coordination of functions and formal elements as an evolutionary relationship in diverse types of literary systems, starting with the elements and devices within the individual work, continuing with the work as system and literary systems of higher order such as schools and periods, and finally reaching the system of literature as a whole, including its shifting boundaries with extraliterary language use. It is persuasive in its theoretical formulation and practical application of the insight that such a description must deal with each level both synchronically and diachronically by identifying each element or system in question in its structure and function by contrast to other simultaneous elements or systems and by determining the location of this element or system as a part of an evolutionary series. But just as we begin to think that literature can be described adequately only through the process of its historical evolution, it becomes clear that a pure intraliterary theory of evolution will not do. For, as Jakobson and Tynyanov themselves observed, even "the question of the concrete choice of direction or at least of the dominant [can] only be solved by an analysis of the correlation of literature and the other historical series."[40] Phase 2 merges into the demand that the interrelation between literature as a system or series and other systems or series of social development be described in a system of systems.[41] This demand, however, remains unfulfilled. One important reason for this is that the theoretical model of phase 2 is insufficient to define this interaction theoretically and to allow it to be described systematically.

The theory of literary evolution of phase 3 ties in at the very point where phase 2 refers to correlating the literary series to other series of the system of systems and its overall development. To define and describe this correlation, phase 3 uses its central theorem: the notion of the linguistic work of art as a sign in aesthetic function. Even on the level of the individual linguistic signs within the work the receiver (reader) can ascribe meaning to these elements of the artifact only through recourse to codes governing the linking of the linguistic symbol with meaning and referent (as the mind's corollary to the extra-linguistic world of objects). If the codes that are binding for the particular linguistic and cultural collective change—if, for instance, in the course of the history of a language the semantic field of a particular word changes—a later reader will ascribe to a given element of a given artifact a meaning other than the one it held for the author and the audience of his contemporaries. If the element in question is an important one for construing the meaning of the work, this concretization receives a structure of meaning that differs from an older one of the same artifact. To this extent an evolutionary series of concretizations can begin even at this level. Changes in the general codes of natural languages are relatively slow, however, and so cannot be the crucial motor force behind literary evolution. What is far more to the point is that the function and the meaning that a particular linguistic element assumes in a particular literary work of art are not adequately covered by the general codes of language. As already shown, such an element becomes aesthetically effective precisely by deviating from customary, hence automatized, usage, thus emphasizing the tension between the carrier of linguistic meaning and its meaning potential and permitting a decision with respect to its specific meaning and function in the work only within the context of the structure of the work as a whole. But whether and how the individual element and device are perceived as deviating and whether they contribute thereby to the construction of meaning of the aesthetic object and how are matters that can only be determined with reference to the state of literary evolution and the currently prevailing norms—with reference, in other words, to specifically literary and aesthetic codes.

Through this projection of the individual element and the individual work onto the general system of literature and onto the codes that govern it, a dual peculiarity of aesthetic norm systems comes into play. An aesthetic norm, unlike a grammatical norm (or a legal or ethical norm), is not set up to be satisfied in every particular. The aesthetic norm is no more than an orienting standard by which one may measure realizations of, deviations from, and violations of the norm, and by combining them construct the work of art and its aesthetic meaning. The aesthetic norm system in its genesis and in its normative function depends on the artistic production. It is a normalizing abstraction of tradition, of certain rules derived from it, of certain works that have been elevated to paradigmatic status, and so on. Therefore, if a work of art succeeds in establishing itself within the tradition, the tradition absorbs not only that work's realizations of the norms but also, more notably, its violations of traditional norms. The norm system must then be altered so as to canonize the deviations as well. To this extent every work of art that is accepted as such by the public and the critics is both passive in its reference to tradition and active as a motivating factor of the tradition or, more to the point, of the tradition's evolution. This also explains why aesthetic norm systems or codes are subject to far more rapid change than codes meant to ensure that the linguistic communication functions as smoothly as possible.[42]

4

The dynamic relationship of a work to tradition is crucial for its aesthetic value. The problem of valuation played no significant role in phases 1 and 2, but it is at the center of the theory and critical practice of phase 3. Mukařovský regards the poetic work as "a totality of values."[43] He starts with the basic question of how "noetic requirements for objectively valid aesthetic judgment" may be reconciled with the fact of the "mutability of aesthetic valuation in time"[44] and attempts to answer it by discriminating among different evaluative premises and different kinds of aesthetic values.

An objective aesthetic value is noetically posited as a value "inherent in the material artistic product," since only this, as artifact, "has continuous, unchanging existence." But because the work as sign takes on meaning only in the concrete semiotic context, this value "has only a potential character."[45] The concrete object of aesthetic valuation is, rather, the work as aesthetic object, as it is constituted as a structured, meaningful, and value-carrying unity in the concrete act of aesthetic perception. "And therefore an aesthetic valuation comprehends the work as an integral whole (unit) and is an individuating act;

aesthetic value in art offers itself as something unique and unrepeatable."[46] At the same time, this act of aesthetic concretization and valuation is possible only because the perceiving subject refers to the system of aesthetic norms and aesthetic values shared with the other subjects of the historic and social collective to which he or she belongs. Considering this, the aesthetic value that in the individuating act of concrete valuation presented itself as something "unique and unrepeatable" is itself a supra-individual, collective, social fact. As a collective value handed down collectively, it is not eternal, but historically mutable.[47]

Mukařovský defines the relation of this aesthetic value to the other, extra-aesthetic values of the same collective as both negative and dynamic. As a sign in an aesthetic function, the work of verbal art can, by means of its individual linguistic signs, actualize a multitude of extra-aesthetic values. But by the aesthetic use of individual signs and because of the integrity of the structure of the work as a unity, direct object reference gives way to the "objective indefinitude of the material reference of the work of art as a sign."[48] As this happens, every extra-aesthetic value appealed to is torn from its "relation to the corresponding existential value" and replaced by the relation and reciprocal tension between the total "complex, contained in the work of art as a dynamic totality of values and the entire system of values . . . that form the motor force of life as it is lived by the collective that accepts the work of art."[49] To this extent the work of art is "actually a conglomeration of extra-aesthetic values . . . and nothing but precisely this conglomeration," and the aesthetic value dissolves in this conglomeration, being "nothing other, actually, . . . than a summary term for the dynamic totality of their interrelations."[50] But precisely through this negativity, the aesthetic value has a positive effect on life as it is lived by the particular collective and the individuals belonging to it and fulfills an important anthropological function in it, canceling the one-sided pragmatic determination and the monofunctional orientation of their value judgments and freeing man as a polyfunctional creature from these constraints.[51]

Mukařovský differentiates this general conception of

aesthetic value and makes it operable by distinguishing three kinds of value. Following step by step the elaboration of this concept in his writings, one may paraphrase it, as Felix Vodička does, as a path "from the evolutionary value . . . via the immediate aesthetic value . . . to universal value."[52] Because these categories and Mukařovský's whole concept of aesthetic value will be discussed more thoroughly in Part IV, I will content myself here with these general remarks.[53] Although certain points of Mukařovský's definition of value may be criticized, his achievement of relating the theory of aesthetic valuation to the theory of literary evolution (and vice versa), and thereby extending the scope of phase 3 beyond that of phases 1 and 2, remains unchallenged. By differentiating between kinds of value (and by the logically prior differentiation between artifact and aesthetic object) he distinguishes more clearly than could be done in phases 1 and 2 between the constants and variables of aesthetic communication; and he distinguishes, too, between the specifically aesthetic qualities of the work of art and its relation to the life of the individual and the life of the collective—not so as to make division between the two but to show the interplay that unites them.

For this special problem of valuation and in general, phase 3, like phases 1 and 2, could apply to higher literary unities the results found in investigating the individual work and its relationship to literary evolution. However, the strong interest in the higher unity of the genre characteristic of phase 2 falls off conspicuously in phase 3, in which theory and practical analysis concentrate chiefly on the author and his oeuvre, as well as on epoch (group, school) and national literature. At all levels, though, the double reference remains—on the one hand, to the concrete and particular work of art as an integral and meaningful structure and, on the other, to the general question of aesthetic function and its relation to other human functions, norms, and values. This double reference is essential for the designation of literature as a system. An art that works with language, literature is by the very nature of its material more closely related (or relatable) to the conceptions, experiences, and expectations of life praxis than music, for example, or other art forms. The tension between the orientation to extra-aesthetic values, norms, and functions and the contrary tendency of the aesthetic function is particularly distinct in this case. It determines the evolution of this art form and is, according to the cultural context and from one evolutionary phase to the next, subject to great variation. For that reason the dominance of the aesthetic function can, under particular historical and social conditions, be put in doubt or even canceled outright by other functions, whether only in the area of reception or in the area of production as well.[54] This does not eliminate the basic dominance of the aesthetic function of literature as art and of the literary work (as artifact and aesthetic object), but it forces the literary scholar as literary historian to remain aware of the tension of the diverse functions and values and to identify its character in every concrete case of literary production and reception. The problem of the varying functions of literature in the historically changing system of systems and the identification of the functions and tasks of literature in varying historic and social contexts become the central theme of theoretical inquiry and literary historical investigation.

Thus, the semiotic premises of phase 3 produce two crucial and interrelated complexes or lines of inquiry for the concept's evolutionary theory and the literary history deriving from it. One is the inquiry into the concretization of linguistic signs, into the general conditions of concretization within the work of art as artifact and in the system of norms and values handed down collectively, and into the historical concretizations themselves—which leads to the unfolding of a semiotically based structuralistic history of literature with special emphasis on the history of reception. Second, there is the inquiry into the specific identification of the aesthetic function in relationship to other functions of people and of their collective life, and into the change of this relationship under historically changing conditions—which could be taken as the point of departure for a structuralist history of literature as a history of functions.

These aspects will be examined later, when I review Felix Vodička's literary history, his theoretical conception of concretization, context, literary tasks, and so on. I shall, therefore, conclude my sketch of the character of phase 3 in its relation to phases 1 and 2. I hope that the outline has shown to what extent each concept can be distinguished from the other two as a theoretical conception in its own right and to what extent each takes off from its predecessor, adopts certain guiding principles and central categories from it, and extends or modifies them, so that all three may be regarded as phases of an evolutionary series.

5

How does this schematic account relate to Russian Formalism and Czech Structuralism and their historical development? We might say that Russian Formalism covers phases 1 and 2, and Czech Structuralism, phases 2 and 3. Although this may be an oversimplification, it indicates that each of the schools does not fully include one of the concepts, and that phase 2 is common to both.

After what has already been said, it is unnecessary to emphasize that saying Czech Structuralism does not include phase 1 neither casts doubt on the continuity between the theories the two schools developed nor interprets "the course of history . . . as a process of evolutionary progress and increasing perfection," as if in phase 3 Czech Structuralism had finally overcome the deficiencies and omissions of Russian Formalism.[55] Fundamental tendencies and categories of early Russian Formalism undeniably still exert influence over late Czech Structuralism. For example, the two basic terms from Shklovsky's early essay—device and defamiliarization—not only remain key terms in Mukařovský's first writings after the founding of the Prague Linguistic Circle, but also remain indispensable for late Czech Structuralist theory and analytical practice (although their explicit use becomes less frequent). But both terms had been taken over as parts of phase 2. The initial restriction has already been abandoned; and the construction of the system[56] is no longer based on the individual, isolated device and its defamiliarizing effect, but on the work of art as a functional system and as a structural totality, which notion is established even more clearly in phase 3, in which the work of art is interpreted as a "sign in aesthetic function." Conversely, the term aesthetic function, for example, crucial for Czech

Structuralist aesthetics as a whole, had already been used in early writings of Jakobson and Jakubinsky. Significantly, this use is only sporadic. What dominates are the terms "poetic function" and "poetic language," while the development of expressly articulated aesthetics[57] and likewise systematic speculation on the relation of the aesthetic function to other functions of human life achieve full development only in phase 3.[58]

What must be qualified is the assertion that phase 3—the semiotic concept—began only after Russian Formalism had run its course. One may object that Jakobson was a semiotician from the start; that semiotic conceptions and categories appeared in his early writings on literature, too; that even the absence of a particular terminology need not indicate the absence of the ideas usually associated with that terminology; and that most basic Formalist terms can be translated into the vocabulary of semiotics without difficulty. All this is true. Nevertheless, the fact that a translation of this sort was not systematically effected at the time by the authors themselves is more than a terminological incidental. It is particularly conspicuous because, after all, Jakobson and other representatives of early Formalism took off directly from modern linguistics, which is to say among other things from Saussure, to whom the later, explicitly semiotic theory of literature and aesthetics (including Mukařovský's) make direct reference. That semiotics established itself as the immediate foundation for the Structuralist theory of literature as late as in phase 3—despite the historically and biographically clear genetic connection—again supports the notion that evolutionary series of this kind cannot be explained as the results of direct influences. They have a dynamic of their own, which is contingent on the nature of the system to which they belong, and which determines whether, when, and how a given historical or biographical fact will become an evolutionary factor within the series. Therefore, explanations why particular suggestions are taken up or not are problematical and should not be misconstrued as genetic. In the present case, the linguistic premises of Jakobson and other early Formalists (and, in parallel, the concentration on the individual device on the part of Shklovsky and others) may well have stood in the way of an early definition and theoretical elaboration of the work of art as a sign. Such a step became an issue for the system only after the work of art as a total unity had become the main theoretical topic, when the primary aim was no longer to describe the work of art in its organization of linguistic elements and technical devices but also in its aesthetic realization as a structured and meaningful aesthetic object.

This supposition is buttressed by the fact that explicitly semiotic notions and sketches by authors who belonged to the Formalist circle or were closely associated with it are most frequently to be found in instances where a particular interest existed in problems of aesthetics and in special aspects of the realization of the work of art as an aesthetic object. This was the case, for instance, of Gustav Shpet, a Russian student of Husserl and an aesthetician who, on the basis of his aesthetic writings and especially his *Aesthetic Fragments* (1922–23), may be regarded as one of the initiators of semiotic aesthetics in Russia[59] and whose writings, lectures, and discussions were a direct stimulus for the Formalist circle.[60] This was also the case of the Department for the History of Literature (founded in 1920 at the State Institute for the History of the Arts in Petrograd) under the chairmanship of Viktor Zhirmunsky, to which belonged—in addition to Shklovsky, Eikhenbaum, Tynyanov, Tomashevsky, and other Petrograd (Leningrad) Formalists— other notable scholars who were associated with the Formalists only temporarily, such as Zhirmunsky himself, Viktor Vinogradov, and others.[61] Within the department a pronounced interest in questions of aesthetics left its mark on the later development of Formalism; this stands out distinctly in *The Formal School in the History of Literature* (1927) by Boris Engelgardt, who also belonged to this circle.[62] Something similar may be said of the group that formed around Mikhail Bakhtin.[63]

A particularly informative example in this context is Sergey Bernstein's "Aesthetic Assumptions for a Theory of Declamation."[64] Bernstein also belonged to the circle of Formalists at the Institute for the History of the Arts in Petrograd. Striking parallels to several fundamental concepts of semiotic Structuralism are obvious from the article's subject: declamation as an artistic realization of the material aspect of the linguistic sign, and thus, concretization of an artifact as an aesthetic object. Bernstein states that "the work of art is above all a *sign*. A sign is a thing that serves the consciousness as the representative of a system of conceptions, which constitutes its *meaning*" (p. 346).

By concretizing the "sensory substratum" of the "work of art as sign,"[65] a declamation must always select *one* of the options (of articulation, emotional coloring, rate of speech, and so on) that are built into the text but the realization of which is left open. Therefore, every declamation is more concrete than the text and, at the same time, only a specific selection from the total potential of the system of conceptions. The particular perspective of the person declaiming determines the choice of what is made concrete; this choice alone permits the fixed text to be structured meaningfully as an aesthetic object.[66] Bernstein does not allow the possibility of a single valid declamatory realization of a poem—not even in the sense of an ideal to which one might aspire—but only of various concretizations of one and the same poem that are equally true to the work. What is here a special case—a theory of declamation—already compactly encompasses a semiotically based, Structuralist theory of the concretization of aesthetic signs and appears in retrospect as an anticipation (developed with respect to a particular problem) of the Czech Structuralist aesthetic of concretization.

The examples cited show that intimations of a semiotic approach can also be found in the literary scholarship of Formalism. It is probably not accidental, however, that most such examples come from a sort of periphery—whether in the sense of group membership, which is to say, more from the fringe of Formalism than from its core, or in the sense of special topics, such as declamatory theory. Chronologically, it should be noted that most of the publications referred to appeared in the late twenties, immediately before the demise of Formalism as a school (and some even after the founding of the Prague Linguistic Circle). This too blurs the lines between phases, complicating the question of what is representative of Formalism in its terminal phase and what should be viewed as peripheral. Still, distinctions can be made. For example, if the special case of Bernstein's "Aesthetic Assumptions for a Theory of Declamation" (1927) is compared with Jakobson and Tynyanov's "Problems in the Study of Literature and Language" (1928), we notice that in the theses semiotic terminology is absent. As already noted, these theses can be regarded as a summation of Formalism and as the transition from Formalism to Structuralism. At the same time it is significant, with regard to sheer terminology, that "Formalism" is mentioned only once, in quotation marks and with a derogatory meaning (in Thesis 1), and that the basic topic is no longer form but "structure," "structural types," and "developmental structural types." The use of the word structure is of course no adequate criterion of the "Structuralist" character of a theory or a program, and was not such a criterion even in 1928, when the word was not yet quite so overextended as it is today. With that in mind, it is worthwhile to consider the attempt of Roland Barthes thirty-five years later to define Structuralism as "structuralistic activity" by reference to its manners of speech and proceeding.[67] The term structure being "by now very worn out" and an insufficient criterion, he suggests: "Pay note who uses *signified* and *signifier, synchrony* and *diachrony,* and you will know whether the structuralist conception is there."[68]

In the theses of Tynyanov and Jakobson the pair of terms "synchrony" and "diachrony" is not only used; it is even the topic of the most comprehensive thesis (4), which formulates the recognition that literature as an evolving system can be comprehended and described only in the conjunction of synchrony and diachrony. Characteristically, however, the other pair of terms Barthes mentions is neither taken up as a topic nor made practical use of; even the word sign (which Barthes notes as one of the usual terms) is not used in the theses a single time. And this despite direct reference to Saussure's Geneva school (Thesis 6)—the reference characteristically being to the school's other famous pair of categories, *langue* and *parole,* as "given norm . . . and individual utterance."[69] If therefore one speaks and can speak of "Structuralism" with reference to the theses of 1928, it is Structuralism clearly bound to phase 2. For example, conceptually and terminologically, it links structure with function, system, synchrony and diachrony, and even with the demand that literature be classified within a system of systems (Thesis 8). But the explicit semiotic system of terms and notions is missing.

However, this is true not only of late Russian Formalism but also of early Prague Structuralism. Here, too, this cannot be a mere terminological incidental. In this context, as for the relation between Russian Formalism and Czech Structuralism in general, Mukařovský's first major publication after the founding of the Prague Circle is enlightening. It is a monograph, published in 1928, on the poetic masterpiece of Czech Romanticism, the long poem *May* by K. H. Mácha.[70] The key terms of phase 1, device and defamiliarization, play a far more crucial role here than in many of the writings from the late period of Russian Formalism. The author of the study of *May* also views the linguistic material as something that defamiliarizing devices must deautomatize and thereby actualize aesthetically so that, organized in this fashion as a form, the linguistic material can fulfill an aesthetic function. This is demonstrated by means of a minute analysis of the poem proceeding layer by layer and with precise statistical acuity. But the statistical results are never ends in themselves. Rather they serve to exemplify the dominant that governs the structure and meaning of the whole: a tendency toward de-reification, achieved by the "organization of the phonic material in closed and uniform phonic units";[71] by the attenuation of the direct information in favor of the semantic potential of connotations; by the "semantic isolation of individual words" as well as of syntactic and thematic units;[72] by the accumulation of oxymora; by the effacement of the boundaries between the objective world and the subject (including the "I" of the hero and the poet), and so on.[73] The textual analysis is complemented by a diachronic comparison of poetic treatments of the same theme by three Czech poets from different periods of the nineteenth century.[74] And this comparison in turn helps support the thesis that new generations of poets must apply new devices and construct novel structures, "in order to create a form that is new and aesthetically effective, that is, not worn out."[75]

The resemblance to Formalism is so unmistakable that one might say—as it often has been—that Mukařovský's 1928 study of *May* was still distinctly Formalistic. But put so vaguely, this classification does not say much. One must at least distinguish between the two phases of Formalism and between Mukařovský's concept of evolution and his descriptive model of the literary work of art. Then one can say that the Formalism of the diachronic comparison still corresponds to a high degree to Shklovsky's early concept of literary evolution as an inherent alternation between automatization and revitalization by means of defamiliarization, while the realization of later Formalism that the literary series must be correlated to other series and integrated into the system of systems does not yet emerge. By contrast, the "Formalism" of the textual analysis is no longer oriented to the isolated device and its defamiliarizing function (as in phase 1), but is directed, in a manner characteristic of phase 2, toward the overall structure of the work as a functional system, which Mukařovský describes in its various levels, relating them to each other and finding in them a constant dominant, which governs the structure and meaning of the whole. And one may say in addition that with regard to synchrony Mukařovský applies this descriptive model more systematically in his analysis of *May* than the Formalists (even in their writings from phase 2), while, at the same time, he grasps less fully and less systematically than several Formalists in phase 2 (especially Tynyanov) the diachronic aspect, the relationship of the particular uses of devices and of the organization of levels to literary tradition.

When the early study of *May* is characterized as still Formalistic, it is usually implied (or stated outright) that it is not yet truly Structuralist. This does not have to do with the substitution of the term structure for the term form, for the term structure already begins to oust the term form in the Formalist writings of phase 2, and the terms alternate in Mukařovský's 1928 study. Nor can the adoption of the descriptive model of phase 2 be considered the crucial point, for it is used in later writings of Mukařovský and other Czech Structuralists, which are accepted as paradigmatically Structuralist. The most suitable criterion proves here, too, to be the absence of the semiotic basis, including the dependence, which follows from it, of aesthetic perception on historically changing codes, on systems of norms and values that are handed down collectively and change as does the social collective. Actually the addition, discussed above, of the explicitly semiotic base in phase 3 was not only and not even primarily crucial for its own sake, but because it raised new questions concerning the particular modes of existence and functioning of literature, and because it made it necessary to refer the work as sign and literature as an evolutionary series to the codes available to the recipient (the reader), which required the theory and analytic description of literature as literature to include the relationship of literature and society, and of changes in both.

In this context it is revealing to note that Mukařovský's recourse to the linguistic theory of signs and his development of a semiotic aesthetic go hand in hand with his increasing awareness of questions of the correlation and interaction between literature and society, between literary evolution and general social change. In the early 1930s it is still chiefly an interest in the "low" phonetic level of the work of verbal art and its aesthetic realization that causes Mukařovský (like Bernstein) to take up anew the topic of the relation of structural poetics to modern linguistics.[76] At the same time, however, literary structure as a "complex of functional relationships" is now expressly transposed from immanence within the individual work to literature as a whole, the location of which is now posited in the "consciousness of a particular collective (a generation, a milieu, and so on)."[77]

This shifting perspective also determines the attitude toward early Formalism as expressed in Mukařovský's review of the Czech translation, published in 1934, of Shklovsky's collection of essays, *The Theory of Prose.*[78] On the one hand, Mukařovský defends the Formalistic concentration on how the literary work is constructed; on the other, he emphasizes that the realization of the structure of an aesthetic object "is connected with the work, but exists in the consciousness of the collective."[79] And picking up on Shklovsky's prefatory remark that, if literature be compared with the cotton industry, he, as a Formalistic scholar of literature, is interested "neither in the situation on the cotton market, nor in the politics of the trusts, but only in the yarn types and the weaves,"[80] Mukařovský observes:

The difference between the perspective of Structuralism to-day and the quoted Formalist thesis may be put this way: The "weave" is still the central topic of interest, but at the same time it is certain that one cannot ignore the "situation on the cotton market," since the development of weaving—in the nonfigurative sense, too—is not only governed by technolog-ical progress in weaving (by the intrinsic laws of the develop-ing series), but at the same time by the needs of the market, by supply and demand; for literature, *mutatis mutandis,* the same thing holds . . . From this perspective every literary fact ap-pears as the result of two forces: the inner dynamic of literary structure and an intervention from without.[81]

When Mukařovský speaks here of the "quoted Formalist thesis" and further on of the "one-sidedness of Formalism,"[82] he is, above all, defining his position as against the conception of early Formalism, which set out to deal only with the struc-tures inherent in literature.[83] For in the later writings of the Formalists, the question of the relationship between the weaves and the needs of the market was posed more and more often. And Mukařovský's own demand, stated in the same review, that the literary series be seen in conjunction with the "multiplicity of series (structures)" in the "domain of social phenomena," while one must still respect the specific function of the series (in this case, the aesthetic function) and the "tendency toward autonomy," which still exists despite all interrelationships[84]— connects directly with the eighth of the theses published by Jakobson and Tynyanov.

But, for the moment, Mukařovský's proposal remained contradictory. What in the first sentence of the quoted passage resembles the program for a modern sociology of literature taking into account work structure is then restricted by classi-fying the extraliterary factors as mere "intervention from with-out." To be sure, the point of the restriction is to avoid both the one-sidedness of most sociological concepts that attempt to de-rive literary evolution wholly from extraliterary conditions and also the "one-sidedness of Formalism." But the extraliterary social factors are still regarded as interferences in the intrinsic development. And the literary work still appears as the simple intersection of series, as the product of depersonalized forces, which finally, despite his strong polemic protest against causal determinism, comes suspiciously close to just that.

It was only in 1934, when Mukařovský began laying systematic groundwork for a semiotic aesthetic, that these contradictions and ambiguities gradually started to be cleared away. Felix Vodička later described this development (especially in view of the theory of literary evolution) in "The Totality of the Literary Process: On the Development of Theoretical Thinking in the Work of Jan Mukařovský."

6

One aspect of this development should be paid special attention here, for it bears importantly on the contemporary debate between Marxist literary theory and the bourgeois aesthetics of reception, as well as on Vodička's own theory of reception: the debate between Prague Structuralism and Prague Marxism in the 1930s, and its effect on the Prague Structuralists' conception of the role of the "socially active subject" as the author who produces and as the reader or critic who receives what has been produced.

Two pieces by the Marxist critic and theoretician Kurt Konrad, both published in 1934, are particularly illuminating in this regard. "The Quarrel over Content and Form: Marxist Remarks on the New Formalism"[85] is, like the 1934 review of Mukařovský's just discussed, a direct response to the just-published translation of Shklovsky's *Theory of Prose*. In his critique of Formalism Konrad also takes on the Structuralism of Mukařovský, conceding and recognizing differences but seeing both schools largely as one unit. From this compaction the general objection results that the new Formalism isolates literature as an autonomous series from "social man, its 'active subject' "; neglects "the relationship of the poet to a shaped reality"; and, "by canceling the component of meaning," sees "in the work of art a finished preparation, something petrified, not a social factor."[86] This objection is doubtless more justified with respect to Shklovsky's Formalism than Mukařovský's Structuralism, in which the component of meaning and the social factor were early paid greater attention. But the systematic deployment of these topics did not actually begin until 1934 and as part of the formulation of the semiotic aesthetic.

In September 1934, at the Prague Philosophical Convention, Mukařovský presented "L'art comme fait sémiologique," a paper in which his semiotic version of a Structuralist aesthetic is outlined for the first time. Konrad's second article, "Again, the Quarrel over Content and Form," appeared the same month. In it he continues to criticize certain aspects of Mukařovský's Structuralism, but he notes in view of the semiotic departure that "the theory of art as a sign" provides a "positive starting point for the interpretation of the social character of art."[87] In December of the same year, the Prague Circle and guests representing various approaches (among them Marxists such as Záviš Kalandra) gathered for a special session to discuss methodological problems of the new concept.[88] And as early as 1936, in *Aesthetic Function, Norm, and Value as Social Facts,* the new theory presented itself full-blown—at least with regard to the nature of the work of art as a sign, to its relatedness to social norms and values, and to its function.

This provided a foundation whose far-reaching difference from the position of new Formalism Konrad criticized in 1934 is unmistakable. Defining the work as a sign at once directs attention to "the component of meaning" (Konrad). But every sign acquires meaning only within a supra-individual and binding communications system. For this reason alone (and also because of the changes in history of the collective conditions), the work of art, for Prague semiotic Structuralism, is precisely *not* a "finished preparation, something petrified" (Konrad), but an artifact with the purpose of communication and constructed by the active subject of the author as a potential for meaning, which artifact in the act of concretization receives from the active subject of the reader (or beholder) the ever novel structure and meaning of an aesthetic object. Precisely because the structuring of the aesthetic object presupposes the active subject, the specifically aesthetic function has the power to activate the other social functions of socially active subjects. And the work and literature as a whole have the power to become a social factor (Konrad).

Both ideas were given theoretical elaboration in

Mukařovský's writings of the late thirties and early forties. On the one hand, he treats systematically the aesthetic function in relation to other functions of man in society.[89] On the other hand, the role of the active subject as mediator between literature and society, and between literary evolution and general social development, is emphasized and treated on the theoretical level.

If in the 1934 Shklovsky review Mukařovský still worked from a contrast between an intraliterary developmental dynamic and the intervention of society from without, and if he still thought of the literary fact as the intersection of two largely abstract forces, in his later writings the active subject of the author moves into this function. In an essay with the characteristic title "The Individual and the Development of Art," written between 1943 and 1945, he states: "Personality is the point where all the external influences that can affect literature intersect; it is at the same time the focal point from which they enter literary development. Everything that takes place in literature happens by the mediation of personality."[90] And, with still greater emphasis on personal activity: "The history of poetry is the struggle between the staying power of poetic structure and the violent interference of personality; the history of the poetic personality, the biography of the poet, describes the poet's struggle with the staying power of poetic structure."[91]

Quoted in isolation this may suggest a sliding back to the cult of the author so firmly rejected by both Russian Formalism and Czech Structuralism. But in the context of the writing of Mukařovský and other Czech Structuralists of the period it is simply the systematic development of one of the chief aspects of the triad producer–work–recipient on which this aesthetic of semiotic Structuralism is based. Parallel to the development of the role of the author, this unity is reaffirmed in the concept of the semantic gesture central to Mukařovský's aesthetics and expounded for the first time in 1938, in his study of "The Formation of Meaning in Mácha's Poetry."[92] Semantic gesture indicates, on the one hand, "the fusion of meaning," which results from the "creation of the intention of a work" by the author,[93] and, on the other hand, the organization of the work "as a dynamic unity from its simplest elements to its most general contours." This unity no longer is conceived "as a form in the sense of the 'outer garment' of the work," but as "a semantic fact, an intended meaning, though it be qualitatively undefined."[94] Precisely because of its dynamic character and its lack of qualitative definition, the semantic gesture presupposes the cooperation of the recipient, who from the formal construction of the artifact concretizes the unity of meaning of an aesthetic object, to which unity the subject of the author, as the unifying principle of the work structure, also belongs.

But this already points to the theory of concretization and reception as formulated in the early 1940s by Vodička— and thus belongs to Part III. Here the purpose has simply been to show, by several examples from the debate between Prague Structuralism and Prague Marxism in the 1930s, to what degree the new semiotic conception offered the possibility of connecting analysis of the structure of a work with inquiry into the work's social function "as a sign that mediates between two parties, the subject who gives the sign and the object that receives it, as members of a particular collective."[95] In the view of the writers of the period, and in our own, "new conception" does not signify a rupture with the preceding concepts, but a new line of thought that takes off from them and yet distinguishes itself from them in both theory and methodology.

In constructing an evolutionary series it seems correct to mark at about the year 1934 the beginning of a new concept or phase. This again supports the attempt to describe the relation of Russian Formalism to Czech Structuralism not as the opposition of two concepts but as an evolutionary series with three concepts or phases. Against the background of this triadic pattern it becomes clearer, too, why the systematic and chronological emphasis varies so greatly in argumentative evaluations of the relation between the two schools. For when the purpose is to stress the difference between them it is useful to identify Formalism primarily or exclusively with phase 1 and Structuralism primarily or exclusively with phase 3, bracketing out, as much as possible, phase 2, which is common to both. Conversely, when, for whatever reasons, the aim is to demonstrate the essential conformity of the two schools, what dominates is concentration on phase 2, or even a projection of the entire development back onto phase 1. Depending on the intention of the particular account, these approaches lead to varying evaluations of the early phase. The accounts may make it their polemical business to show that even Structuralism never overcame the narrowness and one-sidedness of Formalism, in which case the new semiotic concept and the correlation derived from it of the literary system and the social system of systems is played down or passed over entirely. Or they may read the entire later development, including the semiotic concept and its consequences, as having been implicit in early Formalism.

In contrast to the tendency to polarize and the tendency to equate, the proposed division into three concepts as three phases of an evolutionary series allows, with regard to theory and methodology as well as in view of the Formalists' and Structuralists' practical literary investigations, clear discriminations. Obviously this evolutionary series, too, fails to do full justice to the concrete, historic variety of both schools and remains a schematic construction. Being so clearly a construct, however, it may sharpen one's awareness of how much every form of literary scholarship depends as scholarship on constructs, and to how much the perspective of the inquirer contributes to structuring the object of his analysis and theory. This does not free the critic to construct at random and at will, but it should encourage him to see his object afresh and to concretize it, giving it new currency as a meaningfully functioning system.

PART III

Felix Vodička's Theory of Reception and Structuralist Literary History

My account of the theoretical foundation of Czech literary Structuralism so far has been based almost solely on the writings of Mukařovský. This is not coincidental. Unlike Russian Formalism, with its propensity for theorizing in dialogue, its parallel and simultaneous development of varied methodological approaches, and its array of several equally representative personalities such as Jakobson, Shklovsky, Eikhenbaum, Tynyanov, and others, Czech literary Structuralism consistently refers back to the aesthetics and poetics of Mukařovský, even where individual points of his are criticized or where particular areas of the theory are developed independently. His work is the theoretical cornerstone for the entire school both historically and systematically, both for the Czech Structuralists' understanding of themselves and for their reception and evaluation by others. These continual references, and the fact that "Mukařovský's teaching has an originality, clarity, and systematic coherence found only very rarely in the history of literary theory,"[1] give the school as a whole a systematic coherence rare in the history of literary theory.

But even as we acknowledge Mukařovský's special position, we should not overlook the fact that his theory came into being in a Circle and developed within the framework of a school. It is true that the school's younger members built on the theoretical and methodological foundation Mukařovský had formulated, but in the process they opened up new materials and new problems, working out partial theories of their own—some of which Mukařovský later incorporated into his theory. This was especially true of Felix Vodička, the most important literary scholar of the second generation. In his writings Vodička often presents himself as a reporter, an applier, or at best a supplementer of Mukařovský's theory, even in areas where he actually is a greater expert, as with the theory of literary concretization and the history of reception.[2] This reflects his extraordinary modesty as much as his basic conception of the division of tasks within literary scholarship. When, as early as 1942, in his essay "Literary History: Its Problems and Tasks," he distinguishes between the tasks of literary theory (as a poetic within the framework of an aesthetic) and those of literary history,[3] he sees himself primarily as a literary historian, building on theoretical foundations established by literary theoreticans and aestheticians. However, the following characterization forms part of the self-image: "One may say generally that all questions the solution of which is subject to temporal perspectives and which presuppose investigations within a historical context belong in the field of literary history; this would include questions of so-called developmental poetics" (p. 32).

It was precisely in this area, the intersection of "investigations within a historical context" and "questions of developmental poetics" (or theory of literary evolution), that Vodička made his substantial contribution to Czech Structuralism and literary scholarship. As shown in Part II, Mukařovský's theory of the work of art as a sign and his theory of the aesthetic function made possible a Structuralist history of literature as a history of reception and a history of functions. But a corresponding translation of this into literary-historical practice required some intermediate steps in theory and methodology. Vodička played a significant role in developing and formulating these steps, especially through his theory of concretization and his theoretical and methodological reflections on the function of literature, which was later to be called his "theory of tasks."[4]

From the time of his earliest prestructuralist writings,

Vodička was concerned with problems of literary effectiveness, with questions of "echo," "reception," and "concretization."[5] Studies of the echo of Baudelaire in Březina (1933), of de Banvilles in Vrchlický (1934), and on the reception of Béranger in Czech literature (1935) still fall within the scope of the young scholar's historical and positivist training in Romance and comparative literature.[6] The article on Mácha as a dramatist, later termed Vodička's "first sketch of a structural analysis, though conceived outside the framework of a structuralist school,"[7] appeared in 1937 in a commemorative collection the title of which—*Karel Hynek Mácha: Personality, Works, Echo*—documents the lively interest of Czech literary scholarship of that time in problems of reception.[8] And when Vodička first appeared in the journal of the Prague Circle, *Slovo a slovesnost* (The Word and Verbal Art), actively joining the ranks of Czech Structuralism, he did so characteristically with an article about "The Literary-Historical Study of the Reception of Literary Works: On the Problem of the Reception of Neruda's Works."[9]

In this 1941 article and in the chapter on the history of reception in "Literary History: Its Problems and Tasks" (1942), Vodička introduces his theory of the concretization of literary works and his conception of the history of reception. For this theory he borrows the term "concretization" from the Polish phenomenologist Roman Ingarden, divorces it from the systematic context of phenomenological aesthetics, and modifies it in a way that allows him to relate it to Mukařovský's conception of the work of art as a sign in an aesthetic function. On this theoretical basis Vodička outlines his own program for a theory of concretization and analysis of reception "in literary historical practice and in the theory of Structuralism."[10]

The manner in which Vodička cites Ingarden was criticized because it allows and has caused "misunderstandings of Ingarden."[11] To be sure, here, as in any self-characterization by means of contrast, there is danger of a one-sided simplification of one's counterpole. This danger increases if such a definition is later taken over in isolation by others as a feature of Ingarden's thought, thus threatening to establish itself as such. Moreover, Ingarden's book *The Literary Work of Art* (1931), to which Vodička mainly refers, is an insufficient basis for a general evaluation of his concept of concretization. The complementary volume, *On the Perception of the Literary Work of Art* (1937), should have been consulted. Yet consideration of Ingarden's collected works does prove his concept to be amenable to a historic view of literature. But Vodička never denied all this. It was the very hospitality of Ingarden's concept that allowed Vodička to make an explicit connection to him, and in drawing up his own theory and methodology, he first notes the features he and Ingarden share. Ingarden, too, Vodička writes, sees the literary work of art structurally, as a system of hierarchically related layers. For Ingarden, too, the work, fixed as text, requires concretization by readers to acquire meaning and to become an aesthetic object. Ingarden also distinguishes between the work and the sequence of varied concretizations in which it lives and which point to the fact that "there exists a time-bound mode of reading, which corresponds to the overall literary atmosphere."[12]

But, Vodička observes, despite these common views, the different concept of the verbal work of art leads to a different definition of its concretization and to a contrary direction of inquiry in analysis. Ingarden's starting point is his concept of the literary work as a schematic creation, the "spots of indetermination" of which must be filled in by the reader. Since such spots are especially frequent in the higher, thematic levels (of the "matter presented" and of the "schematized views" crucial to them), the variability of concretizations affects these levels. The "identity of the work in the nonschematic parts," however, must be preserved, lest "the artistic substance of the work itself" be "damaged." To this extent the work itself has, in Ingarden's view, a "structure," which is understood as the "polyphonic harmony of aesthetic value qualities," and the aesthetic value of which is posited as "independent of the development of the time-bound literary norm."[13]

By contrast, Prague Structuralism assumes the historic contingency of every structuring of the work as an aesthetic object on all its levels. It understands "work structure as an element of the higher structure of literary development. The higher structure of literary tradition is ever present here as a factor organizing the aesthetic efficacy of a work when it becomes an aesthetic object. For this reason the work is understood as a sign, the significance and aesthetic value of which are only to be established on the basis of the literary conventions of a particular time."[14] The passage quoted underscores to what degree, for Vodička, too, Mukařovský's definition of the work of art as sign is the theoretical foundation of the literary branch of Prague Structuralism. But a transposition occurs in the course of Vodička's argument, one characteristic of him as a literary historian. For him the immediate point of departure is not the semiotic definition, but "literary development" and "literary tradition"; only the recognition that these are the critical factors in every aesthetic structuring leads to the statement that the work of art is "understood as a sign." For the literary historian and his concept of concretization it can remain open whether this "understood as" is to be thought of in the sense of a classification or only as an analogy. For whether, for instance, value and norm systems by the aid of which one determines whether and in what manner something is aesthetically significant are the same as or only comparable to codes that govern what a sign means—all this is of consequence for inquiry into the semiotic character of the corresponding theorems of Mukařovský.[15] Yet it alters nothing in the statement, crucial to Vodička's concept of concretization, that only the projection of the work of art "understood as a sign" onto the collective systems of aesthetic norms and values "understood as codes" allows the structuring of an aesthetic object.

By beginning with literary evolution and tradition in order to return again, after introducing the semiotic definition of the work of art, to the "basis of the literary conventions of a particular time," the passage emphasizes the difference from Ingarden. Since the historicity of every concretization of aesthetic objects is fundamental for Prague Structuralism, the interest of the Structuralists progresses from the structure of the work of art to the conditions for its concretization, which are given outside of the work itself, are collectively handed down, and are historically variable. This concept of concretization differs importantly from that of Ingarden, who expressly allows that such factors do exist and contribute, but for his own part concentrates on the relationship between the work of art and the perceiving subject, aspiring in the final analysis to an ideal concretization, independent of time, realizing "*all* the aesthetic qualities in the work"[16]—even if he posits this only in the sense of a theoretical postulate.[17]

To this extent H. Schmid is right when, in her systematic comparison of these two concepts of concretization, she speaks of a "shift in perspective," with Vodička stressing "on the one hand the conditions under which concretization takes place, and on the other hand the consequence of the perception of the aesthetic object, the aesthetic act of valuation."[18] The only thing problematic is her comment that for Vodička the aesthetic object recedes "to the background";[19] it is easy to misconstrue. Such an impression may arise if inquiry is restricted to those theoretical formulations of Vodička already cited, because they stress his differences from Ingarden, while referring directly to the theory of Mukařovský. But when we consider the overall context of Vodička's literary historical research, we get a different picture, which necessitates distinction between Mukařovský's and Vodička's concepts of the aesthetic object.

For Mukařovský, "the aesthetic object [has its] place in the collective consciousness."[20] This is evidently based on the following line of argument: Because the norms and values that are activated in the act of aesthetic perception are handed down collectively, the meaning ascribed to the artifact by their agency—which meaning is equated with the aesthetic object—must have the same ontological status, and therefore be located in the "collective consciousness."[21] Leaving aside the question how methodically to grasp this collective consciousness, this is already unconvincing on the theoretical level, even and most particularly from the perspective of a consistent semiotic aesthetic. Semiotics distinguish very clearly between collectively binding norms or codes and the individual act and result of coding and decoding. Thus, within the framework of Czech semiotic Structuralism Mukařovský's thesis was countered later by the assertion that the aesthetic object arises in the individual consciousness, while in the collective consciousness it might have, at the very most, potentiality.[22]

Vodička, whose theory of concretization appeared a good quarter-century before this intra-Structuralist critique and just a few years after Mukařovský's first sketch of a semiotic aesthetic, does not explicitly take issue with his thesis of the collective consciousness as the location of the aesthetic object. But even where he refers to Mukařovský or quotes him directly, he conspicuously avoids the term collective consciousness, preferring circumlocutions such as "the aesthetic object that in the consciousness of the members of the particular collective corresponds to the material artifact."[23] Or, "in the consciousness of those that perceive a work, the work exists as an aesthetic object."[24] Or, making direct reference to the individual, "the aesthetic object . . . in the consciousness of the beholder."[25]

In introducing the concept of concretization into Czech Structuralism and focusing his theoretical as well as literary-historical interest on the concretizing process, Vodička above all makes a clearer distinction between: (1) the collective conditions for a concretization; (2) the individual act of aesthetic perception and its result, the aesthetic object; and (3) the communication of aesthetic experience within the collective.[26] For Vodička, the individual as aesthetically perceiving subject remains a part of the collective, sharing with the other individuals of the collective not only certain historic conditions but also the need to communicate these aesthetic perceptions and their results to other members of the collective. This leads to talking and writing about aesthetic experiences and aesthetic objects in the collective or to the literary public.

In this the critic has a special function. He is an individual who from the start experiences works of art with the collective in mind, describes the work with explicit reference to the norms that apply to this collective, and makes public his definite statements. For the literary public, he thereby assigns the work a particular place within the literary system and in the hierarchy of aesthetic values, confirming, modifying, or rejecting the norms and models previously valid and canonized, and creating examples for further individual concretizations of this particular literary work and of literary works in general. He is thus the mediator, not only between individual aesthetic experience and the literary public, but also between the individual work and the momentary state of literary and social evolution. Because of this dual function the statements of the critic are the "most abundant source" the literary historian has for "reconstructing the literary norm" of an age.[27] As the handed-down descriptions of individual experiences with individual works of art, they are also his "only relic, so to speak, of the active and evaluative relation of the reader to the work."[28]

These fixed public statements remain for Vodička mere relics, mere descriptions of concretizations, accessible to the literary historian as "testimony about concretizations"; they are not themselves concretizations or aesthetic objects. If the literary historian wishes to deduce the latter from the former, he must first define the manner of description, and the argumentation on which it is based before he can reconstruct the norms that became active in the concretizing act and the aesthetic object structured in that act. The reconstruction of a work as an aesthetic object thus presupposes the reconstruction of the historical "framework of the description of a concretization," which in turn comprehends the "totality of relationships" that make it possible "aesthetically to view and evaluate a work." For this framework Vodička introduces the term *context,* which he borrows from linguistics. And the theoretical and methodological foundation of reconstructing contexts, the reconstruction of particular literary-historical contexts as developmental phases of Czech literature, and the description of shifting contexts in the reception history of individual works or entire schools (as, for example, Romanticism in the various contexts of different European nations and their literatures) become the chief concern of Vodička's writings as a literary historian, comparatist, and literary theoretician.

To this extent—but only to this extent—one may say that Vodička's interest does not center on the aesthetic object but on the conditions and the consequences of its concretizations. This state of affairs has not come about because his interest in the aesthetic object is slight or because he wishes to put it aside, but because he recognizes that the literary historian is never handed aesthetic objects as such but must infer them by deducing the pertinent literary-historical context. For Vodička, therefore, the attempt to reconstruct such contexts and the description of concretizations within their framework does not indicate a turning away from the literary work of art and its structure. It is, on the contrary, an attempt to make comprehensible and describable for scholarship the structuring of these works of art as aesthetic objects and their functioning. "For this very reason it is the task of literary history to investigate changing concretizations within the reception of literary works, and the relationship between the structure of the work and the developing norm; because this way we are always attending to the work as an aesthetic object, and thus tracing the social import of its aesthetic function" (p. 70).

Theoretical and methodological ambiguities are implied in the dual orientation—to the structure of the work, on the one hand, and to the structure of literary development and the context, on the other. In the passage just quoted, Vodička speaks of the "relationship between work structure and the developing norm"; elsewhere, he says that in a concretization "the structure of the work and the structure of time-bound norms of literature meet" and that by reason of its "special character, [the work of art] possesses the properties of a structure." Formulations of this kind, found not infrequently in the writings of both Vodička and Mukařovský, make us question what is meant by "work structure." If what is meant is the structure of the work as an aesthetic object, then it is not something the work possesses and that meets the time-bound norms but something that is only realized on the basis of these norms in the act of concretizing. Conversely, if what is meant is the work as artifact, structure would be a quality of the work itself after all, even before the work is concretized. But the Prague Structuralists explicitly renounced this conception—for instance, in their disputes with Ingarden. At such points it becomes evident that the division, which Czech Structuralism introduced for sound reasons, between the work as artifact and the work as aesthetic object is not sufficient until one also indicates and shows in practice whether and in what fashion the artifact itself already has the property of being structured, and brings this property with it, as "prestructuring," to the act of concretizing, in which act it assumes a guiding function. In other words, one must go on to inquire how, in the act of aesthetic perception or concretization by the recipient, the "code" generated by the work itself as an artifact, structured by

the author for the purpose of aesthetic communication, inter-
acts with the collectively handed-down, historically changing
norms.

In Mukařovský and Vodička, inquiry into the structuring of the artifact and its guiding function—which is at the
heart of later Structuralist and non-Structuralist theories of
perception and remains controversial—is less important than
inquiry into the structure of the aesthetic object and its relation
to the changing context.[29] But that is true only for their theoretical system. In their concrete analytical work Mukařovský
and Vodička used descriptive models that allowed them to
grasp and describe the elements and combinatory rules of a
given literary work so as to reveal its basic possible aesthetic
effects, and hence to allow them to determine and explain why
in a particular concretization within a particular context a particular selection from these elements and relations came about
to structure a particular aesthetic object.

As we saw in Part I, Russian Formalism had already set
up such a descriptive procedure. The early Prague Structuralists were able to adopt, modify, and extend it. As for its rules of
segmentation and recombination, it was a model that divided
the work as a linguistic creation into several levels, each of
which displayed a particular quantity of particular unities in a
particular sequence. By the return of identical or comparable
elements and relations (by the "recurrence of equivalents") one
could grasp and describe structuring that reached beyond the
strictly grammatical and syntactic or logical construction. Tynyanov, however, had already recognized that the question of
which of these elements, relations, and recurrences would be
perceived as aesthetically relevant *in what way* could only be
resolved and described against the background of the literary
tradition as it developed. In the development of Formalist-
Structuralist theory this aspect was the critical one. Therefore,
it was the only one emphasized in my description of the general
evolution from Russian Formalism to Czech Structuralism. But
in discussing to what extent the potential of the artifact is
describable, the other aspect deserves equal attention: the possibility in the descriptive procedure, to describe as a fixed text
the literary work of art already in its status as artifact, in order

to set up the potential thus registered against the work's concrete historical realizations. This could allow us to draw conclusions regarding the contingency of aesthetic decisions on the respective historical context or to construct hypothetically what various aesthetic concretizations this potential of a work would allow under changing contextual conditions.

To describe the aesthetic potential of a work of art by means of a model of levels was Ingarden's intention, too. Characteristically, Vodička does not take exception to Ingarden's model of levels as such, but merely criticizes the tendency to regard only the higher, thematic levels as variables while neglecting the lower levels of "linguistic sound formations" and the "meaning units" of word, sentence, and sentence sequence.[30] It should be remembered, however, that Ingarden deals chiefly with prose, literature in which the aesthetic organization of the lower levels does not play as critical a role as do meter, sound, and so on in verse poetry.[31] Formalism and Structuralism, on the other hand, with their general opposition to approaches to literature that center on content, had from the start paid special attention to the organization and function of these levels and developed their descriptive model—not by chance—in connection with the "problem of verse language."[32] But it is characteristic that Vodička, in this respect, too, would mediate between divergent traditions and tendencies. In his dispute with Ingarden he does direct attention to the lower levels and to the literary-historical variability of their construction and perception. Nevertheless, he does not concentrate on verse poetry, which, being especially relevant, had also been more thoroughly examined, but tests his descriptive approach on prose, the domain preferred by Ingarden (and most who are focusing on the higher levels). Vodička's book *The Beginnings of Newer Czech Belletristic Prose* (1948), remains a model of how the linguistic and stylistic characteristics, the aesthetic intention and organization, and the social function of the literary prose of an entire, crucial epoch of a national literature can be described in scholarly fashion through analysis of the structure of representative works and with the aid of a synchronically and diachronically oriented model of levels that comprehends the social and literary context as it changes in history.[33]

2

The first chapter of this book, an analysis of Jungmann's translation of Chateaubriand's *Atala,* demonstrates how thoroughly Vodička deals with the lower levels. The same can be said of the analyses in other chapters. Still, the emphasis varies according to the nature of the work under consideration and the purpose of the chapter. The chapter on *Atala,* for example, in its analysis of the low levels, concentrates on vocabulary and syntax, which are thoroughly studied, while the sound level is discussed only in connection with the intonational structure of sentences in prose and poetry. On the other hand, Chapter 3, which treats J. Linda's novel *Dawn Rises on Heathendom* (1818), devotes three subsections to the level of phonetics.[34] But in each case the analysis of the organization of phonemes, words, and sentences is part of a description of a work reaching from the lower levels up to the highest ones of thematic construction and conceptual intention and investigating their reciprocal relationships. Only by these means can Vodička's methods satisfy the theoretical and methodological principle of Structuralism stating that structure can only be recognized and described as the interaction of all the constructive factors of a system, since it follows from the principle that to neglect an entire structural level inevitably causes one to miss the structure of the object described.

In accordance with his striving for wholeness Vodička does not, in characterizing an individual level, simply adduce isolated, suitable examples; he covers a coherent complex as fully as possible. In the chapter on *Atala,* for example, he investigates all 223 complex sentences of the novel's third part, then compares them with 200 coherent sentence complexes from contemporary Czech works. Similarly, in inquiring into the function of neologisms, he discusses all the examples Jungmann marks as such. To consider the basic material in its totality (and in all its complexity) rules out interpretational arbitrariness via selection; serves to verify or refute one's own hypotheses and those of others; and allows statistical comparisons of results. Thus, the data on sentence construction in Jungmann can be compared with those in Chateaubriand, and both with the statistically established usage norms in French and Czech prose of the periods in question. These results can be supplemented diachronically with data relating to the development of sentence construction in older Czech prose, and synchronically by comparison with sentence construction in Czech poetry in Jungmann's time. This provides a broad, reliable basis of information for Vodička's literary-historical discourse on the various functions of various syntactic constructions in various texts, kinds of texts, and contexts.

His concluding section on "thematic construction" seems by comparison disproportionately short and selective. (Only the function of the descriptive passages is taken up in depth.) Even allowing that the conceptual tendency was discussed at the start of the chapter, before the analysis of levels,[35] there remains a discrepancy between the analysis of the lower and higher levels, underscored by the quantitative distribution, which points to a general difficulty with method. The lower levels, being far easier to formalize and scan, lend themselves far more readily to statistical comparison. The layering into sounds, words, and sentences had, as it were, already become current in traditional philology, which had worked out historical and comparative data that structural analysis, too, could make use of. The situation regarding the investigation of meter, rhyme, and rhetorical figure by historical stylistics, poetics, and rhetoric was much the same. But the thematic levels had hitherto been inventoried almost exclusively, if at all, from the point of view of content— for example, in catalogues of motifs. The systematic inventorying of formal characteristics of construction as was needed for comparative structural analysis began late and was sporadic. It was most often undertaken in highly schematized genres such as the fairy tale, and in this area, significantly, work only began under the aegis of Formalism.[36] True, in the decades following the turn of the century interest in questions of plot construction, point of view, and so on, increased, and steps toward formalizing and systematically describing these matters were made.[37] But collections of comparable data were still lacking. Indeed, even the basic prerequisite for them was lacking: a sufficiently broad consensus on what levels or organizational planes were to be regarded as essential, what could and should be formalized and how.

Vodička, whose primary concern in this area was to develop practicable analytical procedure, goes back to early Formalist and Structuralist work as well as to proposals made by non-Structuralist research into narrative. In the last analysis his classification, too, is based on a division between the narrated world and the manner of narrating. He separates thematics as a system of motifs into three "planes"[38]—action, figures, and surroundings—to which correspond three "means of expression"—"storytelling," "characterization," and "description."[39] In the case of *Atala,* only the partial aspect of description is gone into, presumably because in this work descriptions (especially of exotic nature and foreign customs) are particularly significant and because in this area copious material for comparison was available from various contexts, as was a rich tradition of theoretical debate on description in poetry. (Vodička makes direct reference to this tradition.)[40] This concentration on description is bought at the price of neglecting the narrator and his problems.[41] Express reference is made to the "change of the subjects of linguistic utterance" and to the significance of variously handled narrative points of view in "changing the shape of the thematic planes,"[42] but in Vodička's theoretical outline of the descriptive model and in his textual analysis this aspect is not fully treated.

What is more important, and more remarkable than the division into three planes and three means of expression, is Vodička's explicit and reiterated remark that these levels of construction or manners of presentation and the relationships among them are variable components, and that it is only their changeability that makes the structure dynamic. "Structure," in this case as elsewhere, means *both* of the essential and mutually connected aspects of literature as Vodička recognized them: the structure of the work and the structure of literary evolution. The work structure (under this aspect) is made dynamic when "as one reads on" the same motif, the same figure, and so on are "assigned [to various] planes" and thus placed "in ever new associations of meanings." Literary evolution is dynamized in this regard because the organization of the individual planes, their relation to each other, and their assignment to the means of expression in literary production and reception constantly change. Only the recognition and description of such dynamic structures, not the mere setting up of new patterns and divisions, open up "methodically new perspectives for us in studying the historical development of literary structure."[43]

Both problems Vodička addresses here—"reading on," that is, the diachrony of the work as a guiding axis in the process of reading and of concretizing; and "change of the subjects of linguistic utterance," that is, point of view as a factor in constructing meaning—were investigated further and more systematically in the course of Czech Structuralism. Structuralists of the third generation particularly have shown how the construction of meaning in a literary work is accomplished in the continuity of its linguistic unfolding and of the perception of it. From this perspective they have defined and described the work as a "process of meaning."[44] Others have supplemented systematic investigations of the lower levels as the basis of a Structuralist "statistical theory of poetic language" with "motif analysis" of the thematic levels, a "typology of narrators," or a "structural theory of content in prose fiction."[45] Outside the circle of Czech Structuralism, its suggestions have been modified and, in the case of Polish scholars, combined with communications theory to describe the "change of subjects of linguistic utterance" as a differentiation between different senders addressing different receivers.[46] On the other hand, the genre-specific *absence* of a narrator and the genre-specific presence of extralinguistic means of expression (mimetic, gestural, scenic, and so on) allowed new systematic approaches to the Structuralist theory of drama on the basis of Mukařovský's aesthetic theory and the testing of it by means of a semantic analysis of plays. But as we consider later developments we must remember that Vodička's book appeared some decades ago, and that his goal was not theoretically to justify and systematically to establish a general model of levels for the structural analysis of literary works. He was attempting to describe the evolution of particular genres in a particular national literature in a particular era by means of the structural analysis of representative works with regard to their fundamental literary-historical context as reconstructed via such analysis.

We mistake the intention and significance of Vodička's analysis of the translation of *Atala* if we measure it against the objectives and criteria of a general theory of translation, to which Czech Structuralism actually has made substantive contributions.[47] For Vodička, the analysis of translation, too, stands wholly in the service of the goal just named, to the achievement of which he applies the general methodical options with great subtlety and in accordance with his special intention. By choosing a translation as the subject of his book's first detailed analysis, the author can begin by conducting a comparison of versions (Chateaubriand's original and Jungmann's translation) with complete precision on all levels. He can demonstrate significant deviations in the work structure as contextually determined variables and thereby introduce his "starting context"—the literary, linguistic, and social situation in Czechoslovakia during the early Jungmann period—by contrast with the French context of Chateaubriand and the older Czech tradition. At the same time he can illustrate by example two of the basic tenets of his theory: that work structure and the structure of literary evolution are correlated, and that the context of the moment is the framework and condition for literary reception and literary production. For a translation stands between literary reception and production. It is a reception of the original in a context not identical with the context of the original's creation; and it is also a reproduction, oriented to this original as an aesthetic object but at the same time creating a new artifact in a different language and directed to a different context.

In this peculiar intermediary situation the translator must decide (and the literary historian can demonstrate by reference to his decisions) whether the functions of individual elements and devices of the original can be fulfilled in the different context by the same means, or if they must be replaced by new ones better suited to that context. Conversely, he can take over the old elements and devices—although, as a result of different contextual conditions, they will have different effects—in order to achieve deliberately such different effects, according to the degree to which his own intention deviates from the original author's. In this way Vodička shows, for example, that a contemporary Czech reader, because of his native (Hussite, Baroque, Enlightenment) tradition, would have received certain principles of diction, syntax, and thematics very differently from a French contemporary of Chateaubriand whose aesthetic experience and expectations were already marked by Sentimentalism and the subjectivism that accompanied it. In order, therefore, to achieve the same, or similar, effects as Chateaubriand, Jungmann would have to counteract the misleading Czech context with different principles. Conversely, despite his own Enlightenment leanings, Jungmann was able to accept a work so strongly governed by religious mysticism as Chateaubriand's, because in the dissimilar Czech context relatively slight modifications would limit the effect of the pertinent motifs and devices to their *aesthetic* potential, to make them the means of a pronounced poeticity.

Vodička establishes this tendency to poeticity for the purpose of aestheticizing the reader's perception as the consistent constructive characteristic of Jungmann's translation of *Atala* and as the chief intention of his program for "newer Czech belletristic prose."[48] At first this may seem an inappropriate projection of modernist or romantic notions of poetry onto an older age whose literature had previously been seen wholly in terms of a national, sociopolitical engagement meant to "educate the people" (the Czech national rebirth). But Vodička's structural analysis and his evidence of "Jungmann's theoretical attitude to problems of poetic prose"[49] prove that poeticizing is an objective derivable from the concrete contemporary Czech context as a task that in this context could assume an eminently sociopolitical and educational function. For the development or generation of an aesthetic consciousness in dealing with literary texts, including in particular texts of belletristic prose, was for Jungmann and his Czech contemporaries the precondition for the creation of a Czech public as the audience for a native Czech literature of quality, which in turn was the precondition and beginning of a new national culture of language and a new national literature—indispensable features of a national rebirth.

The actual value of Jungmann's translation thus rested primarily on the fact that in the special historical context in which it came into being, emphasis on the aesthetic function assumed a great social import. From the perspective of Czech literary history, too, this emphasis acquires a high evolutionary value. At the same time the very direct orientation to the special needs of this particular context reduces the likelihood of new concretizations in altered contexts: it is unlikely that the work in question can establish a high general value or a history of reception in the sense of a series of documented concretizations within changing contexts.[50] Once the specific objective has been reached—once, that is, an aesthetically receptive reading public for Czech belletristic prose has been created—the conditions for reception alter and, as they change, so do the demands made on production. In the chapters that follow his discussion of Jungmann, Vodička shows how (from the Jungmann era via the preromantic period to the romantic poet Mácha) work structures change with contextual conditions. He supplements the results of this horizontal analysis with a sketch of the vertical division (the literary-aesthetic and social hierarchy of belletristic prose during this time).[51] The literary-historical findings and methodological soundness of Vodička's account of this initial phase of modern Czech literature remain unsurpassed to this day.

3

The fact that Vodička, "historian of reception," starts his book with the analysis of a translation that has no outstanding history of reception points to his special understanding of the aesthetics and history of reception. Both, to be sure, he considers essential components of literary scholarship, but they are only components. The whole must comprise all three principal aspects: literary production by authors; the products, that is, the works; and the reception of the works by readers and critics.[52] The aesthetics of reception, understood in this manner, has to do primarily with the "teleological"[53] orientation of every artistic act of production and of every artistic product to aesthetic reception. If representative documents about concretizations are available, the literary historian will adduce them in reconstructing contexts and also in carrying out work analyses. But a literary historian, even one oriented to the aesthetics of reception, can manage without them. If there is no pertinent documentation, he can set up hypotheses without it, offering reasonable scholarly conjectures as to which peculiarities of a work might achieve which effects under which contextual conditions, or as to why in a particular context (the context of its creation, for example) a particular work has had no effect. To the literary scholar whose concern is for problems in the history of reception, the nonreception of an individual work or of an entire oeuvre can, in this respect, be of no less interest than a very eventful history of reception.

Vodička investigated various types of such nonreception historically and in their theoretical implications. His chief examples are the two authors who might be styled the classics of Czech receptive theory and history: K. H. Mácha and Jan Neruda. As early as his essay of 1942 on the theory of concretization, Vodička begins his set of examples from Neruda with the nonreception of the collection *Graveyard Blossoms* (1857).[54] Such a choice, like his later choice of *Atala* as a starting point for an extended investigation, forces a scholar to begin with aspects relating to the aesthetics of production and of the work rather than with documented concretizations. At the same time, the very failure to achieve intended effects and the consequences an author draws from that failure show clearly how literary production is oriented to reception. This is true not only for authors who set out to satisfy public taste, but also and most especially for a "deliberately revolutionary" poet like Neruda, whose "entire oeuvre is intended to provoke strong reactions from readers and critics."[55] The objective of this provocation presupposes the developments that took place in Czech society and literature from the time of Jungmann and the rebirth to Romanticism and beyond to the first stirrings of a realist countermovement. If, in response to the context of *his* time, Jungmann could see his task as establishing a Czech reading public with a feeling for the poeticity of literary prose, Neruda, a half century later, strives on the contrary to "prosaicize poetic language," meaning thus to combat the equation of "poetry with idealizing" grown habitual in the intervening years of Romanticism.[56] This "plan of the author's"[57] can succeed only if the public and the critics take up the work (receive it), and do so in an independent and reflective way, in the form of a "critical concretization."[58] Because *Graveyard Blossoms* did not fulfill even the first of these requirements, Neruda altered his manner of production (though not its fundamental objective). With his next publications he succeeded in provoking a reception, though still not a provocative one; therefore in the works that followed he introduced additional steering and counter-steering devices. Thus, step by step, a better-functioning interaction came about between the author and the literary public, between production and reception.

Mácha's case is different. Although he was decidedly a romantic poet and active in the romantic epoch of Czech literature, his conception of romantic poetry and his work were almost universally rejected by the Czech public of the time, which was oriented primarily toward educating the people and the ideal of harmonic humanity. Mácha was rejected as an aberration into "subjectivity," "turmoil," and "nihilism."[59] Despite the slight and negative echo, he still held to his poetic system, so his work was hardly accepted by the Czech literary public of the romantic period. Because of far-reaching changes in the literary and social context, however, Mácha's poetry, especially the poem *May,* came to be regarded by succeeding generations as the unequaled masterpiece of Czech Romanticism. Indeed, the marked poeticity of *May,* which lends it a particularly high degree of multiple interpretability, makes possible and indeed calls forth new and often contradictory concretizations, timely programmatic interpretations, and new canonizations of the poem, practically each time any deep change occurs in the native context. Eventually, therefore, this most romantic poem of Czech literature became the banner for an emerging, more realistic, poetic conception, designed with a view to prosaicizing. The group surrounding Neruda called their almanac *May;* and they entered into the consciousness of their realistic contemporaries as well as into Czech literary history under the name of the May Group.

The case typified by Neruda involves an interaction between literary production and reception mediated by the author as the subject of a continuing process of production. Conversely, in the case of the reception of *May* it is the work itself, divorced from the author, that, thanks to its aesthetic power and multiplicity of meanings, provokes a continuing interaction between literary production (as product) and its reception. In considering these matters I should stress (as Vodička does) that, on the one hand, the completed work separates itself from the person of the author, but that, on the other hand (and this is often not seen so clearly), by this very process the author, as the subject that produced and organized the artifact with a particular intention and in a particular way, becomes a structural factor of the aesthetic object and a possible object for structuring in the history of reception.

According to Vodička, the most important intraliterary causes for such concretizations of the author and for "changes in the structure of the 'author' in the currently prevailing estimation" are to be sought, first, in the reaction against automatizations of previous evaluations of an author and, second, in the need of new, not yet canonized schools to establish their own legitimacy by referring to authors who are already canonized, and who now have only to be restructured in a way that accords with the newcomers' needs.[60] Vodička gives an impressive object lesson in how very much such changes in an author's image, too, depend on context. He juxtaposes two characterizations of Neruda by a single leading critic, F. X. Šalda; they come to almost contradictory conclusions because, being distant from each other in time (their dates are 1901 and 1934), they were formulated in two very different literary, social, and political contexts.[61] The example of Neruda also demonstrates the degree to which the concretization of an author can achieve independent status, and how closely such a concretization may approach the independence a work or title can assume as a programmatic icon in the history of reception—the "May type." A twentieth-century poet from the geographically, culturally, and historically very remote context of South America, picked up and thus received for himself as author-subject the name of the Czech poet, whose structure as author seemed to him closely akin to his own and worthy of emulation. With this name he achieved international fame at least as great as that of his "god-father." The poet is a Chilean, Neftalí Ricardo Reyes Basualto, known to the world as Pablo Neruda.[62]

The author—a structural factor in the work, as well as the subject of the production of a series of works and the self-detaching object of their reception—bridges not only these three basic aspects but also the gulf between the individual work of art as the central topic of literary scholarship and the investigation of "higher literary units."[63] Whereas the higher unit of genre receives less attention in Vodička's theory, or in the theories of most of the Czech Structuralists, the higher units of "literary groups, the literary epoch, and national literatures" form a central theme both for his theory and for his literary-historical research. Consider Vodička's article "On the Quarrel over Romanticism, Especially That of Mácha."[64] In the context in which this piece was written—Czechoslovakia in 1962 on the occasion of an official inquest into the issue of Romanticism[65]—assuming a decisive, affirmative stance in favor of Romanticism and of Mácha as a Romantic amounted to an indirect snub of the binding dogma of Realism then current, which, by polarizing Realism and Romanticism, had gone far to discredit the latter. Although it was possible, and even usual, for materialistic criticism to distinguish between reactionary and revolutionary Romanticism, the scholarly debate showed that even this disposition ran the risk of equating Romanticism with German Idealism, and equating both of these with reactionaryism or at least escapism. As Vodička's contribution demonstrates, even knowledgeable and sensitive Marxists fell into this trap—Karel Kosík and Růžena Grebeníčkova, for example, who during the phase in question were making an effort to disassociate Mácha from Romanticism, to present him as progressive and significant, and thus to rescue him. Vodička, on the other hand, boldly observes that, the negative appraisal of Romanticism notwithstanding, clinging to the old schematic contrasts in effect perpetuates the "traditional conception of romanticism" in idealistic scholarship instead of overcoming it as "materialistic criticism" demands.[66] He (here in accord with Kosík) refers to Marx's own definition of the "romantic view" as a justified contrast to the bourgeois view and as the expression of the "individual's longing for fullness" in a society that stands in the way of the satisfaction of that longing.[67] Because that is what the romantic view is, it can even, under particular social conditions, lead to a far quicker and more radical open negation of the status quo than an objectively observing and descriptive Realism, although Romanticism also runs a greater risk of taking refuge in "compensatory imaginings" such as "dream, mysticism, and arcana" or in "mere gesture."[68]

In all this the given social conditions are by no means understood as causes by which a context determines an author. On the contrary, the example of Mácha and his relation to the mainstream of Czech Romanticism gives Vodička the opportunity to differentiate his own concept of the relationship between author and context from that of any deterministic contextual method.[69] He argues that "literary and artistic creation is . . . an active exercise of people who under the social conditions they live in and in the forms of presentation suitable to the condition of society and the accumulated experience of art deal subjectively with objective reality."[70]

The objective conditions of the Czech context in Mácha's time favored literature directly oriented to the commonweal, propagating positive values that serve collective, national tasks. Such was the literature then advocated by the majority of Czech poets and critics. From their point of view Byronic Romanticism, stressing the subjective and the negative, was a betrayal of the common good. But Mácha's choice was subjective. As an individual, artistically creating, subject, he chose the subjective direction, which in the native, contemporary context led to nonreception and disparagement. It was left to later generations to discover from their own experience to what degree this romantic view, decisively sustained, was charged with a progressive, even revolutionary, spirit. Retrospectively, Vodička could write: "In our country in the thirties and forties, to embrace Romanticism publicly, especially Byron's, was publicly to embrace a modern and downright revolutionary conception of literature."[71]

One cannot fail to note the analogy to Vodička's own context. In his country in the 1950s and 1960s, to embrace such an interpretation of Romanticism and of Mácha as a Romanticist was to embrace a modern and downright revolutionary conception of literature (and literary scholarship). Both required courage. Felix Vodička's courage was his lifelong readiness to advocate what he had recognized as true, and to do so without fear or fanaticism, hesitation or pretension, even when the situation made such advocacy difficult and personally risky. With respect to himself he would never have summed up these qualities with the word greatness. For him they were not the expression of a Romanticist's unclear yearning; rather they were rooted in a scholarly ethos that strove for integrity no less in human affairs than in learned questions. But noting these provisos, we may apply to Vodička what he says of Mácha at the close of his paper on Romanticism, taking off from Marx's observations on the romantic view:

> Mácha's greatness lies in setting up the existence of this world against illusion as the only real basis of human life and of a possible human happiness. But Mácha does not stand on the foundation of existing social reality; he does not accept this reality as "ideal." Nor did he make himself "ridiculous" by wishing to return to a past world, or by accepting bourgeois reality and the "bourgeois view." He opposes them with his yearning—however "romantic" and unclear—for the human "face," for the human community.[72]

4

This example alone demonstrates that Vodička's purpose as a literary historian is to place a work, an author, or a literary period in its particular context and thus comprehend it in its historical singularity—and by this comprehension to reveal its significance for the present and raise the issue of the historical contingency of the assumptions on which our own interpretations rest. Putting the matter this way, we cannot fail to see Vodička's proximity to the contemporary historico-hermeneutic theory of reception and to the contemporary branch of literary history oriented to the aesthetics of reception. Hans Robert Jauss conceived his principles for *Literary History as Provocation for Literary Scholarship* in 1967—without knowledge of the Czech Structuralist theory of reception. But in the revision of 1970 he does refer to Vodička's writings on concretization (1941 and 1942), calling them the contribution that "most sharply identifies . . . the methodological problem involved in stepping from the effect of a work to its reception . . . with the question of the changes in the work realized in the course of its successive aesthetic perceptions."[73]

Historically, then, there is no direct line of descent. But beyond the extensive systematic analogies, one should remark, as a parallel condition of the two contexts in which these theories arose, that Jauss, like the Prague Structuralists, developed his conception of literary perception and evolution while working directly with tenets and theorems—some taken over, some critically modified, some rejected—of both Russian Formalism and Marxist literary theory and criticism.[74] Mukařovský's work led to his establishing a semiotic aesthetic, which was to serve Vodička, too, as a theoretical basis for his concept of reception. Jauss's concept of the history of reception does not build on a semiotic and Structuralist aesthetic; rather, it is linked to the German tradition of hermeneutics as a theory of understanding. The contrast is no unbridgeable gulf, but it does lead to different directions of inquiry, systematization, and methodological procedures.

Historical hermeneutics, for example, direct attention a priori to the conditions of one's own understanding and the historical process through which these conditions have come about. Thus, Jauss starts out from his own "horizon of expectation," and passes backward from it through the series of the historical receptions of a work until he reaches the work's "horizon of origin." The purpose of this procedure is, first, to actualize the potential meaning of the work through the process of merging horizons, and second, to mirror the history of reception as a history of progressive understanding that feeds into one's own.[75] By contrast, semiotic Structuralism begins with the work as a verbal system and asks how, as a sign made of signs, it can in different communicational situations attain meaning and be structured as an aesthetic object. In Prague Structuralism this approach, too, leads via the collective conditions of perception and their changes in history to a historicization of the entire system, including the construction of evolutionary series reaching into the investigator's own present. The principal intent in forming such series in this case is not, however, to reconstruct a kind of prehistory for one's own understanding, but to investigate the relationships between work structure and the structure of literary evolution. Naturally, Jauss, too, is interested in these relationships, just as, conversely, Vodička again and again reflects on the historical contingency of his own "horizon of expectation." But these matters are weighted differently in each system; in Prague Structuralism the historic reconstruction of the conditions for one's own understanding is not the linchpin of the entire system as it is in Jauss's historico-hermeneutic approach.

The emphasis is almost reversed in their treatment of problems of values. Jauss, like the Czech Structuralists, stresses the historicity of all aesthetic perception; to this extent he understands aesthetic valuation as a historical variable.[76] But the theoretical definition of aesthetic value, the question of what types of value must be differentiated and how to apply them in one's own judgments, are not at the heart of his theory and methodology. They are very much so for Prague Structuralism, in which the complex of problems they raise was discussed constantly from the time of Mukařovský's early aesthetic writings. This discussion in part assumes functions that in the other system are filled by the debate on the problem of historical understanding. For it was precisely in the course of this discussion that Czech Structuralism came to see that decisions about the evolutionary value of a work, for example, demand the construction of series and evolutionary lines, which already in turn presupposes, in matters of selection and correlation, acts of valuation made from the scholar's own historically distanced position.

More pronounced and also more significant for the discussion of a theory of literary reception are the differences in attitude toward literary production, particularly toward the author as the producing subject. Among Jauss's purposes in formulating his principles of literary scholarship as a history of reception not the least was to challenge the aesthetics of production that had so long predominated in aesthetic theory and literary scholarship. This explains Jauss's radical break with production aesthetics of any kind whatever and his deliberate honing of a sharp polemical "provocation." Under similar circumstances the Russian Formalists had made a similar provocative break with literary approaches fixated on the author. Their procedure had been first to redirect attention from the producer's person to the product, the made work of art and its artistic devices, then, by inquiring into the function of these devices, the work of art, and literature in general, increasingly to investigate and theorize about the domain of reception as well. Marxist literary theory and history, by contrast, were and remain among other things the theory and history of literary *production.* Conceiving literature as a reflection that typifies and presents perspectives dependent both in content and form on the author's sociopolitical position, Marxist theory places problems of production and of the author (as "the socially active subject" of production) at the center of interest. To be sure, this approach, too, addresses the question of the function of literature and thus the problem of effect—but the problem is seen in specifically social terms. Indeed the Marxist criticism of Formalism had already taken up both crucial issues: it accused the Formalists of ignoring the character of literary production as a reflection of social reality and also of underrating the social function of literary effect. These considerations still exist. Marxist scholars have used the conspicuous recent shift of attention in "bourgeois" literary scholarship to the aspect of reception as an occasion to recall such options in Marxism and to elaborate them; and they have formulated their "critique of the problem of reception as dealt with in bourgeois conceptions of literature"[77] as a demand that reception theory be strictly linked to production theory as a doctrine of the literary reflection of the social process.

R. Weimann considers the most important yield of Jauss's method of the aesthetics of reception to be "comprehending the historical dimension of literature via its actual, history-making effect." At the same time he criticizes Jauss for skipping over "the literary process—objectively tied to society— of creative expression and of the concrete depiction of a reality that in itself is a process."[78] And he postulates that a Marxist scholarship of literature could never "take the dimension of the history of effect seriously enough; but it will study the history of effect side by side with and after the history of [a work's] genesis."[79] The collection of essays on the theory of reception in literature published in 1973 by the Academy of Arts and Sciences of the German Democratic Republic begins with a chapter on the unity of "literary *production* and reception," placing in the center the author as the subject producing the works and the author's relationship to social reality. A fundamental difference between the Marxist and the "bourgeois" theory of reception is claimed by the Marxists to lie in their own far greater concentration on "problems of literary production of data for reception" (*Rezeptionsvorgaben*).[80]

These problems and the discussion of data for reception[81] that produce preconditions for the reception are by no means unknown in non-Marxist reception theories. Wolfgang Iser in his theory of the implied reader makes a systematic inquiry into authorial strategies whereby data for reception are built into the work structure.[82] And even where recent concepts of the aesthetics of reception, in an effort to polemize against the "data" of particular traditions, detach the aspect of reception too much and at the expense of the aspect of production, it is really only with regard to such exaggerations that a reminder is needed that literary reception and production are mutually interdependent. For this reason Jauss could, in his dialogue with Marxist critics, concede the "*partiality* of the method of the aesthetics of reception," and at the same time insist that the aspect of reception is not to be subordinated to the aspect of production, and that the aspect of production cannot dogmatically be equated with the notion of mirroring.[83]

It is not my intent to summarize the arguments on either side of this debate and to evaluate them critically. I refer to the matter for the sole purpose of pointing out the continuing timeliness of Vodička's theory and history of reception. In this connection I regret that, in the Marxist writings cited, the receptive theory of Czech Structuralism is not considered at all.[84] The collection of 1973, which offers a broad overview of Marxist and "bourgeois" receptive theories, mentions neither Vodička's name nor the receptive theory of Czech Structuralism, not even under the subheading "The Problem of Reception from the Structuralist Point of View," which gives the theoretical suggestions of Russian Formalism their critical due, but then skips ahead to French Structuralism.[85] This is more than a mere scholarly lacuna. For by passing over this very early and very extensively developed theory of reception, the Marxist authors of the collection fail to remark, among other things, that a debate between Marxist and Structuralist literary theory had existed for decades. They ignore the fact that this discussion had very early played an important part in directing the theoretical and literary-historical interests of the Czech Structuralists to the very problems that the Marxist contributors to the collection accuse Structuralist and "bourgeois" reception theories in general of neglecting.

We have seen that Mukařovský, in writings dating back to the 1930s and 1940s, defined the "socially active subject" as the "intersection" between literature and society, between literary production and literary reception, and that this definition arose in the framework of an open dialogue between Structuralist and Marxist literary theory. When decades later, after the emergence of French Structuralism, Sartre and others complained that Structuralism (without national qualification) is ahistorical, apersonal, and in the last analysis inhuman, that it replaces the socially active subject with abstract structures or evolutionary schemata, Czech Structuralists pointed out repeatedly and with complete justification that these charges could not be leveled at Czech Structuralism, in the theory and literary-historical scholarship of which the historico-social aspect and the role of the socially active subject had always played a crucial part.[86] But the language barrier alone sufficed to keep these Czech accounts of Structuralism, like much of the work of this school, virtually unknown outside the native Czech context. Even those few foreign-language presentations of the theory of Prague Structuralism and its development that do include discussions of these problems have been unable to dispel the prejudiced notion that for Czech Structuralism, too, the concept of the individual remains highly abstract and void of its social contents.[87] Such overviews have necessarily had to be very short and thus abstract. They have concentrated on Mukařovský and his theoretical writings, without taking into account the school's full development, including the contributions of the second and third generations. What was and still is lacking, above all, is an adequate picture of the school's literary-historical practice. This alone would provide a sound basis for judging whether and with what success the school has been able concretely to describe the interweaving of literature and society and the activities of socially active subjects in the area of literature.

5

The insistence on concrete historico-social situations and evolutions is one of the chief reasons why the understanding of Czech Structuralism remains, outside Czechoslovakia, fragmentary and one-sided. Concrete investigations into the relation of work structure to contextual structure, literary production to literary reception, and the social import of both, taking into account the particular historical context and its continuous change, could be conducted most thoroughly in the area where the inquirers had the best command of their subject and the precisest sense of nuance: in their native literature and history. One cannot fail to notice how most of the Czech Structuralists, with almost ascetic self-restraint, concentrate on the native context. This is especially striking if one compares them with Russian Formalists like Shklovsky, who generalizes much more freely and easily, interpolates digressions, and often, without the slightest care for contextual differences, documents his theories with motley sequences of examples from the Russian avant-garde, Cervantes, Tolstoy, Conan Doyle, folklore, and Laurence Sterne. By contrast, even Mukařovský, theoretician and aesthetician that he is, chooses examples almost exclusively from the literature of his native land. But, for all their richness, the Czech and Slovak literatures and their cultural and socio-historical contexts are little known beyond the Czechoslovakian frontier. The material selected, therefore, was a further obstacle to making the school known.

This is true also in Vodička's case, most especially with regard to his literary-historical investigations. It applies also to his more theoretical contributions. His effort to test every theorem against the concrete literary-historical material, and his conviction that such testing is possible only with precise knowledge of the momentary production and reception conditions, led him to concentrate increasingly on Czech literature and its history. Even in his early work as a scholar of Romance and comparative literatures (as in the comparatist chapter on *Atala*), non-Czech examples and their contexts served for conducting source studies and making methodological generalizations and, most of all, for illuminating the contrasting native Czech situation and evolution. Despite its universal nature, the theory of reception outlined in Vodička's early years initially and in subsequent developments drew almost all its examples from Czech literature. From the time of his *Beginnings of the Newer Czech Belletristic Prose* (1948) on, Vodička emerged more and more clearly as the historian of Czech literature. This culminated in his official functions as director of the Academy Institute for Czech Literature and in his work as coauthor and coeditor of *The History of Czech Literature* published by the Academy of Arts and Sciences.[88]

Vodička's concept of the literary process, which lies at the base of his literary-historical work from the 1950s and determines its methodology, is usually called a "theory of tasks."[89] It is an attempt to write literary history as a history of functions and to show how the historically altered context of literary tradition and social situation poses or opens up particular tasks for literature; how such tasks are articulated in the literary public and in the dialogue among authors, readers, and critics; how the manner in which handed-down literature is concretized and canonized changes according to the tasks imposed; how the individual author as an active subject in his society translates possible tasks into intentions of his own; how, on the basis of his intention, he produces artifacts formed in such a way that in the given context (but also, because of their aesthetic potential, in other, different contexts) they can be concretized as aesthetic objects; and how, as significantly structured objects, such aesthetic objects fulfill specific functions in specific contexts, becoming factors of literary and social evolution. In this respect this theory only elaborates what, in 1941, Vodička had already sketched out for the area of reception, which was illustrated by the reception of Neruda, and what was demonstrated in such exemplary fashion in *The Beginnings of the Newer Czech Belletristic Prose*. For his later work the era of the national rebirth remained Vodička's favorite—though by no means his only—field for demonstrating what he meant by investigating literary tasks. In this era the new sociopolitical formation of the nation and the creation of a new literature in the vernacular interacted directly, making it possible to show forcefully how, precisely because of its specific *aesthetic* function, literature can become *socially* effective, assuming and performing a multitude of social tasks.[90]

Thanks to this approach, the interest Czech Structuralism had early expressed in the concrete sociohistorical context could be developed in a manner that permitted Structuralist suggestions to be related to the tendencies and demands of Marxist literary theory and literary history. The mediation between them can be criticized for leaving many questions moot, but in the given context Vodička perceived a task he had recognized before, the urgency of which he had acknowledged. The theory of tasks allowed him to keep faith with his conception of "literary history, its problems and tasks"; to present literature as a means of human knowledge and expression that in its social reference and its historicity is unique; to make it timely and, at the same time, by means of careful reconstruction of literary-historical contexts and the tasks associated with them to cast doubt upon the one-sided readings that in their moment of timeliness attain the status of dogma. The theory also allowed him to continue to do these things as he proceeded with his typical conjunction of theoretical and methodological reflections and literary-historical analysis of entire evolutionary complexes, such as particular periods of Czech literature or the overall evolution of Czech literature in relation to the literatures of the world.

How true to his principles Vodička remained to the last is impressively illustrated by a high-school textbook on *The World of Literature,* "written by a collective of authors under the direction of Felix Vodička," the first volume of which was printed in 1967.[91] Roughly one fourth of its barely two hundred pages is devoted to a general, problem-oriented introduction, the construction of which fully corresponds to the course of inquiry customary in Prague Structuralism: It leads from the "Aesthetic Assimilation of the World," the relation of literature to the other arts, and the "Functions of Literature" (chapter 1), via the "Structure of the Literary Work" (chapter 2) and the larger "Literary Units" (chapter 3), to the "History of Literature," with its problems of "Evolution" and the "Literary Process" (chapter 4, parts 1 and 2). Only when this introductory groundwork in theory and methodology has been laid does an outline of the history of literature follow. It takes the reader from literature's origins (in folklore, and in the ancient and Oriental cultures) to Realism in the early nineteenth century, using the most typical examples from European literatures to represent each phase, supplemented by the corresponding developments in the native Czech and Slovak literature. Simplifications occur, as of course they must when topics and problems of such vast scope are condensed for a brief presentation to young students, but the book is by no means only a didactic application of Structuralist theory. The section on "Functions of Literature," for instance, contains a concise and remarkable new theoretical differentiation and independent elaboration of the Czech Structuralist theory of functions.

Anyone reading this book with a knowledge of modern dilemmas in the production and reception of schoolbooks and literary histories can appreciate the meaning of such an enterprise and the knowledge of literary history and theory, not to mention the scholar's personal courage, such a work presupposes.

This book, which Vodička edited so late in life, deserves to be commended in terms like those in which, the year it was printed, Miroslav Červenka praised the *Beginnings of the Newer Czech Belletristic Prose*:

> When literary theory these days does not simply get lost in reports on the views of others or compare theories with other theories, it contents itself, more and more, with projects in which concrete material figures only as "example"; enthusiasm for the perspectives that follow when new methods are applied delivers nothing more than proposed possibilities; method-

ological unrest is gradually changing into a methodological craze. There is a growing danger that attempts to synthesize will become rarer and rarer, and that literary scholarship will disintegrate into pure theory on the one hand and, on the other, the mere arranging of useful facts in publications such as handbooks and dictionaries. In terms of relating the theory of its subject to that subject's history, *Beginnings* remains to this day an unsurpassed masterpiece, a classic.[92]

This quotation, at the close of my discussion of Vodička, which is a report on the views of others and compares theories with other theories, is intended to delineate with all due clarity the limits of what I have been trying to do. The more distinctly one sees them, the better one can appreciate Vodička's own achievement as an attempt to synthesize, systematically to integrate the theory of his subject, literature, with that subject's history. For Vodička, the word systematic always applies to the attempt to show the complexity of the object and of the relationship between its theory and its history—not an attempt to cover that complexity by rigid clinging to a closed system. That is why he asserted again and again that he had never had a system and had never wanted to establish one. This is not to say that he renounced systematic working and thinking. On the contrary, it reflected his determination to inquire with scrupulous integrity into literature, its history, and the tasks of the literary scholar as a socially active subject, and so to stand the test of dealing with systems in the spirit of Schlegel's aphorism, which I have chosen as an epigraph for this book: "It is equally fatal for the mind to have a system or to have none. Therefore, it will have to decide to combine both."

PART IV

Czech Structuralism
and the Present Debate
about Aesthetic Value

My purpose in this final part of the book is to recall a number of ideas, inquiries, and projects of the Czech Structuralists in order to enlist them as possible participants in our current efforts to understand problems of aesthetic value, aesthetic function, and other related issues. In my general introduction I have already dealt with cultural, linguistic, and methodological problems that underlie this attempt. These problems have also dictated the thematic structure of this essay. Each of its seven sections concentrates on one or more issues treated by the Czech Structuralists as well as by more recent theorists. But the discussion moves freely within each section and from section to section, shifting occasionally to other related topics and authors. If such a procedure seems too digressive or not sufficiently systematic, I can only hope—with reference to the epigraph from Schlegel's *Fragments*—that it is justified by the complexity and the dialogical nature of the topic itself.

1

The concepts advanced by the Prague Structuralists are of continuing significance, especially in the current American and European debate about the social role of literature or, more specifically, about how the aesthetic qualities of literature relate to its social functions and to its cultural and historical variability. In this regard the concept of value is of crucial importance. But, as Barbara Herrnstein Smith has recently observed, literary studies in America—and not only there, it might be added—have "for the past fifty years" experienced an "exile of evaluation."[1] Czech Structuralism is one of the few recent schools of literary theory and criticism that has elaborated and tested a coherent theory of aesthetic value. Unfortunately this theory, put forth by Jan Mukařovský during the 1930s, is hardly known in the United States. In West Germany the theoretical writings of Mukařovský have been in print since the 1960s in a well-known paperback series and were thoroughly discussed in the theoretical debates of the 1970s.[2] In the United States, however, where former members of the Prague Linguistic Circle such as Roman Jakobson and René Wellek became leading scholars and repeatedly referred to the achievements of the school, the major works of Mukařovský have not received due attention.[3] The debate about literary theory in this country has now moved "beyond Structuralism" and has become bogged down in a battle of attrition that centers on Poststructuralist concepts. Because of this shift in focus the crucial problem of aesthetic valuation and its connection with social and historical change has continued to be neglected. A discussion of the Czech concept from this vantage point may be of some help in the common effort to overcome such blindness.

I will discuss the Czech proposals mainly in connection with recent Anglo-American and German contributions. That might in part reflect my own Slavic–German–American biography and scholarly orientation; but my neglect of French ideas, which may seem particularly surprising and questionable in a discussion about Structuralism, has mainly to do with the neglect of Czech literary Structuralism in the French debate. Compared with the strong impact Russian Formalism and its transformations in Russia (for example, the work of Roman Jakobson, Vladimir Propp, and Mikhail Bakhtin) have had in France, Czech literary Structuralism did not play any significant role in the development of French Structuralism. And because French Structuralism became the international mainstream of

Structuralism, the polemics during its development and now concerning Poststructuralism have focused on the French version, thus further impeding acknowledgment of the earlier and different Czech concept. Therefore, I will assume knowledge of the French critical discourse on the part of my readers and will only occasionally indicate differences between Czech and French Structuralism, and I will concentrate on Anglo-American, East European, and (East and West) German contributions to the present discussion about aesthetic value and literary evaluation.

Barbara Smith's attack against "The Exile of Evaluation" that I just mentioned and her claim that "not merely the study of literary evaluation has been, as we might say, 'neglected,' but the entire problematic of value and evaluation has been evaded and explicitly exiled" are specifically directed against the American "*literary* academy" (my italics).[4] Such a qualification is in order because the problem of evaluation and the general theory of value have been by no means exiled from America or from the American academy. It is sufficient to consult a survey such as Nicholas Rescher's concise *Introduction to Value Theory* and its informative bibliography to notice how the center of gravity in general value theory shifted from Germany to the United States at the beginning of our century.[5] The pioneering American debate about valuation, led in the first half of the century by John Dewey, Ralph Barton Perry, and others, has remained productive and internationally influential throughout the period of the alleged exile. To understand this seeming contradiction one has to realize that the exile involves not so much a neglect of the value problem nor even the exclusion of general value theory from aesthetics and literary studies but rather a widely shared resistance against becoming involved with the relativity of literary and aesthetic values. As D. W. Fokkema observes in his essay "The Problem of Generalization and the Procedure of Literary Evaluation": "Since Dewey the United States has had a great tradition of empirical research into value problems," but at the same time "historical relativism never got a strong foothold in the New World," which may be the reason that the debate about the historical and social variability of aesthetic values "is a protracted affair in the United

States" and why in this country "warning[s] that historical relativism will lead to an anarchy of values" are popular, persis-
tent, and effective.[6]

It is hardly accidental that both Fokkema and Smith,
criticizing such neglect or resistance, mention Czech Structuralism as the school which "must be credited with having made
us aware of the problem of literary evaluation"[7] and Jan
Mukařovský as the initiator of this achievement whose "explo-
rations of the general question of aesthetic value were both
original and substantial."[8] Both, however, content themselves
either with mere citation, as Smith does, or with a very short
remark about Mukařovský's view on the relationship between
aesthetic value, norm, and function, as Fokkema does.[9] In order to explain the connection between Mukařovský's concept of
aesthetic value and his general theory of aesthetics and literature, I will briefly sum up some of his basic assumptions which
I have discussed in Part II.

One of Mukařovský's earliest theoretical writings dealt
with "The Poetic Work as a Totality of Values" (1932).[10] This
value-centered concept merges with his semiotic theory of literature, which he initiated at approximately the same time.
Literature as verbal art is based on language, which is itself a
system of conventional signs constituting and communicating
meaning only in correlation with collectively shared codes and
norms. This leads Mukařovský to the discrimination between
two different aspects of the literary work, two different modes
of its existence. The first, which he calls "the work as a thing" or
"the artifact," is the text handed down as a selection and arrangement of verbal signs, constructed by the author for an
aesthetic purpose or function. This artifact, however, can fulfill
its function only when perceived by a responsive reader who
transforms the signs and their relationship into a system of
structured meaning, which can now be regarded—and
evaluated—aesthetically. This second aspect is the work as an
"aesthetic object."

One may object that such a dependence on the perception of the individual reader makes this approach, and its concept of aesthetic evaluation, extremely subjectivistic. But
Mukařovský emphasizes the dependence of the individual

reader (as well as the individual author) on norms and values shared by social collectives. The book in which he sets out his new semiotic aesthetics has the telling title *Aesthetic Function, Norm, and Value as Social Facts.*[11] The aesthetic norm does not, however, require that one adhere to it strictly and thus is different from legal, moral, and grammatical norms. It serves more as a tool to generate expectations that can be confirmed, modified, or rejected. At the same time aesthetic norms refer to concrete works acknowledged in the respective society as a canon of masterpieces and models. When a work that deviates radically from the given canon is accepted by readers and critics as valuable, the norms themselves have to be changed in a way that allows them to accommodate the new work. And this modification has repercussions for the production of works to come as well as for older works, which now have to be perceived in a new setting of expectations and standards.

Such a view of literary evolution as a continuous interaction between tradition and innovation, between production and perception, had been put forth by Russian Formalism. Mukařovský goes beyond Formalism by systematically elaborating the semiotic basis for such interaction, by focusing on the correlation between literature and society, and by stressing the connection between the evolutionary process and *aesthetic* evaluation. The literary work, as a "sign made of signs," actualizes a multitude of extra-aesthetic experiences, expectations, norms, and values characteristic of the respective society and its readers. It is, however, constructed and perceived as a work of art, and its aesthetic function subordinates all elements and meanings to its own structure, reflecting on its own construction and aesthetic purpose. In this respect, it is an "autonomous" and "self-reflective" sign. All actualized references are cut off from their familiar, pragmatic context and brought together in a new, complex artistic whole, which requires our imaginative response by making us aware of the controversial relations between structure and meaning, between language and reality, and between our own conflicting functions in society. Therefore Mukařovský can state that the "aesthetic value . . . dissolves into different extra-aesthetic values and in fact is nothing but the general term for the dynamic totality of their interrelations." He can add, however, that this seemingly empty phenomenon serves crucial human functions as an organizing principle. It makes us, who usually act "monofunctionally," aware of our ability to be "polyfunctional." It proves our ability to be creative, to be imaginative and thus to go beyond the given reality, to emancipate ourself in this imaginative realm from pressures but also to become innovative within the social realm. We enjoy the play with different possibilities (or even impossibilities). Our view of society, of our selves, and of human life becomes broader, more intensive and dynamic.

Such is Mukařovský's general view of the aesthetic function and its constant human (anthropological, social, individual) value. One should add, however, that in his various writings on this topic, spanning half a century, his own definitions of the relation between aesthetic function and aesthetic value (or function and value in general) differ in a way which may cause misunderstandings. Thus, in the early essay "The Poetic Work as a Totality of Values" we can read: "The function of poetry is its effect on society with the direction toward a particular value."[12] This statement implies that the function is targeted toward the value as its aim. Soon afterward, however, he states: "By function we understand the active relationship between an object and the end for which this object is used. Value then is the utility of the object for this aim."[13] Here he seems to define value as merely a measure of whether the function reached its goal. The ambiguity results probably from Mukařovský's speaking, here and elsewhere, about two different notions of aesthetic value, one indicating if and how well a work fulfills the aesthetic function, and the other referring to the value of the aesthetic function itself. Indeed Mukařovský usually discusses the latter notion under the heading "aesthetic function," but when he speaks about "aesthetic value" he usually means the ability of an object to perform the aesthetic function (and the degree of this ability).

To make this general concept of aesthetic value methodologically operable he discriminates between three basic kinds of aesthetic value: the actual (or immediate), the general (or universal), and the evolutionary. The actual value is constituted in the act of communication between the artifact and the reader who concretizes the work according to the norms available in his cultural context, which is itself made dynamic. This context can be the one in which the work was written, or a later period, or a different culture. Each time the result will be a different aesthetic object with different actual aesthetic values. It can happen that a work which had high actual value in a particular context never does obtain such value in other contexts. There are, however, works which have the potential to become valid aesthetic objects and models under very different cultural conditions, and this quality Mukařovský calls the general or universal aesthetic value. In spite of this name his notion should not be confused with conceptions of historically unalterable, eternal values of a work of art. To the contrary, Mukařovský insists that the general value is based on the capacity of an artifact to produce *different* aesthetic objects and values under changing conditions. The third kind, the evolutionary value, measures the differences between the structure of the respective work and the structure of the surrounding literary system at the moment of its appearance or, in more general terms, the innovative deviations of a work compared with preceding works and the conventions dominating its contemporary context. And it is this kind of value, Mukařovský adds, with which the literary historian primarily works when he reconstructs and evaluates literary evolution.

Precisely because of this connection with literary history the third category drew early and strong criticism, even from within Czech Structuralism. In the mid-thirties, René Wellek, who at the time was a member of the Prague Circle, rejected Mukařovský's notion by arguing that deviation and newness as such are neither values nor necessarily of evolutionary significance. He held that the decision whether deviations indicate evolutionary trends could be made only retrospectively from a historical distance. Wellek concluded that such a perception is more historical than aesthetic and its value is not an aesthetic value.[14] The same argument was later accepted and elaborated by younger Czech Structuralists in the 1960s, who proposed excluding this third category from the typology of aesthetic values because it was neither aesthetic nor a "value in the full sense of the word."[15]

This controversy deserves a critical review. The statement that innovation as such is not a value needs qualification. Attempts to define a value as such or in the full sense of the word are insufficient without the additional question, a value for whom? As the history of literature and art shows, innovation (as novelty, originality, modernity, and so on) has been a crucial value for many artists and critics or even for whole schools (for example, many Romantics and most Futurists). Yet Wellek is certainly right to claim that the evolutionary significance of deviation and innovation can be perceived and evaluated only from a historical distance. But the strict separation between a genuinely aesthetic approach and a nonaesthetic, historical one does not do justice to the complexity of both our aesthetic and our historical experiences. Our awareness that a work of art belongs to a historical past and that it anticipated later developments does not necessarily cancel our aesthetic perception; it can even add a new dimension to our aesthetic appreciation. One of the main achievements of Mukařovský's aesthetic theory is his conceptualization of the aesthetic function as an organizing principle, "dynamizing" other, extra-aesthetic functions. The historical function—or our functioning as historical beings with historical consciousness—enters together with other extra-aesthetic functions into this mutually dynamic relationship in the process of aesthetic perception. It is not a matter of exclusion but rather one of dominance. If we regard an artifact from the vantage point of a historian, our reconstruction of an evolutionary series will indeed be dominated by the nonaesthetic, historical function and evaluation. If, however, we perceive the artifact "against the background of other preceding works" (Tynyanov) and through our awareness of changes in the artistic tradition since its appearance, the construction of an evolutionary series can very well intensify our aesthetic perception of an artwork as an aesthetic object with "evolutionary aesthetic value." In this respect the notion of "merging horizons," developed later by historico-hermeneutic aesthetics (Gadamer, Jauss), indirectly strengthens Mukařovský's position rather than that of his critics.

Whereas those critics attacked Mukařovský for being too historical, others more recently have criticized him for not being historical enough. Hans Robert Jauss, who mentioned Mukařovský briefly in his programmatic lecture "Literary History as a Challenge to Literary Theory" (1967),[16] discusses him more extensively in his book *Aesthetic Experience and Literary Hermeneutics* (1977, 1982).[17] Having praised him for his emphasis on the reader (or the "perceiver") and on historical change, he goes on to criticize him for persisting "to set against the immanent historical dialectic of aesthetic function and aesthetic norm the aesthetic value as a third constituent, objective and independent of the perceiver."[18] Quoting from Mukařovský, Jauss alleges that the Czech theorist contradicts himself by demonstrating "the variability of aesthetic value" while also claiming an " 'objective (i.e., independent of the perceiver) validity of aesthetic judgment.' "[19] But the quoted half-sentence, isolated from its systematic context, is misleading. The entire passage in Mukařovský's book *The Aesthetic Function, Norm, and Value as Social Facts* is: "The problem of aesthetic value must thus be examined by itself. Its basic problem concerns the validity and range of aesthetic evaluation. Starting from this point, we have equally open paths in two directions: an examination of the variability of the concrete act of evaluation, and a search for the noetic premises of the objective (i.e., independent of the perceiver) validity of aesthetic judgment" (p. 60). Mukařovský speaks here only about different directions of investigation, about a "search," and about the theoretical examination of the "noetic premises" of such an allegedly objective and independent value. And though he takes such a search for this ideal seriously, he clearly rejects its concrete possibility. He explicitly states: "Even if we search among the noetic possibilities and hypotheses of *objective* aesthetic value it is impossible to escape the grasp of the social character of art" (p. 70; Mukařovský's italics). "For us there can be no doubt that art created by man for man cannot create value which is independent of man" (p. 63). And: "Thus aesthetic value is changeable at all levels, and passive inertia is impossible; 'eternal' values vary and interchange, however, now more slowly, now less detectably than less lofty values. But even the very ideal of unaltered duration of aesthetic value, independent of external influences, is not at all times or under all circumstances the highest or only desirable possibility" (p. 62).

I will return to both Mukařovský's view on the search for objective aesthetic value and Jauss's controversy with him. I wanted only from the beginning to show that Mukařovský's position clearly regards aesthetic value "at all levels" as variable in response to social differentiation and historical change. In this respect I fully agree with Jochen Schulte-Sasse, who in his book *Literary Evaluation* compares different theories of literary reception from Russian Formalism to the so-called Konstanz school and concludes that Mukařovský's earlier concept of aesthetic evaluation is theoretically more stringent and more genuinely reception-oriented than Jauss's more recent use of the notion of aesthetic value.[20]

There is an additional advantage. Jauss, rooted in the German tradition of historical hermeneutics and *Geistesgeschichte,* is mainly interested in how particular themes or paradigmatic solutions are differently perceived and handled in changing historical contexts. The Czechs also investigate such problems; but as Structuralists they have in addition elaborated methods to describe systematically the structure of a work on its different correlated levels from metrics, sound instrumentation, and grammatical patterns to imagery, thematics, and worldviews. Applying these methods systematically they have shown, for example, why and how for the aesthetic value of a lyrical poem sound and rhythm are often at least as crucial as thematics, on which philosophical and sociological analyses usually concentrate. And whereas most theories of reception focus on written works (thus the label "reader-response") Czech Structuralists also pioneered in the study and theory of oral poetry and in the modern theory of drama, including its aesthetic values as a staged performance.[21]

In all these fields they stress the interaction among the verbal construct, the individual perceiver, and the collectively shared socially and historically variable conditions. This aspect of Prague Structuralism is praised as its highest achievement in recent studies on literary evaluation, for instance, Schulte-Sasse's book or Karl Menges' article "Theories of Aesthetic Response and the Question of Literary Evaluation." After reviewing critically the reception theories of Roman Ingarden,

Norman Holland, Jauss, and Stanley Fish, Menges comes to the conclusion that even the most recent shift in Fish's theory from the focus on the individual reader to the role of "interpretive communities" has been "anticipated already by Prague Structuralism, especially in the semiotic investigations of Jan Mukařovský."[22]

Menges refers here to the essay "Art as a Semiotic Fact" (1934), in which Mukařovský explains that the artifact has to be "perceived by a public which, following certain collective norms" transforms it into an aesthetic object which is therefore "located in the consciousness of the entire community."[23] Significantly, in quoting this sentence, Menges (or the printer) commits a Freudian slip, Freudian in a direct sense: "consciousness" becomes "*un*consciousness of the entire community." The slip reveals an ambiguity in Mukařovský's statement. He assumes here, as elsewhere, a kind of collective consciousness—which is a dangerously vague notion particularly with regard to developed, complex societies with their social stratification and varied audiences.

In the discussion in Part III of Felix Vodička's contribution to the concept of literary reception and its history I have explained how he clarified Mukařovský's ambiguous notions of collective consciousness and reception by discriminating among collectively shared norms or codes, the concretization itself as an act performed by the individual reader, and the communication of such individual aesthetic experiences and evaluations in the context of public debate. The third aspect, the need for public communication and mediation, explains why for Vodička the critic plays a crucial role: as mediator between his or her own individual and the collective aesthetic experience, as mediator between the individual work and literature as a system (the state of the arts), and as mediator between the aesthetic and the social functions of art. One might add with regard to the public communication of aesthetic experiences and evaluations that the dependence on such social discourse (or, in Bakhtinian terms, on the "controversial polyphonic dialogue" within and with society) disproves the traditional maxim *de gustibus non est disputandum.*[24] On the contrary, the dispute about aesthetic values is vital for the functioning of art and its production (or continuous reproduction) of aesthetic value.

One might also add that the critic's role as a mediator becomes more important than the traditionally emphasized function as a judge. Actually, the legal judge does not merely pronounce verdicts, but also substantiates them by placing and interpreting the case within the framework of valid norms. For the aesthetic judge, who has neither the power of the legal system nor the rigidity of legal norms at his disposal (even though he may use the support of institutions and authorities) and who has to compete in the public discourse, the adequate placement of his case and the persuasive interpretation are the more urgent. Referring to Fish's notion of interpretive communities, one could call the critic an evaluating interpreter who is placing the work within and for an interpretive community.

The intricate correlation of placement, interpretation, and evaluation is evident in a realm which is usually neglected in general discussions of aesthetic evaluation, and which I would like to call evaluative generic placement. To classify a novel with a crime in its plot as a good detective novel places it in this generic line, and may disqualify it as an object of aesthetic value due to the assumed hierarchy of genres (provided that the detective genre in this hierarchy ranks relatively low, as trivial literature). Or take another example, in which the synchronic and the diachronic dimensions of such placements are obvious. Our interpretation and evaluation of one of Chekhov's major plays will differ radically depending on if we place it in the code and mode of comedy or tragedy, farce, realistic drama, or poetic orchestration of moods. And if these plays are placed in the so-called Aristotelian tradition with its stress on dramatic action, directors, audiences and critics may miss dramatic qualities—which happened indeed at the moment of their appearance. Only when the newly founded Moscow Art Theater of Stanislavsky and Nemirovich-Danchenko changed the theatrical conventions to match this new kind of play did it become possible to concretize it on stage as an aesthetic object which now earned high critical praise, emphasizing the previously attacked lack of action as a quality of particular aesthetic value.[25] Applying Mukařovský's three kinds of aesthetic values to this case, we can say the structural difference between Chekhov's play and the dominant conventions was so radical that at first many contemporaries were unable to concretize it as an aesthetic object with actual aesthetic value, far less as one with evolutionary value. The directors and actors of the Moscow Art Theater, by changing the system of aesthetic norms and values, were able to concretize the artifact on stage as a meaningfully structured aesthetic object, thus demonstrating its actual aesthetic value in the contemporary Russian context, transforming mere deviations into groundbreaking innovations of high evolutionary value, and initiating series of new, different concretizations in different cultural contexts—thus proving the high general aesthetic value of Chekhov's plays.

I have chosen this example to indicate how the categories of evaluation elaborated by Czech Structuralists can be applied to works, authors, and contexts better known to most of us than Czech literature and history. The Czech Structuralists themselves, anxious to scrutinize the relations between the literary text and its cultural context as thoroughly as possible, preferred to concentrate on their own literature and culture. Their studies on the Czech romantic poet K. H. Mácha, already discussed in Parts II and III, have to be mentioned here, once again, as striking examples of aesthetic evaluation as placement and indications of the relationship between actual, evolutionary, and general value. Mácha's Byronesque poetry deviated so radically from the mainstream of Czech Romanticism, with its focus on national revival and popular education, that his compatriots refused to make the effort to concretize his work during his lifetime. It did not acquire actual aesthetic value in its contemporary context. The following generation, however, discovered him as the nation's greatest romantic poet and acknowledged how strongly this outsider had changed the poetic system of Czech literature (giving his work high evolutionary value). And from then on each important change in the Czechoslovakian context brought forth new interpretations and evaluations of this poet, asserting the general aesthetic value of his work.

The combination of aesthetic evaluation with historical placement also sheds new light on Vodička's own evaluation of

Mácha in the essay "The Quarrel about Romanticism, Especially That of Mácha." The re-evaluation of the romantic poet by early realist writers and critics did not question his historical or aesthetic placement as a Romantic. The situation, however, was radically different when a century later Czechoslovakia, as part of the Socialist bloc, had adopted from the Soviet Union the notion of Realism as a doctrine—or as what Vodička in his essay calls the "panrealistic theory."[26] As he exemplifies in his own quarrel with contemporary Czech criticism, Realism was now conceived as a "method and an aesthetic category . . . different from Romanticism as a 'historical category.' " Such a general method, allegedly "used by poets and artists in all kinds of systems, classes, and periods," then became a requirement for writers and for works accepted as great works of art with actual and general value. When in the early 1960s Czech scholars, critics, and writers were asked the question, "Is Mácha's poetry romantic?" what seemed to be a task of mere historical placement was actually and primarily a requirement for evaluation—one with strong contextual, political implications, because Mácha remained canonized as one of the great representatives of Czech literature.

In such a situation the easiest solution would have been (and was) to declare Mácha a Realist. A more sophisticated response was to acknowledge the poet's Romanticism but to excuse it as an unavoidable result of his historical conditions. Vodička, unlike other leading critics, rejected both solutions and emphatically insisted on Mácha's Romanticism. Placing him historically and aesthetically in the framework of Czech and European Romanticism, he conclusively demonstrated that such an evaluative placement did not diminish but on the contrary enhanced the actual, evolutionary, and general value of Mácha's achievement. Under Vodička's own historical and political conditions, this was a daring demonstration of the extra-aesthetic, social (here, even directly political) function of aesthetic evaluation correlated with historical placement. As such it is also a proof that the assumption of a radical separation between the aesthetic and the historical attitude—put forth in the critical rejection of Mukařovský's notion of evolutionary aesthetic value—fails to recognize how historical awareness can intensify our perception of aesthetic value and vice versa. To quote again Vodička's own formulation of the task of literary scholarship as literary history: "It is the task of literary history to investigate changing concretizations within the reception of literary works, and the relationship between the structure of the work and the developing norm; because this way we are always attending to the work as an aesthetic object and thus tracing the social import of its aesthetic function."[27]

2

The focus on the social import of literature and its aesthetic function suggests that it might be useful to make a comparison between Czech Structuralism and the Marxist approach to literature from the vantage point of aesthetic evaluation. As noted in Part II, Mukařovský developed his semiotic theory of literature in continuous debate with Czech Marxist critics from Konrad to Kosík. This mutually challenging debate was, however, silenced at the end of the Prague Spring; and more recent theories put forth in socialist countries conspicuously ignore this precedent. Even Marxist theorists who thoroughly question new "Western" or "bourgeois" concepts and whose own less dogmatic approaches share many aspects with Czech Structuralism avoid any dialogue with (and often any mention of) this pioneering school. The same tendency is particularly strong with regard to the theory of aesthetic value.

Literary theorists from East Germany can serve as an example. Robert Weimann, one of the first and most sophisticated responders to the challenge of the new "Western" theory and history of literary reception, outlines a program for the theory of aesthetic value in his "History and Value in the Comparative Study of Literature," delivered at a colloquium on the methodology of comparative literature held in Budapest in 1971.[28] After asserting that the traditional focus on literary production should be complemented by the investigation into literary reception, he continues:

> In this context the concept of *Wirkungsgeschichte* indicates a sociological dimension of value which comparative literature

will have to consider in methodological and practical terms. I am using the phrase "sociological dimension of value" because the specific function or structure and the social nature and impact of the work of art do not necessarily contradict one another. On the contrary, once the artwork's impact on society and its inherent qualities achieve a meaningful correlation, its sociological dimension can potentially be considered as an index of value. (p. 42)

This statement corresponds strikingly with concepts put forth by the comparatist Vodička or by Mukařovský. But instead of referring to them Weimann adds, "It was under the influence of Marx that Sartre, I think, first made the point that in order to be complete, the process of literary creation involves both the work of the author and the cooperation of the reader" (p. 42). After mentioning Arthur Nisin, Robert Escarpit, and Hans Robert Jauss, he concludes his survey of existing proposals without any reference to Czech Structuralism, with its theories of literary reception and aesthetic value (as well as its debate with Marxist critics).

In the same year that Weimann's draft of a program appeared, another literary scholar from East Germany, Rita Schober, published an elaborate Marxist formulation of "The Problem of Literary Evaluation."[29] Like Weimann and other recent contributors to Marxist literary theory, Schober discriminates her own approach from a reductive concept of the reflection theory as mere mirroring (which she rejects as naturalistic). Literature does not directly mirror a "world of objects" but creates a "world of values." Using language, which always has a referential dimension and carries an "ideological freight," the author produces the work as a "polyfunctional polystructure," which can function only if the reader, as an active "receptor," perceives the work as a meaningful whole. As such the reader can now apply it as a model for comparison to his or her own world. For the contemporary reader this will be historically the same world as for the author. Later readers will recreate the model in a way that enables them to apply it to their own context and will at the same time acknowledge "the historical process lived through since its appearance." Each perception has to take into account "the time of production" as well as "the time of reception."

Schober's concept of the problem of evaluation is clearly a relational one, in which traditional Marxist views are combined with communication theory and with some recent theories of aesthetic perception or reception. Evaluation is conceived as an act always involving an evaluating subject, an evaluated object, and a framing system of references. In the case of literature the system of references is twofold: on the one side, the literary work is perceived and evaluated in relation to mirrored reality; on the other side, as a work of art, it is related to previous works of literature and to the whole literary process. The act of literary evaluation is itself twofold: first, the evaluation of the world presented or referred to within the work; second, the evaluation of the work itself. The latter evaluation is "evaluation of the second degree, evaluating an 'evaluation' objectified in the work of art itself as its 'aesthetic value' " (p. 32). Schober acknowledges that this could seem to lead to "subjective relativism," and she explicitly admits that "the starting and the end point of any evaluation is the subject." Value is always "realized in the individual act of evaluating." Nevertheless, the criteria constituting such individual acts are "mainly social, that is, objectively conditioned." They remain, however, historically changeable; later generations of readers will perceive and evaluate the same work differently. Thus, some works which had a strong impact and were highly valued in their contemporary context may later lose this actual value and have at best historical significance, whereas other works remain topical and valid and initiate pleasure in very different cultural contexts, thus establishing in the course of history a record of "objectively secured evaluation."

The parallels with Prague Structuralism are even more obvious than in Weimann's program. Schober explicitly mentions Formalism and Structuralism, but she reduces Russian Formalism to its early and rather one-sided position and she claims that Structuralism "from Jakobson to Barthes" has rejected evaluation as a "misleading task"—simply ignoring or omitting that at least one crucial part of European Structuralism, the earliest Czech version, elaborated a stringent Structuralist theory of aesthetic value and literary evaluation. Instead, she ends by advancing the doctrine of progressive history as evidence for progressive Marxist evaluation, both culminating in "the method of Socialist Realism" as the only "adequate praxis of art" (pp. 47–50).

Unfortunately, the neglect of the Prague school is also characteristic of American and English Marxist literary theorists and critics. Even a representative book such as Fredric Jameson's *The Prison-House of Language,* with its subtitle "A Critical Account of Structuralism and Russian Formalism," moves from the Russian Formalists directly to the French Structuralists without taking Czech Structuralism into account.[30] The same is true for contributions dealing especially with aesthetic evaluation, such as Terry Eagleton's essay "Marxism and Aesthetic Value," included as the final chapter in his book *Criticism and Ideology.*[31]

Eagleton introduces his book with a complaint that as an English Marxist trying to construct a materialist aesthetics he is almost unavoidably "disenfranchised from debate" and that his chapter on the problem of literary value is merely a "clearing ground on which a genuine discussion of these matters could be conducted." Czech Structuralism, now also disenfranchised from debate, would have offered an excellent though rather indirect chance for a debate of these matters. Eagleton characterized his own approach as a "double refusal"—of Marxist or non-Marxist concepts reducing literature to a mere mirroring of the given historical moment and of "reductive operations of formalism" (p. 166). This way of putting things recalls Mukařovský's position in 1934 when he articulated his own recently introduced semiotic Structuralism in an open debate with Shklovsky's reductive Formalism on the one side and the positions of Czech Marxist critics on the other side. For Mukařovský the value of a literary work depends on its ability to challenge the total view of society and our relation to it as well as on its innovative deviation from literary tradition and convention at the moment of its appearance. Eagleton conceives the value of a text as "determined by its double mode of insertion into an ideological formation and into the available lineage of literary discourse" (p. 186). Mukařovský defines the aesthetic function as negative and empty insofar as it only organizes other, extra-aesthetic functions, elements, and values, cutting them off from their pragmatic entanglement and integrating them into the structure of the work where they gain a new, specific meaning. For Eagleton the literary work's "aesthetic effect is itself the index of a certain bracketing, whereby the work dissolves and distantiates the real to produce it as a signification. The aesthetic is that which speaks of its historical conditions by remaining silent—inheres in them by distance and denial" (p. 177).

Such dialectics between the inherence in and the distance from the particular historical conditions in which a work was once produced revive the old question that troubled Marx and Engels in their evaluation of artworks of the past. If one defines the work of art as a mirroring of its historical and social conditions and their ideology, one has to explain why works of the remote past can still have aesthetic value for us—that is, for later readers who live in radically different sociohistorical contexts. The traditional Marxist answer is to separate the ideological significance—directly relevant for the author's contemporaries and historically relevant for us—from the aesthetic value, which could not be rationally explained but had to be admired as the product of a creative genius. Eagleton attacks both sides of the argument. He points out with shrewd irony that Trotsky's evaluation of Dante and Lenin's evaluation of Tolstoy fall back upon "the Romantic category of individual 'greatness' " (p. 174). And he rejects the reductive explanation of a work merely as a product of a certain social milieu. "It is not that Dante's work is valuable because it 'speaks of' an important historical era, or 'expresses the consciousness' of that epoch" but because it "internally distantiates" itself from the "complex ideological conjunction" in which it inheres and which it produces, thus rendering "its depths and intricacies vividly perceptible."

Eagleton's rejection of the recourse to creative genius does not imply disinterest in the role of production. On the contrary, he demands from a genuinely materialist approach that it "re-enact the founding gesture of Marxist political economy and reconsider the question of aesthetic value on the side of literary *production*." At the same time he states: "Literary value is a phenomenon which is produced in that ideological appropriation of the text, that 'consumptional production' of the work, which is the act of reading." Thus it seems that both sides of the communication, the author and the reader, are fully taken into account. But the theoretical and methodological importance of the reader's response is minimized when Eagleton, at the very beginning of his essay, refutes all "reformist moves towards 'reader participation'" as tautologies which "we may leave aside." Instead he proposes to scrutinize "the value-question" not in the interaction between reader and text but on the "level of the text's own historical self-production in relation to its ideological environs" (p. 168). By narrowing the focus to the text, not only does the reader slip out of sight; the author as producer also recedes, because the text appears now as a product of its "own historical self-production." Although this quotation speaks at least of a *relation* to the ideological environs, soon ideology itself, or "the ideological," becomes that which genuinely "produces" (p. 177).

It is this narrowing of the communicative process and the conceptualization of the text as the product of an almost substantialized "ideological" which has to be objected to, not the concern with ideology as such or the attempt to show how a literary work represents a particular ideological formation and at the same time distances itself from it. But for an adequate understanding of this process and its aesthetic significance (and value) one has to consider the effect of it on the reader and the reader's response to this ideological and aesthetic challenge— instead of "leaving aside" concepts of reader-participation. This is even more urgent for an explanation of why and how such challenges of a literary work can be continuously reactualized as aesthetic values in the course of history and in the transition from one culture to another.

In this respect it is worthwhile to mention at least briefly a collective attempt of other British Marxists to apply Eagleton's proposals critically. In their article "History and Literary 'Value': The Case of *Adam Bede* and *Salem Chapel*,"[32] Peter Widdowson, Paul Stigant, and Peter Brooker take Eagleton's (and Althusser's) analysis of ideological structures in literary

works as a starting point but criticize Eagleton for not sufficiently discriminating between "authentic" and "mediocre" literary works and for presenting merely a "broad, skeletal
reference . . . to the ideology and social relations which are
specific to particular moments in history" (pp. 4, 5). They scrutinize more intensively the specific historical conditions and
show that both novels distantiate ideology, but the mediocre
novel of Mrs. Oliphant simply "criticizes ideology in terms of
ideology," whereas George Eliot's authentic novel exemplifies
"more intrinsically how ideology is reproduced" as an "explan-
atory power" and an "imaginary account of real relations" (p.
37).

That Mrs. Oliphant's novel is mediocre and has less (or
no) literary value compared with George Eliot's could probably
have been proven without such ideological scrutiny or by
merely referring to a skeletal ideological frame. Nevertheless,
the critics succeed in pointing out how differently the two novelists deal with the ideology of the same sociohistorical context
and how the genuine work reproduces, explains, and thus to a
certain extent overcomes the established ideology. But this can
prove, at best, the validity of this work as a historical example
for the laying bare of ideology. It does not explain the specific
aesthetic (or literary) quality of this achievement, far less the
impact of such structural display of ideology on the enrichment
and evolution of literature as verbal art—its evolutionary aesthetic value. And the more closely the critics focus on the particular ideological formation in the particular historical
moment, the less they are able to exemplify if, why, and how
the "momentary" actual value of the work in its original sociohistorical context can be reactualized under radically different
historical, social, and ideological conditions. To use their own
formulation, we learn about the novel's value in "the historically
precise 'real relations' in which it *stands*" (p. 38, my italics); but,
to use the terms of Mukařovský's value categories, we do not
learn why and how such actual value can be accumulated and
be transformed into a general aesthetic value in the *process* of
history in which the genuine work of literature and its genuinely literary value do not "stand" but move, as a continuously
renewed and modified response to changing historical condi-

tions and ideological formations. Hence, when the three authors announce that to overcome shortcomings of Eagleton's approach they "would rather suggest the need for a criterion of value which accounts necessarily for the artistic, ideological, and historical threads which weave a 'text' with its 'context' " in the "dialectic between the internal world a work presents and the historically precise 'real relations' in which it stands" (p. 38), they actually propose as a program what Czech Structuralists half a century earlier had proposed and elaborated theoretically and tested in textual analysis and historical investigation.

Czech Structuralists investigating the "threads which weave a text with its context" were, however, mainly concerned with the artistic (or aesthetic) and the historical aspects of this process and less—at least less than Marxist literary theory and criticism—with its specifically ideological function. Though Mukařovský, Vodička, and other Czech Structuralists were fully aware of the impact of ideology on literary production, perception, and evaluation, they did not elaborate a coherent theory of the interaction between literature and ideology. Regarding the complex relationship between literary structures and ideology, the crucial innovative contribution came from another contemporary Slavic group which was also semiotically oriented and whose theory also took shape in a kind of "double refusal" of reductive Formalist and reductive Marxist positions. I refer to the group of Russian literary theorists around Mikhail Bakhtin; and I refer deliberately not simply to Bakhtin but to the group as a whole, because the decisive role of ideology was systematically discussed mainly in the two early works, *The Formal Method in Literary Scholarship: A Critical Introduction to Sociological Poetics*, published in 1928 as the work of P. N. Medvedev, and *Marxism and the Philosophy of Language*, published in 1929 as the work of V. N. Voloshinov.[33]

The Formal Method attacks Formalism, not as Marxists usually did and do for overemphasizing the "specificity" of literature, but for not being specific enough. Formalism (and Medvedev identifies Formalism with its early, extreme position) misconceives language as a kind of neutral material which the artist forms into a meaningful construct. But language as speech is never a neutral repertoire of words and linguistic rules; in its everyday use it communicates by utterances that select, interpret, and evaluate reality or our attitudes toward it. The interaction of such evaluative views and opinions, articulated as voices in a polyphonic and controversial (or "heteroglossical") dialogue, form the ideological discourse which surrounds us as users of language and to which each utterance or special discourse refers and contributes.[34] The ideological realm separates us from unmediated reality but at the same time refers us to it. Hence, we can neither directly mirror reality, as reductive Marxist concepts claim, nor use language without becoming entangled in its referentiality and in the ongoing ideological discourse—as reductive Formalism assumes.

For Bakhtin the most adequate literary response to this polyphonic dialogue and its challenge is the genre of the novel. Itself polyphonic and "dialogical" in its interaction of controversial voices reported or mediated by the voice of the narrator, it is at the same time a critical and self-critical (critically self-reflected) dialogue with the surrounding society and its controversial ideological discourse. Bakhtin's theory of the novel—particularly his studies on Dostoevsky and on Rabelais and the Carnival, and his comprehensive theory and history of the genre, "The Discourse in the Novel"[35]—have finally found the broad international acknowledgment they deserve. Some of his basic notions, such as the "polyphonic dialogue" or "the Carnivalesque," permeate recent literary theory and criticism. But the understandable fascination with these aspects of his theory tends to detract from his emphasis on ideology as the crucial link between literature, language, and society, which was put forth in the early books of the group and which also serves as a basis for Bakhtin's concept of the novel. In "The Discourse in the Novel" he states: "The novel begins by presuming a verbal and semantic decentering of the ideological world, a certain linguistic homelessness of literary consciousness, which no longer possesses a sacrosanct and unitary linguistic medium for containing ideological thought; it is a consciousness manifesting itself in the midsts of social languages" (p. 367). The statement alludes to Georg Lukács' famous characterization of the novel as the most adequate "expression of transcendental homelessness" in his *Theory of the Novel* (1916, 1920).[36] Bakhtin, during his years in Leningrad (1924–1929), had started a translation of Lukács' book into Russian but gave up his project upon learning that Lukács no longer liked his early (more Hegelian than Marxist) masterpiece.[37] Like Lukács, Bakhtin conceives of the novel as a modern counterpart to the epic that appeared under particular sociohistorical conditions (though Bakhtin traces the novel back to its Hellenistic beginnings).[38] He, too, is concerned with ideological thought and social languages. But whereas Bakhtin emphasizes language and the diversity of social languages and voices, Lukács tends to neglect the constitutive role of language, of the "Word in the Novel."[39] In general Lukács considers the pluralism of modern society, in which the individual experiences "transcendental homelessness," as a transitional (though historico-dialectically indispensable) stage which should be overcome and will be overcome by the revolution. In his writings after the early *Theory of the Novel* he claims that the expected new stage has been initiated by the newly established Soviet state and its socialist society, which can and must command a unified ideology and a unified language. This is one of the reasons why the author of the early revolutionary book on the novel could so soon become one of the leading promoters and theorists of Socialist Realism.

In 1934, the same year in which the First Congress of Soviet Writers established Socialist Realism as the only acceptable, unifying, and sacrosanct literary doctrine, Bakhtin, in exile beyond the Ural mountains, wrote "The Discourse in the Novel," courageously insisting on the value of diversity and controversial "heteroglossia."[40] He did so explicitly; but as the cunning theorist and analyst of innuendoes in discourse he often used mere allusions or proposed mere reformulations. Thus he merely alludes to Lukács' "homelessness." Or, at the end of the same essay, he proposes a reformulation of the traditional and at this time particularly topical requirement that "the novel must be a full and comprehensive reflection of its era" (p. 411). Obviously he refers here to Hegel's famous characterization of the novel as the product and adequate expression of the modern prosaic era, in which its task is to achieve what the epic did for older societies—that is, to represent the "unified totality" of the world in its given stage of development.[41] This Hegelian definition was reinforced by Marx, Engels, and Soviet criticism (including Lukács). Bakhtin, avoiding names, refers to this traditional concept when he speaks of the imperative which emerged in the wake of the polyphonic modern novel (since *Don Quixote*) and which "was later often hailed as constitutive for the novel as a genre." He proposes, "The imperative should be formulated differently: the novel must represent all the social and ideological voices of its era, that is, all the era's languages that have any claim to being significant; the novel must be a microcosm of heteroglossia" (p. 411).

Bakhtin's own proposal is hardly less imperative. He does not reject or reduce the task of representing society as a complex whole, but it has to be represented in *language* as a controversial ideological dialogue. All claims to mirror reality directly and objectively have to be laid bare as "utopian pretensions."[42] Language itself as speech becomes the genuine object of representation and the main issue of analysis. The controversial polyphony of social and literary discourse is conceived and evaluated not as a transitory shortcoming which should soon be surmounted but as an individual and social value worth fighting for.

Though this controversial diversity is manifest in the coexistence of different individual voices and social languages, Bakhtin, as a semiotician, traces its genuine source back to the process of semiosis itself. The connection of conventional signs with meaning and reference generates ambivalence, interpretability, and controversy. But this ambivalence is for Bakhtin neither an imprisonment in language which separates us from reality nor an erosion of value. On the contrary, he defends it as a valuable human condition which makes it possible and necessary for an individual voice to respond to the ongoing dialogue and thus to participate in social and historical reality. One can say with Rainer Grübel that for Bakhtin "the ambivalence of semiosis is the value-equivalent to the freedom of meaning. Where the process of signification becomes unambiguously fixed in its valuation, the freedom of interpretation gets lost."[43] In a very direct sense Bakhtin correlates the freedom of speech as a basic human right and value with the freedom of interpretation, tracing back both to the ambivalence of semiosis, which requires dialogue and evaluative interpretation.

This freedom (or this ambivalence), however, would lead to an "anarchy of meaning"[44] if the response itself is not structured in ways indicating meaning and evaluation. Responding to this danger, Bakhtin the semiotician becomes a semiotic Structuralist—in the broad sense in which Roland Barthes later defined "Structuralist activity." For Barthes this "activity, whether reflexive or poetic . . . reconstruct[s] an 'object' in such a way as to manifest thereby the rules of functioning (the 'functions') of this object," thus transforming or recreating the object into a meaningfully structured "simulacrum."[45] For Bakhtin this activity is also a combination of the cognitive and the creative. It relates (as for Barthes) to our perception of real objects as well as to the construction and perception of imaginative objects and worlds. It unifies otherwise disintegrated elements or aspects into meaningfully structured wholes. And it is, as Bakhtin emphasizes, always an evaluative activity as well.

Bakhtin's notion of the "chronotope" is an illuminating example of an evaluative structure that refers to the perception of reality as well as to the construction of fictional worlds. Michael Holquist, in his introduction to *The Dialogical Imagination,* refers to this notion as "a category that no brief introduction (much less glossary) can adequately adumbrate,"[46] and yet describes it aptly in his glossary as a "time-space" category that stresses the interdependence of both dimensions and enables us to read "texts as X-rays of forces at work in the cultural system from which they spring" (pp. 425, 426). The only thing missing in connection with the topic under discussion is the strong evaluative aspect of this structuring principle. Bakhtin stresses it himself by adding to his essay "Forms of Time and the Chronotope in the Novel" (written in 1937–38 but not published until 1975) "Concluding Remarks" that, significantly, begin with one of his most explicit statements on value:

> A literary work's artistic unity in relationship to an actual reality is defined by its chronotope. Therefore the chronotope in a work always contains within it an evaluating aspect that

can be isolated from the whole artistic chronotope only in abstract analysis. In literature and art itself, temporal and spatial determinations are inseparable from one another, and always colored by emotions and values. Abstract thought can, of course, think of time and space as separate entities and conceive of them as things apart from emotions and values that attach to them. But *living* artistic perception (which also of course involves thought, but not abstract thought) makes no such divisions and permits no such segmentation. It seizes on the chronotope in all its wholeness and fullness. Art and literature are shot through with *chronotopic values* of varying degree and scope. Each motif, each separate aspect of artistic work bears value.   (p. 243; Bakhtin's italics)

The relationship between a work and an actual reality is apprehended as an evaluating relationship. It is a twofold process of reference and evaluation: each element, as a sign, has a referential dimension and at the same time "bears value"; but each is also and primarily a part of the artistic unity of the work which, as a meaningfully structured whole, refers to the actual reality and to the principles of structuring and evaluating reality. The unity itself, however, is the result of "living artistic perception." Although Bakhtin speaks here about artistic perception and the artistic unity of the work, for him both the artist's creative perception and its result, the work as an artifact, need the response of the reader, his or her "living" concretization of the artifact as an aesthetic object related "in all its wholeness and fullness" to the reader's own actual reality, thus actualizing and evaluating also this context and its values. The similarities with Mukařovský's concept of aesthetic evaluation—particularly with his notion of actual aesthetic value—are obvious. But to understand what both concepts of evaluation have in common and in which respects they differ, additional qualifying remarks about Bakhtin's approach are needed.

Comparing Bakhtin's approach with Lukács' I said that Bakhtin stresses the constitutive role of language. This emphasis on language should not be confused with linguistic approaches to literature. On the contrary, he repeatedly and emphatically distances his own concept from such approaches. "Descriptive linguistics" (as well as "behaviorism") can describe only the "mechanism" of "utterances" as reactions and that of the dialogue as a chain of reactions; but such mechanical analyses apply to true as well as to false statements and to works of art by geniuses as well as to talentless products. They cannot define the specifically aesthetic qualities and values of literary works, nor can they describe the particular relationship of literature (as fiction) to reality, nor can they adequately deal with the claims and evaluative implications of literary utterances:

> Every utterance makes a claim to justice, sincerity, beauty, and truthfulness (a model utterance), and so forth. And these values of utterances are defined not by their relation to the language (as a purely linguistic system), but by various forms of relation to reality, to the speaking subject and to other (alien) utterances (particularly to those that evaluate them as sincere, beautiful, and so forth).
>
> Linguistics deals with the text, but not with the work. What it says about the work is smuggled in, and does not follow from purely linguistic analysis.[47]

This is not the place to discuss whether Bakhtin's opinion about linguistics does justice to all kinds of linguistic analysis, including more recent developments in speech-act theory, discourse analysis, and so on. What matters are the caveat against linguistic claims to grasp the specific qualities and values of literary works, and Bakhtin's use of these polemics to distinguish his own approach. His own focus is on the implications, claims, and valuations of speech in literature and on its different forms of relationship to the speaking subject, to other speaking subjects, and to the reality in which and about which such utterances are spoken. The speaking subject itself is conceived and evaluated not only as a subject of verbal expression but also and mainly as a subject of dialogic response. It is hardly an exaggeration to say that responsiveness was the starting point and remained the basis for Bakhtin's approach to literature, literary criticism, aesthetics, their ethical foundation, and his concept of value.

Significantly, his first publication, a short programmatic declaration of the young scholar printed in 1919 in a provincial journal but almost unknown until its posthumous republication in 1979, is on "Art and Responsibility."[48] The Russian word *otvetstvennost'* which Bakhtin uses has the denotative meaning "responsibility." But the noun *otvet* from which it is derived means "answer, reply, response"; and the verb *otvechat'* means both "to answer, to respond" and "to be answerable, responsible."[49] Though Bakhtin is exploiting particular semantic possibilities of the Russian language, the correlation of the two meanings in one word or its derivations and the semantic transition from response to responsibility is, of course, not specifically Russian and appears in many languages—for example, besides English, in the French *réponse–responsif–responsable* or in the German *Wort–Antwort–Verantwortung* (with "word" as the root). It is precisely this transition of the word from response to responsibility (or answerability) which Bakhtin emphasizes in his early article.

Even this early Bakhtin is already concerned with the tension between diversity and unity. Unity remains mechanical and external as long as there is no "internal unity of meaning." But such an internal unity depends "in three realms of human culture—science, art, and life" on the ability and willingness of the individual "to appropriate them to one's own unity." The unity of the individual itself is, however, only guaranteed as a "unity of answerability." "For what I experience and understand in art I have to answer (be responsible for) with my life" (p. 5). Bakhtin admits this is a troublesome task. Most of us—artists as well as beholders—tend to make life and art easier by separating them and by ignoring the one within the other. But, he insists, such a division neither is a given limitation of art itself nor can be justified by appealing to artistic inspiration or the ideal of pure art. It results from our own insufficient response and responsibility and is, therefore, our own guilt: the unity is actually a "unity of guilt and answerability." Acknowledging this responsibility as well as the existing separation, the article concludes with this imperative: "Art and life are not one, but they have to become united within me, in the unity of my responsibility" (p. 6).

Thus, from its very beginnings, Bakhtin's approach emphasizes the crucial role of responsiveness (or answerability). After acknowledging this one can reconstruct his concept of literary evaluation as a process of evaluative responses on different interacting levels. Within the literary work itself we have a first level of represented values, explicit evaluative judgments or actions and mental reactions implying evaluations by different characters ("speaking subjects") in response to other such subjects and to given or imagined reality. In the novel (or narrative literature in general) these voices are not only reported but also answered and more or less explicitly evaluated by the narrator, whose own voice joins and at the same time mediates the polyphonic dialogue. Both levels with their multifaceted interplay of evaluative stances are integrated by the author into the work as a whole and are colored by their functions within this whole, the structure of which also implies evaluation (see my remarks on the "chronotope"). As such a meaningfully structured whole the work of literature is on the one side an evaluating and value-setting artistic response to reality—as social, cultural, existential reality and as a reality which can be questioned and transcended by creative imagination. On the other side this artistic response is itself oriented toward the evaluative response of readers. The literary work as an artifact can have effect and can survive only when readers are able and willing to respond to it, and in this response to reconstruct its imaginative world together with the values represented or implied within it. In doing so, the reader has to evaluate these values—a process which generates tension between this value system and the reader's own, leading to their mutual reevaluation. At the same time the reader is aware of responding to an artifact, that is, to a construct invented and made by an artist for the purpose of being perceived and evaluated as an aesthetic object. Hence the evaluation also comprises the ability of the work (and its author) to fulfill the aesthetic function, to be aesthetically effective (maybe even innovative), and so on. The reader registers and evaluates if and how the work is able to intensify our aesthetic responsiveness and through it our perception of the world. The evaluation of extra-aesthetic values merges with the aesthetic evaluation of the work itself. And this evaluative aesthetic response merges into the personal responsibility to respond and to unify the otherwise separated realms of art and life. Aesthetic response and evaluation appear in the last analysis to be grounded in the ethical responsibility for responsiveness, which proves to be the fundamental orientational value of the Bakhtinian concept.[50]

The similarities with the concept of evaluation in Czech Structuralism are strong—just as the differences in voice and focus are apparent. The emotionally charged, suggestive, generously generalizing voice of the Russian thinker reminds us of the provocative statements of early Russian Formalism (attacked by Bakhtin's own group) rather than of the quiet, cautiously elaborated, sometimes dry explanations of his Czech fellow semioticians. Each cultural context with its particular tradition of scholarly and public discourse colors the voice of the individual and the social language of the group.

The Czechs and the Russians also subjected different fields to systematic scrutiny. The Czechs elaborate a coherent theory of aesthetic value, whereas Bakhtin's concept of value and evaluation has to be reconstructed from scattered remarks and from his own evaluations. Bakhtin and his group are far more systematic about ideology in language and literature, whereas Mukařovský and other Czech Structuralists deal with it rather indirectly, mainly by investigating the variability of functions, norms, and values as social facts or by analyzing the impact of an author's worldview on the structure of his work (for instance, Mácha's rejection of the established value system and its impact on the construction of his poem *May*). And whereas the Czechs are very systematic in their analyses of individual works, Bakhtin avoids this kind of analysis. Even his extensive and pioneering studies on Dostoevsky contain not a single thorough analysis of one of Dostoevsky's great novels— leaving such applications to later followers.[51] Instead, Bakhtin focuses on Dostoevsky's poetics, on his ability to represent and to initiate the polyphonic dialogue, and on his crucial role in the development of the novel as the most adequate and dominant genre in modern literature and society.

Most significant for the two conceptualizations of aesthetic value are their differences in emphasis or direction— toward the author or toward the reader. At first glance their similarities seem to dominate. Both groups reject the concept of an objective aesthetic value as a quality owned by the artifact.

Both conceive of such values not as a measurable quantity of the object but as relational—as resulting from the relation of evaluating subjects to evaluated objects.[52] And both acknowledge as evaluating subjects the author (in his evaluative response to reality, literary tradition, and so on) as well as the responsive and imaginative reader. But Bakhtin clearly privileges the author; he speaks preferably about "artistic" perception, about the author's worldview and poetics, about the author's mastery in constructing his works and exploring the possibilities of literary discourse.[53] Even his long essay on the hero deals, significantly, with "The Author and the Hero in Aesthetic Activity"[54] and not with the reader's "Interaction Patterns of Identification with the Hero" as works by representatives of current *Rezeptionsästhetik* do.[55] And though he and his circle shrewdly describe (and even systematize) the effects of different types of discourse on the reader, they do not try to elaborate coherent theories of reader response and do not write histories of a work's or an author's reception.[56] It is precisely in such theories and histories that Czech literary Structuralism excels. Its theory of aesthetic value focuses on the response of the reader who concretizes the artifact as an aesthetic object, actualizing in this process the potential of values inscribed in the text as well as the reader's own values and evaluative assumptions.

Although it emphasizes the reader's response as the crucial moment in which aesthetic value is actualized, Czech Structuralism does not go as far as Bakhtin does to make response and answerability the central orientational value of its theory of aesthetic value. Bakhtin demanded a unifying personal response not only for art and life but also for "science, art, and life," thus binding together the scientific, the aesthetic, and the existential response and responsibility.[57] And he tried in his existence as a scholar concerned with art to live up to this imperative under extremely adverse conditions. They were hardly more favorable in Czechoslovakia when Vodička—before and during the suppression of the Prague Spring—publicly stood up for this movement, thus risking (and losing) his scholarly career and his personal well-being. He went through this experience fully aware of his responsibility and "guilt" that his example as scholar and academic teacher encouraged, endangered, and consequentially ruined the careers of some of his best former students or colleagues. Such a personal response was, as Bakhtin's certainly was, an indirect proof of their own theoretical assumption that the historic subject (as artist, as reader, as critic or scholar) is not simply determined by historical circumstances but is challenged to respond to them—with possibilities of personal choice and resulting personal consequences from such choices. It goes without saying that other leading scholars in the same environment and under comparable pressure responded differently.[58] This should not entitle us, who live and work under very different conditions, to condemn them for striving to survive as scholars and persons, but rather should help us see the responsible responses of Bakhtin and Vodička as more valuable.

It might seem out of place to mention such personal responses to political circumstances in a book which deals with the theories and other scholarly achievements of these persons and their groups. But for those who share the concept of responsiveness and responsibility in art, life, and scholarship, such personal decisions *are* an integral part of their scholarly achievements, one of particular significance and value. To mention in this connection the Russian Bakhtin together with the Czech Vodička does not imply any kind of comparative evaluation. I refer to these matters to help clarify what the concept of answerability means and implies—and not to measure who realized it better. In the same sense by comparing the two circles or their approaches to the problem of aesthetic value I do not mean to establish priorities (in the evaluative or even in the chronological sense) for one group or the other, for one scholar or another. The plurality and diversity of simultaneously available and valid responses to identical or similar problems and tasks constitutes and maintains the controversial polyphonic dialogue which both circles have investigated so thoroughly and to which both have made crucial, groundbreaking contributions.

3

The preceding section started with Marxist theories of value and, using the problem of ideology as a link, shifted to

Bakhtin and his circle. Marxist criticism is recently experiencing a certain revival (though hardly a "Marxist cultural revolution") in American universities.[59] American journals now feature new interpretations and extensions of Marx's own value theory that combine Marxist notions with deconstructionist and feminist readings.[60] More relevant with regard to Czech Structuralism and its theory of aesthetic value are approaches that connect their Marxist basis or heritage with general communication theory. As Marxists such scholars can claim that Marx's own theory of value (particularly his notion of exchange value) was already a relational and communicative concept. At the same time, their explicit grounding in communication theory eases an understanding or a dialogue between their approach and non-Marxist concepts of aesthetic value also based on communication theory. An interesting case of such a discourse and transition is the so-called post-Lukácsian Budapest school.[61]

I have mentioned Lukács as the author of *The Theory of the Novel* and as a leading promoter of Socialist Realism. It is in these two functions that Lukács is best known in the United States. Far less well known are his writings on general aesthetics, which nevertheless represent an important position in Marxist aesthetics.[62] In his native Hungary the philosopher and social theorist Agnes Heller, one of his closest collaborators during the last years of his life, put forth a Marxist theory of value including aesthetic value that referred to his aesthetics. Her first work published in English translation in the United States was the essay "Towards a Marxist Theory of Value."[63]

Heller conceives of values as means to help organize reality, insofar as they are primarily "orientational values" with the "good-bad category" as a starting point. Such general categories of preference have to be attributed to objects thus valorized as goods ("goods values") which then can serve as means ("means values") to reach a goal ("goal values"). These kinds of values function in all realms of human activity including art. Aesthetic valuation starts from the discrimination between "beautiful" and "ugly," and aesthetic value is defined as "the value of beauty objectified in art" (pp. 29, 52). Such general assumptions could be shared by non-Marxist theories of aesthetic value, including Mukařovský's. He also conceives of the aesthetic function as a principle organizing our perception of reality. And though he rejects aesthetics that deduce aesthetic value from beauty as a metaphysical concept, he also considers beauty as a basic category of aesthetic evaluation. True, he stresses more strongly the negating aspect of the aesthetic function. But Heller likewise admits that aesthetically valid works "help to organize reality even *against* ruling systems of preference."

Despite such similarities, however, differences prevail regarding the approach to all three dimensions of aesthetics: artistic production, its product, and its perception. For Heller, as for Lukács, the main issue remains the author as the person who expresses his or her individuality in the work to a degree that "the individual and the creation become a homogenous unity" (p. 53). It is no wonder, then, that "genius" is declared the condition for genuine art and for the "permanence of the validity of art." Regarding the validity of the artwork itself, Heller still discriminates between its content, which has to represent the "value hierarchy manifested in the individual . . . from the level of the species being," and its form, which has to be a "self-closed perfect form." Both requirements strongly remind us of Lukács: the former of his stress on the typical (as in the merging of the individual with the general in the Hegelian sense of "Das Allgemeine im Besonderen"), the latter of Lukács' increasingly dogmatic rejection of intentionally open and experimental forms in favor of "self-closed perfect" classics. Thus, Marx's question of why a work conceived as a mirror of its age can remain aesthetically valid for later generations is answered once again by combining genius, typical content, and closed form.

Heller's answer to the related question of how the Marxist emphasis on historical change could be reconciled with the claim to make objective (and not merely historically relativistic) evaluative judgments is rather revisionistic. The usual answer would be simply to refer to the objectivity of history leading to Socialism-Communism and hence to one's own position. But in this respect Heller criticizes even Marx himself for "coming into conflict with his own ontology." Due to "given circumstances . . . in his own time" he "justly considered communism as the only alternative." But later experience has taught us that "capitalism found the mechanism by which the forces of production, could, in a certain respect, develop freely" (p. 68). Hence Marx's view of history as an unambiguous though dialectical progress toward Communism has to be modified into a concept of history as an open, controversial "unfolding." As a result "the foundation of the Marxist criterion of value" is not simply the guaranteed historical progress, but "the commitment to the revolutionary struggle" and its goal (p. 69).

If one takes into account the circumstances under which this essay was written (Hungary, 1970), this is a rather liberal view of the relation between evaluation and history. The concept of aesthetic value may still be Lukácsian rather than post-Lukácsian. But aesthetic evaluation is now connected with a relatively open general theory of value in which authors and readers have to evaluate within a process of unpredictable historical change.

This relative openness was taken up and extended by John Fekete, himself a descendent from the Budapest school, in his "Value and Objectification: Notes for an Agenda."[64] Trying to "clarify the concept of literary value and evaluation in relation to a general theory of value," he refers back to Heller on several basic points. He defines value as "a category of orientation, a primary, underivable and universal category of social praxis." He emphasizes the priority of "value creation" (in opposition to the tendency to focus on value regulation, distribution, and consumption). And he discriminates between two "orders of social objectifications which mediate between the social and the subjectivized personal orders of value." Language belongs to the first class, literature to the second, which "permits both social and personal distance from the first order of objectifications and their boundaries and . . . therefore institutes the horizon of self-conscious value autonomy." These assumptions are characteristic not only of the Budapest school; they concur partly with many different positions and traditions, including Czech Structuralism and Soviet Russian semiotic Structuralism (with its theory and analysis of literature as one of the "secondary modeling semiotic systems").[65]

This concurrence makes it sometimes difficult to understand if Fekete's polemics against "structuralist entrapment," "structural bias," the "structural model," and so on refer only to specific versions or to Structuralism in general. For example, he calls "a forgetting of value, that is, a forgetting of value creation in favor of regulation, a forgetting of the internal relations that articulate the medium of value as a combination of creation and regulation" a "structural topographic bias." That might be justified with regard to some versions of Structuralism (especially the French), but hardly for all of them and certainly not for Czech Structuralism—which neither "forgot value" nor neglected the role of the creative artist, and which in fact did conceive of aesthetic value as a "combination of creation and regulation." One has to admit (as I did in the comparison with Bakhtin) that Mukařovský's concept of actual aesthetic value starts from the reader and focuses on the reader's evaluative concretization of the artifact. But the constitutive part of the author as the creator of the artifact and as the evaluative historical subject is fully acknowledged. And the notion of evolutionary aesthetic value even emphasizes the author's ability to create an artifact which transcends the contemporary boundaries of the literary system.

Fekete himself qualifies his insistence on the priority of value creation when he states:

> This is not to argue in any simple sense that writers produce value and meaning. A theoretical account of the aesthetic functions developed in literary production would be possible, but would not offer sufficient conditions for valuation. These functions still need to be socially validated and realized, and, as social aesthetic value, may amount to more, or less, than their hypothetical measure prior to reception. The truth is that aesthetic value and meaning live only in the reception of art; the meaning and value of art is the history of its reception, particularly as the anticipated conditions of the reception of art become formative principles in its composition. (pp. 16–17)

What Fekete says concurs in a remarkable way with what Mukařovský set out in his theory of aesthetic function, value, and norm as social facts, and what Czech Structuralists did when they described hypothetically the "anticipations" inscribed in literary works and then tested the concrete evaluations of these works in the history of their reception. Even Fekete's stress on the creative qualities and values of literature—for example, in its ability to transcend given limitations by "fictionality" or "the imaginary, the positioning of things that are not"—coincides with Mukařovský's specification of literary fictionality.[66] And they correspond with Vodička's reminder that literature and its valuation are "induced not merely by traditional conventions but also by the striving for new concrete works which respond to ambiguous though internally felt and articulated conceptions of literary beauty not yet realized."[67]

To acknowledge such similarities helps to identify short-comings on both sides. Although Czech Structuralism did not neglect the role of the author as creator of the artifact and as mediator between art and reality, the question of how artists create value and how they objectify their evaluations as indications of and for evaluation remained theoretically and analytically underdeveloped compared with their theory and analysis of aesthetic value actualized in literary reception. Despite the concern with literary reception as well as with literary production, the internal relations between value creation and value perception were not sufficiently clarified. This enhances the urgency of Fekete's agenda. But Fekete's own concept of value creation remains too unspecific. Is it limited to the artist as creator or does it include the active, imaginative reader (and if the latter is the case, what is the relation between value creation and value regulation on each side)? If writers do not produce value "in any simple sense," how do they do it in a more complex sense? What does Fekete's notion of a creative aesthetic value "a priori" mean? A merely temporal priority of production with regard to reception would be a truism; a kind of "a-priorism" taking such value out of time and change would be a very questionable assumption that would require a stronger defense. Of course, an "agenda" is expected to articulate tasks and questions rather than answers; but even as questions within an agenda such issues need further elaboration.

These reservations do not invalidate Fekete's own caveats, two of which are particularly worth heeding in our context:

192

the warning against a one-sided concern with value regulation, distribution, and consumption at the expense of value creation; and the reminder that "there is always a danger when analogies are turned into identities." Particularly suggestive but also dangerously ambiguous are analogies between aesthetic and economic value when economic terms are applied without clear discrimination between analogy and true identity. Fekete calls "the economic discourse on value" an early form of "the structural model." Again, the notion of "structural" would need qualification—especially in its combination with "early," which probably means early French Structuralism and not the still earlier Czech version. The treatment of aesthetic value in economic terms is, of course, also a strong tendency in Marxist contributions, including the most recent Poststructuralist versions.[68] But the main target of Fekete's criticism in this case is probably neither Structuralism nor Marxism but rather Barbara Herrnstein Smith's "Contingencies of Value," although Fekete acknowledges the proper importance of this essay as an "admirable agenda-setting article" (which it truly is).

The second part of Smith's article has the title "The Economics of Literary and Aesthetic Value."[69] The economic aspect is one of the most prominent features of her approach but the use of economic terms is not always made sufficiently specific. Economy regulates exchange; hence such a functioning of any system can be called its economy. Economy has also to do with production, distribution, and consumption of goods and values; and because literature is also produced, distributed, and consumed, the two realms can be compared and literature can be described—more or less analogically—in economic terms. But literature is also itself an industry with a market in a very direct, nonfigurative sense, and this reality of literary life (as the Russian Formalists would put it) can also be designated by the phrase "the economy of literature." Both terms can also be used separately to describe the relationship between literature and economy—as a system within a system with full or relative autonomy, or in the sense of the more or less strict dependence of literature on the respective economic system (for instance, the different functioning of literature in a market economy or in a centrally planned economy).

Smith generously exploits this broad range of possibilities. The resulting ambiguity might be an intended polemical device to provoke those who regard concern with the economic aspects of art and literature as irrelevant or irreverent. But even if one accepts such a polemical justification, the unspecified use of economic terms can blur or weaken otherwise cogent arguments. When, for example, Smith calls all value "the product of the dynamics of an economic system," such a formulation could mean that literary value depends on the economy as well as merely that any kind of value results from an interaction between subjects and objects (which is probably what Smith means in this context).[70] Nor does Smith strengthen her argument by her sweeping polemic accusations. She is surely right to criticize the "tendency to isolate or protect . . . works of art and literature from consideration in economic terms" because this has had "the effect of mystifying the nature—or, more accurately, the dynamics—of their nature" (p. 13). But is that really a specifically "idealistic, humanist, genteel" tendency? Hardly less mystifying is the tendency of many proponents of "materialist" and "democratic" positions to isolate the aesthetic value of classics from economic, social, and historical variability by declaring them immutable creations of genius; in addition, Smith's label "humanist" (even with the added "traditional") is questionable. Humanism—in its historical, professional, ethical meaning—allows very different approaches, including the consideration of art and literature in economic terms—as an economy, and in relation to economy. Mukařovský, who would have certainly considered himself a humanist rooted in the humanist tradition, comes to mind with his reply to Shklovsky's "economic" simile comparing literature with the cotton industry. Whereas Shklovsky had claimed that literary scholarship should investigate only the "yarn types and weaves" (of literature), disregarding the "situation on the cotton market" or "the politics of the trusts," Mukařovský stresses the need to investigate both, "since the development of weaving—in the nonfigurative sense, too—is not only governed by technological progress in weaving (by the intrinsic laws of the developing series), but at the same time by the needs of the market, by supply and demand . . . From this perspective every literary fact appears as the result of two forces; the inner dynamics of literary structure and the intervention from without."[71]

Shklovsky uses economy as a simile, but he uses the simile to *exclude* economic considerations from the tasks of literary studies. Mukařovský, on the contrary, discriminates between the figurative and the nonfigurative meaning (using both) and stresses the need to investigate the interaction between intrinsic and extrinsic factors, between the structure of literary works (their "weaves") and the market.

After Shklovsky's *Theory of Prose* (1925)—for whose Czech translation (1934) Mukařovský wrote the foreword from which I have been quoting—Russian Formalism did investigate problems of literary economy as a market, or what it called the everyday "life of literature."[72] Significantly, most of these investigations concentrated on so-called trivial literature. The problem of aesthetic evaluation in general or its application to "trivial" literature in particular remained neglected. It was taken for granted that such writings did not claim or at least did not have aesthetic value, and that aesthetic value was an inherent quality of great works of literature. Czech Structuralism confronted this problem more systematically, adding a general theory of literary evaluation and aesthetic value and investigating how aesthetic values are generated in the interaction between "supply and demand" of literary production and literary reception interacting on the "market."

Smith goes further by attacking traditional attempts to discriminate strictly between great and trivial literature and to exclude the latter from considerations about aesthetic evaluation. This tendency is also criticized and transcended in Jochen Schulte-Sasse's book on literary evaluation. Opening their theories of aesthetic value and literary evaluation to all kinds of literature, Smith as well as the Czech Structuralists (and Schulte-Sasse) emphasize that within the reception history of a literary work its perception, interpretation, and evaluation continuously change. Yet, although he insists on such variability and rejects the deeply rooted and fervently defended concept of an immutable objective aesthetic value possessed by the artifact as such, Mukařovský nevertheless acknowledges the important function of such an assumption as a theoretical "postulate" and as a driving force in literary production to create artistically perfect works of enduring aesthetic value. Smith, who also stresses dynamics and mutability, merely denigrates this striving for "transcendence, endurance, and universality" as "the humanist's fantasy" which "beguiled" American critical theory (p. 10).

Fortunately, Smith's basic arguments are valid despite her polemic exaggerations. The use of economic terms can be helpful where economics refer only to exchange, interaction, or interdependence, as when Smith states that "what may be recognized as the economics of literary and aesthetic value" is "the various forms of interdependence." This interdependence is first of all between subjects and objects: perceiving an object or artifact, the subject "foregrounds" some of its properties and "suppresses" others, thus "constituting it as a different configuration" according to his or her own interests or needs. But constituted "entities" can themselves "also produce the needs and interests they satisfy and evoke the purpose they implement." At the same time the process is one of classification. The subject constitutes the new entity "in terms of some category" which is expected to fulfill particular functions. This enables us "to refer its value to the extent to which it performs those functions more or less effectively" (pp. 12–13).

This cogent description of the process corresponds to the Czech concept of evaluative concretization, to what I have said on evaluative placement, and to Mukařovský's view on value as a measure for how well a particular object performs a particular function. The additional observation that objects or configurations constituted in such processes can also produce the interests or needs they satisfy can be illustrated by referring to the relationship between landscape beauty and horticulture which Mukařovský mentions in his book *Aesthetic Function, Norm, and Value* (pp. 15–17). If we start with Smith's formulation of "an object or artifact," we can say that for Mukařovský the *or* is a crucial point of discrimination and transition. He discriminates between artifacts as artistic constructs produced and perceived to have an aesthetic function and other (natural or manmade) objects which originally serve other functions but can also be perceived from an aesthetic vantage point. Thus

196

nature can be aesthetically perceived as a beautiful landscape. To apply Smith's terms, the "subject" selects and classifies a segment of nature as an "object" worthy of aesthetic contemplation and evaluates it with the respective expectations. Some properties of the segment are foregrounded, others suppressed. What was originally a part or segment of nature now constitutes a new entity as a particular configuration which can be evaluated in its more or less effective performance of the aesthetic function. This new experience stimulates the interests and "needs" it satisfies. Our aesthetic pleasure—already extended from the realm of art to the realm of nature—induces us to transform our natural environment into gardens and parks, that is, to create configurations of natural elements designed and cultivated for the purpose of being aesthetically enjoyed. In terms of Czech Structuralism, the aesthetic function, exploiting and integrating nonaesthetic elements, functions, and values, expands its social range. The social aspect of this expansion is also crucial for the mutability of such configurations and their evaluation. Gardens and parks are not only shaped by individual taste; they are also and very strongly influenced by aesthetic norms shared by social collectives. And because such norms are social and historical facts, the French garden with its symmetrical patterns and pruned trees differs radically from its romantic English counterpart, and the international distribution and dominance of such models remains variable socially, culturally, and historically.[73]

This example opens up the perspective in two directions. The first leads from the aesthetic experience and evaluation of an individual (the subject) to aesthetic function, norm, and value as social facts. The second exemplifies how aesthetic perceivers (consumers) become creators (producers) of aesthetic objects with aesthetic value and points to the internal relation between the consumption, regulation, and creation of aesthetic value. Mukařovský's book, as its title suggests, is mainly concerned with the first aspect, but in his work and even more strongly in the later development of Czech Structuralism, the process of literary perception and evaluation is always conceived as a genuine interaction between the reader and the artifact as a construction of a creative (and evaluative) writer.

Smith's article focuses almost exclusively on regulation and consumption, on the "Cultural *Re*-Production of Aesthetic Value" (p. 23, my italics). To return to Shklovsky's (and Mukařovský's) comparison of literature to the cotton industry, her essay offers stimulating insights into the "situation of the market" (particularly though not exclusively the American market) and into the politics that regulate the evaluative process—particularly the "evaluative authority" of the "literary and aesthetic academy" (pp. 7, 23). But it neglects the choice of yarn and the ways in which it is woven, that is, the stuff that literature is made of as well as the impact intrinsic factors have on the development of technical methods of "weaving" in the evolution of literature. Shklovsky and early Formalists were interested only in such internal factors, in the "literariness" of literature, polemically excluding what they conceived as external forces. Smith tends to become polemically one-sided in the opposite direction.

Thus it is not surprising that, of the three kinds of aesthetic value discriminated by Mukařovský, the evolutionary value, concerned with literary structures and their internal modifications, does not appear in Smith's essay—not even as a controversial issue. Yet she thoroughly discusses what Czech Structuralism would call the actual aesthetic value and its variable realizations under changing conditions and regulations. The third category, the accumulation of actual aesthetic value in continuously new concretizations and evaluations as the universal or general aesthetic value of a work, appears in the essay in connection with her stimulating observations about literary classics and the function of literary canonization.

In Czech Structuralism the concept of the literary classic has been less a topic of special inquiry than a part of the theoretical discourse on general (or universal) aesthetic value or of investigations into the reception history of works canonized as national classics. Smith approaches the topic first by attacking the notion of the classic and of the allegedly immutable canon of masterpieces put forth in Anglo-American criticism (by T. S. Eliot, Northrop Frye, and others). Then, in her last chapter, she elaborates her own concept of the continuous re-evaluation of classics and canons as part of the "Cultural Re-Production of Values."

The condition for such a continuous re-production is, as she observes, the survival of the original artifact. The chances for survival grow if a work gets high actual value in its original context: "An object or artifact that performs certain desired/able functions particularly well at a given time for some community of subjects . . . will not only be better protected from physical deterioration but will also be more frequently used . . . and thus will be more readily available to perform those or other functions for other subjects at a subsequent time" (p. 27). One could add that examples like K. H. Mácha's show that this community is not necessarily contemporary society (and Smith mentions the possibility of a work being " 'rediscovered' as an 'unjustly neglected masterpiece' "). But even in such cases the artifact has to survive. Once this has happened and the work has acquired actual value, Smith anticipates "two possible trajectories." The first is the loss of actual value if under changing conditions an artifact is no longer able to perform its original function or if this function is no longer desired. Such works can then, at best, be valued as relics for their archeological or historical interest. The alternative is that works continue to perform their original function or "some desired/able function" under different conditions, each time reconstituted differently with "newly foregrounded or differently framed or configured properties" (pp. 27–28).

This description obviously shares with Russian Formalism and Czech Structuralism the acknowledgment of diversity and mutability in the correlation of functions with constructive principles, as elaborated in Russian Formalism by Yury Tynyanov. He investigated this correlation theoretically and historically with regard to specific devices, individual works, genres, and the evolution of literature as a system. In his study on the evolution of the Russian ode he indicated that such functional changes occurred not only due to general historical developments but also for internal reasons, for example the automatization of once effective devices.[74] But as a leading representative of the later stage of Russian Formalism he also stressed the role of external factors such as changes in social demands or in the communicative situation (for instance the shift from oratorical performance in large halls to private reading). Czech literary Structuralism, which in many respects continued from where Tynyanov left off, elaborated this concept by focusing mainly on the change in external factors but understanding them as one side of the internal relations and interdependences which induce literary evolution—including its continuous modifications of the relationship between functions and constructive principles. Smith tends even more to concentrate on such external conditions as constitutive for the interaction and its change. What all these approaches have in common, and what makes the crucial difference between them and traditional concepts which defend the notion of an immutable universal aesthetic value, is the emphasis on diversity and mutability and on the need for continuously new and different reactualizations and re-evaluations—as a *proof* (and continuous broadening) of the enduring aesthetic function and value of classics and not, as alleged, as a relativistic denial of such value.

In this respect Smith explicitly opposes not only Anglo-American concepts of the literary classic but also the one put forth by Hans Georg Gadamer in his book *Truth and Method*.[75] Gadamer, who as one of the main representatives of modern hermeneutics and reception aesthetics stresses the role of historical change, makes an exception for the "classic," to which he attributes the ability to "interpret itself," to "speak directly . . . to the present" and thus not to depend on historical mediation. Gadamer's claim of exceptional status for the classic has been criticized by Hans Robert Jauss, another leading representative of contemporary German historical hermeneutics. In his *Literary History as a Challenge to Literary Theory* Jauss generally shares Gadamer's views, but he rejects Gadamer's treatment of the classic as a "work containing a timeless truth." This is not the place to enter into a discussion about whether Gadamer really means a *timeless* truth and whether his concept of recognition excludes the possibility of anticipating "ways to future experience" as Jauss alleges.[76] What matters here is that Jauss (like Smith and the Czech Structuralists) accepts a gradual rather than ontological difference between classics and other aesthetically valuable works. To deny a special, immutable kind of aesthetic value neither degrades classics nor, as some of its defenders claim, jeopardizes the whole notion of endurable aesthetic value. On the contrary, it strengthens this notion by relating it to the ability of a work to acquire new significance and new actual aesthetic value in changing cultural contexts.

Jauss insists on such mutability of classics mainly for the purpose of keeping them within the historical-hermeneutical "fusion of horizons" and the "dialectics of question and answer."[77] Smith is more interested in the social and cultural functions of classics, and she adds valid observations in this area, indicating for instance the functioning of classics as "banner(s) of communal identity," as a "reservoir of images, archetypes, and topoi," and as stylistic and generic examples that "shape and create" their respective culture, thus also "perpetuating the conditions of [their] own flourishing" (pp. 28–29).

More controversial or at least worth questioning is her view of the complex problem of whether classics support or challenge established value systems and those in power. Her conclusion is:

> The texts that survive will tend to be those that appear to reflect and reinforce establishment ideologies. However much canonical works may seem to "question" secular vanities such as wealth, social position, and political power, "remind" their readers of more elevated values and virtues, and oblige them to "confront" such hard truths and harsh realities as their own mortality and the hidden griefs of obscure people, they would not be found to please long and well if they were seen to undercut establishment interests *radically* or to subvert the ideologies that support them *effectively*.   (p. 30; Smith's italics)

Such an opinion and evaluation seems directly to contradict Mukařovský's conclusion in his chapter on value in *Aesthetic Function*:

> Only a tension between extra-aesthetic values of a work and life values of a collective enable a work to affect the relation between man and reality, an affect which is the proper task of art. Therefore we may say that the independent aesthetic value of an artistic artifact is higher and more enduring to the extent that the work does not lend itself to literal interpreta-

tion from the standpoint of a generally accepted system of values of some period and some milieu.   (p. 93)

The evident divergence can be partly explained as a result of historical changes in aesthetics and literary theory during the half century which separates the two statements. Mukařovský's aesthetics are thoroughly connected with Modernism. Modernist theories and programs of art tend in general to stress radical innovation, defamiliarization, and so on. They validate deviation, negation, resistance. The stronger such tendencies are in a particular work the higher its "independent" value and hence its ability to endure and to fulfill the same or similar functions in other contexts. But in the transition from Modernism to Postmodernism aestheticians and theorists have learned to question such modernist assumptions in two respects: first, they have become more skeptical about the proclaimed ability of literary masterpieces to change "radically" or at least to subvert "effectively" established powers and the ideologies that support them. And second, they have had to acknowledge that many modernist theories too one-sidedly focused on the (undoubtedly important) critical properties of great art at the expense of its assertive functions and values. This other side of the coin, so to speak, had again to be reintegrated and re-evaluated—which includes, of course, the critical evaluation of such possibilities and their social, cultural, and political ramifications. It should go without saying that Smith's treatment of classics belongs to this last version; its difference from Mukařovský's quoted statement is not as radical as may seem at first glance.

But there is a deeper and more complex contradiction involved, which has to do with the underlying problem of literary canonization (also discussed by Smith in this connection) and which needs some methodological comments. Russian Formalism had shown that literary evolution works as a continuous formation, reshuffling, and replacement of hierarchies and canons. Not only can works be promoted to the status of models with allegedly unquestionable authority or lose this privilege, but they can also be rediscovered, re-evaluated, and re-established "on the mountain crest" (to use the formula of the Formalists, who also compared this process with sons who, to get rid of their fathers, rediscover their grandfathers and uncles). Such helpful insights and felicitous remarks, however, are not specific enough to qualify the particular character of *literary* canonization.

In the more recent international and interdisciplinary debate about canon and canonization these notions have been scrutinized in very different fields—religion, law, literature, social behavior—and have been applied to very different kinds of entities, including texts, genres, persons, rules.[78] To keep the notion operable, qualifications and restrictions are indispensable. With regard to literature I would recommend using the notion of a canon mainly for texts (works) and—with some caution lest differences be effaced—for authors and genres. One could, of course, also speak of canonized norms, rules, or values, but for literary theory and analysis such an extension of the notion seems to me to obscure more than it clarifies. If we concentrate on literary works, the crucial problem is that canonization involves the ontological status of the work in two senses—both as an artifact or verbal construct and as an already concretized and evaluated aesthetic object. Any kind of literary concretization foregrounds some elements and aspects and suppresses others; this is particularly true for literary canonization. It is always "partial," in a double sense: the canonizing authority as a "party" is interested in the canonization of only those "parts" of the text which support its own reading and its own ideology and power (in this respect I fully agree with Smith). But because literary canonization canonizes the work as a whole (and not only selected statements or episodes that satisfy the authority's views and needs) the canonization saves and privileges the whole artifact, together with the elements and possibilities that were neglected in this particular canonical concretization.

This potential of the artifact is one of the crucial factors inducing its continuous reinterpretation and re-evaluation. Another driving force is change in external conditions or in the communicative situation. The reading of the same artifact has to be adapted to different needs and expectations to maintain its validity, its actuality, and its canonical functions. A third important aspect is the reappraisal of earlier readings and evaluations; in order to function as a canonical work, this work and its functions have to be commented upon continuously. This commentary becomes itself part of the canonization, and each new interpretation and evaluation has to justify itself not only as a valid reading of the text but also as a valid (assertive or critical) contribution to the preceding commentaries.

Smith acknowledges the latter two factors—the continuous "re-configuration" of canonical works and the reference to their "pre-evaluations" or their "own evaluational history" (p. 23). She is far less specific about the contribution of the work in its aesthetic function. Therefore she underestimates the hidden potential of an artifact, which, once the work is canonized, can become activated in history—particularly when history itself is used as justification in the politics of canonization.

As Marx showed in "The Eighteenth Brumaire of Louis Bonaparte," revolutionary movements as well as established powers need both tradition and history to support their own actions and authority.[79] This is particularly true for ideologies claiming to be the fulfillment of human history, even if this fulfillment requires radical revolutionary transformations. Such claims may falter if works previously canonized as great achievements of human history or national heritage are excluded from the canon. Of course, some of them could be omitted, even banned or blacklisted, because the canonization of some models and the blacklisting of their opponents often go together. But, as experience teaches, such indexing often has to be revised, even by the same authorities or within their system. It may better serve one's ideological and political interests to recanonize the respective works or authors by reinterpreting and re-evaluating them from one's own authoritative position. For this purpose those elements which could subvert one's own ideology have to be marked as erroneous (idiosyncratic, historically obsolete, and so forth), whereas shared views and more general aspects have to be emphasized. This is precisely what Lenin did with Tolstoy or Trotsky did with the *Divine Comedy*. Such procedures do not, however, eliminate the subversive elements from the classical text. Their availability is actually perpetuated and strengthened by the very process of recanonization, which publicly acknowledges the privileged status of the artifact as a valid work of art. As such it is supposed to be read, and each reading has to reconsider *all* parts of the text to decide how to integrate them into a meaningfully structured and valid aesthetic object. As a result, the partiality of canonization, which tries to prevent divergent or even subversive readings, is counteracted by the potential of the artifact. And if critics—Smith among them—are right to caution against overestimating the ability of canonized works to challenge effectively established authorities and powers, one should not underestimate such subversive possibilities either.

This is true not only for openly political recanonizations but also for evaluations claiming to be purely aesthetic. As Smith observes, there is a "tendency among humanistic scholars and academic critics" to "glaze over or background" "alienating" features of the canonized work to transfer "the locus of interest to more formal or structural features" (p. 28). Once again, the evaluation of Tolstoy can serve as an example. After Lenin had recanonized Tolstoy for partisan readers by dismissing constitutive aspects of his worldview as erroneous, and after Henry James had ascribed *War and Peace* to the class of probably lifelike but certainly artless "large loose baggy monsters,"[80] Eikhenbaum and other Russian Formalists transferred the locus of interest to more formal and structural features and re-evaluated Tolstoy as a great artist. In their continued investigations, they tried to demonstrate that this art grew out of the tension between Tolstoy the artist and Tolstoy the moralist, social critic, and teacher,[81] whereas later humanistic scholars and academic critics often try to separate the two aspects in an attempt to "save" the artist and the enduring aesthetic value of (some of) his works. Such an exclusion is hardly possible for Tolstoy as author; it is even less possible to exclude respective elements or passages from an individual work. One might declare those chapters and epilogues of *War and Peace* in which the author discusses in general terms his views on history and historiography as merely ideological, aesthetically detrimental and hence superfluous. But that does not remove them from the canonized text (nor does it remove all the other such authorial generalizations that continuously interfere with the narration). What is said in such generalizing chapters about history as the integration of human differentials, or about time, space, and movement in the lives of individuals, families, and whole nations, remains indispensable for an understanding and evaluation of the historical and fictional characters, of the plot, of the whole work as a meaningful message and as a great artistic achievement.

Thus the problem of literary canonization is thoroughly connected with the question of how literary artifacts are transformed into aesthetic objects and evaluated as such under changing conditions and with changing results—a process central for Czech Structuralism, its concept of concretization, its theory of value, and its investigations into the reception history of works and authors. This correlation makes the study of literary canonization an urgent task, fortunately so identified by Smith in her agenda. She has good reasons in this respect (as in general) to emphasize the impact of institutions and regulations on the distribution and consumption of literary value, because these aspects, though crucial for literary life in social reality and history, are often neglected in academic discourse. As Fekete points out, however, by focusing mainly on the literary market her essay does not pay enough attention to value creation, at least not on the side of literary production, where it is created by artists who construct the verbal artifacts with evaluative potentials which have to be concretized and actualized by responsive readers. Such lopsidedness, although justifiable with regard to antagonistic traditions and tendencies in aesthetics and literary theory as well as to her tendency to treat literary value in economic terms, may also be an indirect cause of her not being specific enough about the aesthetic functions and values (the specifically literary properties) of literature in its production, distribution, evaluation, canonization, and so on. To ask for such specification is not to suggest a return to the narrow notion of "literariness" as defined in early Formalism; and it should not detract attention from nonaesthetic functions and values of literature. On the contrary, as Russian Formalism in its later stage of development and Czech Structuralism throughout its existence have stressed theoretically and demonstrated analytically, one has to understand the problems of literature in its aesthetic function and value to be able to describe adequately its nonaesthetic functions and values and its social range in variable social, cultural, and political contexts.

4

The emphasis on variable results neither eliminates nor sufficiently answers the question of whether the process itself combines variable factors (individual idiosyncrasies, historically changing aesthetic norms) with constant factors (such as general principles of human perception). This implies the additional question of where to locate such constants—in the work as an artifact, or in the reader, or in both, or outside both. In Czech Structuralism this problem is discussed mainly under the heading of "anthropological constants." This notion is still controversial, even among former members of the Structuralist movement and other experts in this field.

The main traditional approach, characteristic not only of "formal aesthetic axiology," is to explain such "constancies" as "inherent qualities of the objects and/or some set of presumed human universals." Smith, who quotes Hume's essay *Of the Standard of Taste* as a classic example, strictly rejects any kind of universal value inherent in the object and insists on the variability of all kinds of values, but concedes nevertheless: "Given a more sophisticated formulation, Hume's belief that the individual experience of 'beauty' can be related to 'forms' and 'qualities' that gratify human beings 'naturally' by virtue of certain physiological structures and psychological mechanisms is probably not altogether without foundation." (p. 16).

Mukařovský's "anthropological constants" are precisely such presumed human universals or physiological structures and psychological mechanisms governing and gratifying naturally our perception of forms, including aesthetic objects. Whereas variable aesthetic norms and values refer to our social nature, such general principles of perception are conceived as rooted in the general anthropological nature of all human beings and therefore recurring as constant factors independent of socially and historically changing circumstances. Mukařovský proposes a sample of such anthropological conditions distributed among different types of arts: "for temporal arts—rhythm, based on the regularity of blood circulation and breathing"; for "spatial arts—vertical and horizontal, right angle and symmetry which can be derived entirely from the structure and usual positioning of the human body"; for "painting—the complementarity of colors"; and for "sculpture—the law of the stability of the center of gravity."[82] He conceives of them as basic norms, which do not, however, require strict compliance. On the contrary, it is the tension and the free play between complying and deviating which are aesthetically gratifying. In this respect they resemble conventional aesthetic norms, which specify and diversify their application. But whereas socially variable conventional aesthetic norms tend to be automatized relatively fast and therefore have to be modified or replaced for the sake of aesthetic effectiveness, anthropological constants remain a basic standard which can always be reactualized. They are, so to speak, a continuity within the continuous change. They can serve as a common denominator—a kind of universal human code—actualized, for example, in our perception of works from foreign cultures, whose conventions and codes we do not know.

As significant as this notion might be (particularly with regard to Mukařovský's category of universal aesthetic value), the abstractness and the tentative character of Mukařovský's remarks leave the concept ambiguous and rather confusing. They seem to suggest or at least to allow an immediate socially and historically unmediated approach to art and an immutable aesthetic value. But that would contradict Mukařovský's insistence on the mutability of *all* kinds of aesthetic value, including the so-called universal or general aesthetic value. In addition, the conception of such anthropological constants provokes the question of whether they refer only to the *anthropos* as the producing and perceiving subject or if they are also incorporated into the artifact and thus become constant qualities and values of the work itself. Mukařovský gives no clear answer to this question. These inconsistencies or ambiguities have caused controversy among experts in the ongoing debate about Mukařovský's notion of anthropological constants.

Herta Schmid's article "Anthropological Constants and

Literary Structure" is a case at hand.[83] Schmid studied at Prague, knows very well the theory of Prague Structuralism, and is in many respects a follower of this theory. Nonetheless she criticizes Mukařovský for overemphasizing deviation, negation, and emptiness. She also challenges Mukařovský for focusing too one-sidedly on the interaction between literature and society, between literary perception and historically changing collective norms and values. She does not deny those relations, but considers them less significant than the immediate perception of the wholeness (*Ganzheit*) and the gestalt of the work of art. Such a perception and the notion of the anthropological constant become for her almost identical: "The ability and the urge to apprehend such subjects as a whole and as gestalt is thus the essential *anthropological constant* to which artistic creation and perception refer . . . This is, however, not a norm, but an *absolute law* which has to be observed by the aesthetic object" (p. 50; Schmid's italics).

Schmid admits that Mukařovský himself explicitly rejected "the notion of wholeness in the gestalt theory" because he conceived his own concept of structure as more dynamic (p. 49). But she claims that he, "without being conscious about it," assumed nevertheless a "gestalt-wholeness" which bears "its own gestalt-law as its own standard" within itself (p. 55). Because this "law" is conceived of as valid for aesthetic perception as well as for artistic production, the work can now be interpreted as an adequate gestalt of the author's intention, which has to be concretized by the reader—and can be concretized adequately due to an assumed "isomorphism between subject and object" (p. 50). She concludes that "the intention of the originator" becomes the standard for "the adequate aesthetic concretization" (p. 57). Mukařovský's whole concept of aesthetic value, with its emphasis on mutability, "has to be revised" in favor of "absolute validity" based on the work itself as an "achieved aesthetic whole." The reader can (and must) perceive this aesthetic quality and value directly, independent of collectively shared and historically changeable norms and values which thus appear "as a danger and as a hindrance to perceiving the work as an aesthetic gestalt" (pp. 50–51).

The resemblance to traditional concepts of an absolute,

inherent, objective, immutable, unmediated aesthetic value is striking. With regard to the American scholarly debate of the last decades, approaches such as that taken by E. D. Hirsch in his *Validity in Interpretation* come to mind.[84] The most direct contemporary reference to Czech Structuralism is to Roman Ingarden and his phenomenological theory of the literary work and its perception. As I explained in Part III of this book, Mukařovský and Vodička borrowed from Ingarden the discrimination between the work as an artifact and as an aesthetic object, as well as the concept of concretization. But they absolutely rejected his idea of an immutable objective aesthetic value as an intrinsic quality of the artifact itself and his correlated assumption of a fully adequate ideal interpretation and evaluation. Herta Schmid reactualizes and enhances such ideas, with direct reference to Ingarden, phenomenology, and gestalt psychology.[85] It is therefore not surprising that Czech Structuralists—who after emigration were able to continue to work within their theoretical framework, like Mojmír Grygar, who lives and teaches in Amsterdam—fervently reject Schmid's revision as a misinterpretation of Mukařovský and accuse it of "throwing back the discussion to its pre-Structuralist stage."[86]

For Grygar, in his recent article "The Theory of Art and of Evaluation in Czech Structuralism," Schmid's emphasis on gestalt denies the importance of "meaning" and thus brings back the old "fundamental controversy between the 'aesthetics of form' and the 'aesthetics of content' " which Czech Structuralism had successfully overcome. Due to this neglect of meaning and the overemphasis on the gestalt the reference to social reality, crucial for Czech Structuralism, also drops out of sight. And aesthetic value is conceived as an absolute, immutable gestalt quality of the artifact, whereas Czech Structuralism had thoroughly and cogently refuted such concepts in favor of variable concretizations and evaluations in correlation with socially variable, historically changing norms and values.

Such harsh criticism notwithstanding, Grygar regards Schmid's interpretation of Mukařovský as representative of one of two extreme positions which have developed within the discussion about Mukařovský's theory of aesthetic value:

On the one side Mukařovský's thesis of the "emptiness" of the aesthetic function and the aesthetic value is pushed to the extreme by denying the aesthetic any quality of its own; i.e., the aesthetic is perceived as a kind of parasite which can exist only due to extra-aesthetic values. One denies the existence of a universal and enduring aesthetic norm which refers to the anthropological constants of human beings; and the value of art is conceived in direct proportion to the significance of extra-aesthetic values which this art makes manifest. (p. 173)

As a characteristic and important representative of this tendency Grygar names the Czech theorist Robert Kalivoda, whose article "The Dialectic of Structuralism and the Dialectic of Aesthetic" (1966) is indeed a stimulating attempt to combine, or rather mutually to test and to complement Marxist and Structuralist aesthetics.[87] The other extreme, with Herta Schmid's article as the example, "relates the aesthetic function exclusively to the anthropological constants, whereas the variable social functions, norms, and values which prevail in art are considered to be secondary and accidental." The aesthetic function not only has to warrant the autonomy and timeless validity of art but is even interpreted as something "antisocial" due to its radical negation of social norms. And aesthetic value appears strictly "tied to the gestalt quality of the work of art" (p. 174).

Grygar concedes that both divergent tendencies can refer back to statements made by Mukařovský during different stages in the development of his theory and that they thus mark "two extreme poles between which Structuralist aesthetics oscillates." To isolate one of them or to make it "absolute leads to a relapse into concepts of aesthetic theory which Structuralism wanted to overcome" (p. 174).

This is true, and the two tendencies indicated by Grygar are indeed characteristic for the discourse about Czech Structuralism and its theory of aesthetic value—as well as for discourse beyond this specific issue. Also characteristic is the oscillation between the two poles. One has, however, to discriminate between oscillation as a constitutive aspect of aesthetic experience (which then has to be theorized as such) and an oscillation within one's own definitions or descriptions of this phenomenon or other related phenomena. Mukařovský's concept of anthropological constants remains itself tentative and oscillating, and Grygar's attempts to clarify it generate new inconsistencies. Stating correctly that for Mukařovský and Czech Structuralism even "the category of enduring and universal value can obviously not be defined as something absolute and immutable," he speaks in the same paragraph about "the *immutable* and universal qualities of the aesthetic value" (p. 169; my italics). Although the anthropological constants first appear as immutable (which constants should be by definition), he suddenly declares: "The so-called anthropological constants are not something once and for all given, immutable, absolute" (p. 174).

The reason for this shift is the observation that man is both a biological and a social being and that "the sphere of the social" is continuously "transcending the purely biological conditions," thus keeping man and his culture "unfinished" (p. 174). This is a crucial point with important implications. Regarding Mukařovský's own definitions this redefinition transforms categories originally conceived as constant into "so-called" constants and actually into variables—although very slowly changing variables. At the same time Grygar does not discuss the implied question: whether those anthropological constants which Mukařovský proposed—such as symmetry, right angles, complementary colors, basic rhythms—really change and if so, how. It is clear only that Grygar himself conceives what he still calls anthropological constants as (slowly) mutable norms. He therefore comes to the conclusion that "in all the changes of artistic norms and values . . . the aesthetic *function* itself remains the only constant" (p. 173; my italics).

In general one can say that Czech Structuralism from Mukařovský to Grygar conceives of a hierarchy of norms which inform aesthetic perception and evolution. In accordance with the nature of the *anthropos* as a biological, social, and individual being, three levels of norms are assumed: anthropological constants (or, more correctly, anthropological conditions) shared by all human beings; socially and historically widely variable conventionalized aesthetic norms; and individual preferences, expectations, and so on. Defining concretization as an individualizing act, Czech Structuralists did not deny the interference of individual factors up to and including purely personal idio-syncrasies. But they excluded them from their own systematic investigations as arbitrary and scientifically not generalizable. The focus was clearly on the middle category, on collectively shared, conventionalized, and historically fast-changing aes-thetic norms. Unlike the intentional disregard for purely indi-vidual factors, the anthropological category—with regard to origin and stability, hierarchically the first—was (and still is) considered crucial for Mukařovský's theory of aesthetic per-ception and evaluation. Despite this theoretical significance the notion was not nearly as thoroughly elaborated in theory or tested in analysis as were the aesthetic norms as social facts.

In addition to this tentativeness, which triggered contro-versial interpretations, the term "anthropological constant" it-self might invite misconceptions in two directions: the one confusing constant with static; the other conceiving anthropo-logical as separable from social. Examples of constants like symmetry or the vertical position refer primarily to human stature and may suggest static rather than dynamic concepts, which might imply that constants, as opposed to dynamically changing variables, are something static. This is, of course, not the intention of Mukařovský. But to exemplify their dynamic nature one would have to describe them as they *function*—which he did not do, although in general Mukařovský's ap-proach is functional and stresses dynamics. If one tries, how-ever, to describe such constants functionally, the question arises whether it would not be more appropriate to leave such static categories behind and to focus on the dynamic functions them-selves as the basic anthropological phenomena, and to approach them as activities in which the *anthropos* expresses himself as both a biological and a social being. Grygar's shift toward the aesthetic function as the only genuine constant and his obser-vation about the interaction between the expanding social and the given natural sphere of the *anthropos* point in this direction. It might be worthwhile briefly to digress from the debate about the Czech concept of anthropological constants and their im-pact on literature to consider the investigations of Structuralist anthropologists into the dynamic interaction between biophysical constants and variable social norms and values within symbolic configurations and performances.

Victor Turner's book *The Forest of Symbols,* based on his research on the rituals of the Ndembus in Africa, conceives of symbols as the basic units of rituals.[88] He deals with symbols taken directly from the natural environment and referring symbolically to the nature of men and women as biological, social, and cultural beings. An example of such a symbol in Ndembu culture is the "milk tree," with its white latex symbolyzing breastfeeding, mother-child relations, matrilineage, and so on. The "major empirical properties" of such "dominant symbols" are "(1) condensation, (2) unification of disparate meanings in a single symbolic formation, (3) polarization of meaning" (p. 30). This combination enables the symbol to bring "the ethical and jural norms of society into close contact with strong emotional stimuli . . . Norms and values, on the one hand, become saturated with emotion, while gross and basic emotions become ennobled through contact with social values" (p. 36). Psychoanalytical approaches to ritual tend to focus one-sidedly on the sensory pole, underestimating the fact that symbols also "refer to social facts that have empirical reality exterior to the psyches of individuals." Anthropologists often examine only the cultural and the structural framework, leaving aside "processes involving temporal changes in social relations." As opposed to such a "static analysis," anthropologists who investigate rituals "within the framework of structural theory and of cultural anthropology respectively" take into consideration both poles of meaning and the tension between them. For them the "essential nature" of symbols and symbolic "constellations" is that they are "dynamic forces." Within this field of tension "the anthropologist treats the sensory pole of meaning as a constant, and the social and ideological aspects as variables"; but the focus is on their interdependence, which the structuralist anthropologist seeks to explain.

Like the Czech Structuralist aesthetician, the English Structuralist anthropologist discriminates between constants rooted in human biophysical nature and norms and values as social facts which vary with social, cultural, and ideological differences and with "temporal changes in social relations." At the same time Turner's conceptualization of such constants as the emotionally loaded sensory pole that saturates established norms, and values which themselves ennoble gross and basic emotions—a formulation strikingly reminiscent of the Aristotelian concept of catharsis—is more dynamic than the anthropological constants listed by Mukařovský. It is, however, precisely this emphasis on dynamics that resembles Mukařovský's general theory of art.

To indicate only some of the similarities: (1) For both Structuralists the individual symbol or sign generates different and frequently controversial meanings, thus initiating a dynamic relationship to reality and to other symbols or signs in the same symbolic configuration. (2) Within such symbolic configurations the semantic potential of each symbol is superseded and dynamically intensified by the structure and meaning of the constellation as a whole. This generates and maintains an internal tension between all parts of the whole. (3) Temporal or sequential symbolic configurations—and ritual as well as literature belongs to this category—produce in addition a particular sequential dynamism which can intensify emotions and can be used for purifying or cathartic effects in rituals or genres such as drama, with sequential urgency compressed in a restricted time span for performance and perception. (4) Both internal tensions are complemented (and complicated) by an external or interactive tension when the perception of the configuration is projected onto the surrounding natural and social context ("the world we live in"). Familiar elements, norms, and values are actualized but also challenged, displaced, and transformed in the symbolic constellation according to its own intentions, needs, and rules. (5) And finally, both systems—the social macrosystem and the symbolic microsystem—are prone to temporal changes. The awareness of such changes serves as a background against which not only works of literature in historically conscious cultures but also—as Turner shrewdly observes—rituals in archaic societies are performed and perceived. And this tension between tradition, its reactualization, and its innovative modification adds a diachronic (temporal, historical) dynamism to the other, synchronic, dynamics.

Only as such a complex, dynamic interplay do ritualistic

symbols and performances fully display their semantic potential and their "critical properties of condensation, polarization,
and unification of disparities." And, as Turner points out, only
as such an internal and contextual interaction do they become
"intelligible and explicable" in their function as "an independent force which is itself a product of many opposed forces"—
a formulation quite in harmony with Mukařovský's description
of the aesthetic function in relation to nonaesthetic functions,
norms, and values.

Having pointed out so many similarities between Turner's view of rituals and Mukařovský's view of art, it is all the
more urgent for me to stress that art and ritual are two different kinds of symbolic activities. For Turner the main function
of the ritual is to "adapt and periodically readapt the biophysical individual to the basic conditions and axiomatic values of
human social life" (p. 43). This emphasis on adaptation is almost completely opposed to the emancipatory function and
value of art stressed in Mukařovský's aesthetics. But this opposition needs to be qualified in both directions. On the one hand,
in stressing the adaptive function of rituals, Turner also emphasizes their critical potential. He observes that the participants in Ndembu rituals "interact by observing, transgressing,
and manipulating for private ends the norms and values" expressed in the symbols of the performed ritual (p. 44). On the
other hand, Mukařovský's theory belongs to the kind of modern aesthetics which strongly and sometimes one-sidedly
stresses the critical and emancipatory abilities of art. Yet even
such theorists—including Mukařovský—are well aware that literature can be used, like ritual, to adapt and to readapt the
individual to the norms and values of the respective social
order. As with many functional discriminations, that between
adaptive ritual and emancipatory art has to be seen not as an
exclusion but rather as a continuum between two poles with
gradual transitions and shifting dominance.

Literature can become ritualized in the very sense that
Turner describes. This happened, for example, with the Soviet
Russian novel during the Stalinist period. Together with the
establishment of Socialist Realism as a doctrine a certain master
plot (or, in Turner's terms one could say a symbolic constella-

tion) of represented protagonists, events, and goals was elaborated and continuously repeated to demonstrate the integration of the individual into the socialist collective and thus into the perspectives of history as defined by the Party. Katerina Clark, who has recently investigated and interpreted this process, calls her book, appropriately, *The Soviet Novel: History as Ritual.*[89] Of course, the use or abuse of literature for indoctrination and adaptation is not limited to Stalinist literature. It is possible under very different social and political conditions, and it is possible with works produced under those conditions for this purpose as well as with works inherited from the past and canonized for such aims.

This digression into anthropology should not itself digress into a discussion about the ritualization of literature. It started with the anthropological constants proposed by Mukařovský; the reason to digress from them to Turner's observation of rituals was to show that even in the framework of Structuralism anthropological constants can be defined and described far more dynamically. Of course, Mukařovský introduces these constants precisely to indicate some relatively stable norms of perception, stable because they are rooted in human nature and not merely based on changing conventions. This more general (or universal) character makes it, however, more urgent to demonstrate how they function. One has to describe them in different media (symmetry in painting is quite different from symmetry in a novel; rhythm in poetry is quite different from rhythm in sculpture), and how they function aesthetically, as principles informing our aesthetic perception and evaluation.

For one such principle, rhythm, in one particular medium, poetry or "verse language," such an approach was elaborated by Yury Tynyanov in his book *The Problem of Verse-Language* a decade before Mukařovský's proposals.[90] Later semiotic Structuralists (particularly Soviet Russian semioticians and their followers) have thoroughly investigated phenomena such as the horizontal and vertical axes as principles of construction, perception, and evaluation in different kinds of works, media, and "world models."[91] Compared with such contributions and with other concepts he himself proposed,

Mukařovský's list of anthropological constants remains tentative, abstract, and insufficiently dynamic. To apprehend the dynamics of artistic production and aesthetic perception that he otherwise emphasizes one has to leave these proposals behind and to focus on the aesthetic function itself. Thus it is not surprising that Grygar, who defends Mukařovský's notion against Schmid's revision, nevertheless goes beyond the so-called constants proposed by Mukařovský and considers the aesthetic function to be the only genuine anthropological constant.

Grygar refers in this connection to the evolution of human nature and to the fact that the sphere of the social in human life and cultural activity continuously transcends the given natural conditions. This is indeed a crucial source of dynamics on the anthropological level. Turner has shown how such a dynamic interaction between the biological and the social sphere and the transcending of purely biological conditions work within ritualistic symbols and performances. In art and its aesthetic perception the transcending and transgressing has to reach out even further. Artistic creativity produces something that is not provided by nature or already existing in social reality. Aesthetic perception enjoys and evaluates the products of such creativity as something *made*—and well made. In this respect the previously discussed discriminations between rituals and art have to be complemented or supported by an ontological distinction between the reality status attributed respectively to ritualistic or to artistic symbolic configurations. Rituals are conceived of as a symbolic reenactment of a preestablished reality with which the participants merge. In aesthetic function the focus shifts to the symbolic configuration itself as a reality which is perceived and appreciated as something artfully made.

Participants in rituals can also consider such performances as something created and well executed. Etiological myths, legends, or tales explain how particular rituals were initiated (created, made) by founders of the community or the cult, by the legendary ancestors, or by "wise men." The participants can, as Turner witnesses, consciously observe and enjoy how well they execute their ritual. This latter possibility tends, in my opinion, toward an aesthetic attitude. But only when the main function of the ritual—the individual's adaptation to and merging with preestablished reality—is replaced by observing and enjoying the symbolic performance per se, does the aesthetic function become dominant. For a fully developed aesthetic experience it might even be necessary to go beyond mere observation and enjoyment to observe and to appreciate one's own pleasure.

On the other side one has to remember that aesthetic experience is not limited to artifacts created by artists. The landscape example has been discussed. As the history of the aesthetic perception and evaluation of nature shows, such an approach was initiated by the experience with art; and even when (later on) it has become pure admiration of a natural object, many beholders tend to apprehend beautiful or sublime views of nature as something created by a great artist—be it God, Nature (with a capital N), or the beholder, who with his or her aesthetic sensitivity selected and in some respect composed this attractive aesthetic object.

One could, however, challenge the whole emphasis on the making of an artifact by objecting that it shares the one-sided modernist (and Formalist) overemphasis on how a work of art is made. Russian Formalists indeed liked titles—and corresponding approaches—such as "How Gogol's 'Overcoat' Is Made" (Eikhenbaum), or "How *Don Quixote* Is Made" (Shklovsky). The specifically formalistic aspect is the stress on the "how," whereas the precondition of this "how," the acknowledgment that the work of art is something "made" by somebody, is a far more general assumption. Actually, the awareness that the "made" and the "how" belong together and inform together our aesthetic experience and evaluation is as old as the earliest Western theory of artistic production and aesthetic perception. Aristotle discusses this problem in the fourth chapter of the *Poetics*.[92] Investigating in this chapter the origins of poetry, he points out two causes for the creation of poetry. The first is the human capacity to imitate (*mimeisthai*); the second is the ability to enjoy (*khairein*) such imitative productions or products. To the confusion of later commentators he mentions in the next paragraph an additional cause "also natural to us": our sense of melody (*harmonia*) and rhythm.[93] All these causes or aptitudes are conceived of as anthropological constants ("rooted in human nature"); all are bound together as special aspects of mimesis; and all are constitutive for the creation, construction, and evaluative perception of poetry.

Between the two statements just quoted Aristotle makes a brief remark which actually is crucial for the later development of a more specific concept of the notion of the aesthetic. He admits: "If by any chance the thing depicted has not been seen before, it will not be the fact that it is an imitation of something that gives the pleasure, but the execution or the colouring or some other cause." For Aristotle this aside serves to integrate such an exception into his general theory of poetry as mimesis; for us who know the later development of art and aesthetic theory this statement opens up possibilities of nonmimetic poetics and aesthetics. These possibilities include modernist concepts, among them the Formalists' focus on how a work of art is made. The Formalists themselves acknowledged this Aristotelian connection. Recent systematic studies of their theory and its sources have investigated this link, correctly pointing out that it was not Aristotle's theory of mimesis that attracted the Formalists, but rather the Aristotelian "Formalism" with its "acknowledgment of the constructive autonomy of poetry and the resulting necessity for internal analysis."[94]

Hence one can say that Aristotle as well as Russian Formalists, mimetic as well as antimimetic poetics and aesthetics have validated the fact that the perceived object is something artfully made by somebody who is able to create such valid objects. This is first of all an awareness of the perceiving and evaluating subject; seen from this vantage point it is, nevertheless, also an appreciation of artistic creativity. That seems to bring us back to Fekete's caveat against neglecting value creation. But whereas Fekete emphasized the creation of value (which is the condition for all kinds of value consumption), we are speaking now—in addition—about the value of creation (as artistic creativity). Artful and imaginative creation itself becomes validated as it is perceived with and through the work of art. The perceiving subject enjoys not only the product or the creativity of its producer but also his or her own ability to appreciate it, to participate in it. The aesthetics of reception (*Rezeptionsästhetik*) and the aesthetics of artistic production, which in recent aesthetics or theories of literature were often in danger of being separated or even being opposed to each other, interact in the process of the evaluative aesthetic experience.

5

Czech Structuralism conceived of aesthetic perception and artistic production as two interacting factors and treated both within the framework of Mukařovský's theory of aesthetic function, norm, and value. More recent representatives of reception theory, who initially referred to Czech Structuralism mainly with regard to its concepts of reader response or the theory and history of literary reception, had therefore to consider critically Mukařovský's general conceptualization of aesthetic experience. In this section I will take up Hans Robert Jauss's critique of Mukařovský's concept of the aesthetic function. Before doing so, however, I must say something about the development in Jauss's own theory of aesthetic reception.

The recent work of Jauss—especially *Aesthetic Experience and Literary Hermeneutics,* which appeared in two different editions in Germany in 1977 and 1982, the first of which was translated into English[95]—represents an important shift in his views from those put forth in his programmatic inaugural lecture at the University of Konstanz in 1967, "Literary History as a Challenge to Literary Theory." Retrospectively he recognizes a certain "partiality" in the early concept of the aesthetics of reception that he had so energetically and successfully promoted from 1967 on.[96] He suggests that his earlier method too rigidly separated aesthetic reception and production. In his recent book he proposes a "triad" of "fundamental aesthetic experiences," *starting* from "poiesis" as the "productive side," followed by "aisthesis" as the "receptive side," and merging into "catharsis" as their "communicative achievement."[97]

This shift in (or the broadening of) focus is accompanied by a reorientation toward Aristotle, whose *Poetics* Jauss now quotes as a basic source. Although he rejects Aristotle's concept of art as imitation, Jauss nonetheless fully shares and even emphasizes Aristotle's notion of aesthetic pleasure. Aesthetic pleasure becomes for Jauss the fundamental notion that unifies his triad of poiesis, aisthesis, and catharsis. In an illuminating historical survey and reappraisal of this notion, Jauss traces its evolution from Aristotle, Gorgias, and Saint Augustine through what he calls the "history of decline of pleasure in the experience of art" up to Modernism and today.[98] He concedes that his rehabilitation of aesthetic pleasure is also a kind of self-correction. For, in unison with most modern aesthetics, his own initial theory of reception overemphasized the critical attitude and assumed "aesthetic reflection" as the basis of all reception at the expense of aesthetic pleasure (p. 28). He also attacks this lopsidedness in Adorno's aesthetics of negativity (pp. 13–21); and negativity is decisive for his controversy with Roland Barthes, whose *La plaisir du texte* Jauss acknowledges as another recent "advocacy for the rehabilitation of aesthetic pleasure." But he criticizes Barthes for his distinction between *plaisir* as "affirmative pleasure" and *jouissance* as "negative aesthetic 'bliss,'" for slipping back "into the circle of negativity and affirmation" with a clear modernist preference for the negative (p. 29).

This is not the place to ask whether Jauss does full justice to Barthes and Adorno.[99] What is important for my discussion is the connection between these arguments and Jauss's ensuing critique of Mukařovský. The subject of this critique is not the notion of aesthetic pleasure but Mukařovský's concept of aesthetic function and aesthetic value. "Pleasure" appears in only one of the quotations from Mukařovský's book *Aesthetic Function, Norm, and Value* that Jauss uses to criticize Mukařovský for not drawing "a clear demarcation" between the aesthetic function and other functions. Jauss introduces this quotation with the remark that Mukařovský "only in passing mentions the ability of the aesthetic function to evoke pleasure and thus 'to facilitate acts to which it belongs as a secondary function.' "[100] Actually, Mukařovský does not make this remark in passing but in the systematically important conclusion of the first chapter in which he sums up the distinctive features of the aesthetic function. In this connection he states that one such "important feature of the aesthetic function is the *pleasure* which it evokes"—with "pleasure" in italics to underscore the centrality of this notion (p. 22). This centrality is emphasized in the second chapter (about the aesthetic norm) when the author repeats: "The aim of the aesthetic function is the evocation of aesthetic pleasure" (p. 28). And with regard to his third basic category, aesthetic value, he adds that "aesthetic value . . . indicates the degree of aesthetic pleasure."[101] Therefore, if one accepts Jauss's claim that aesthetic pleasure has been ignored or neglected in modern aesthetics and that it urgently needed rehabilitation, one should exclude Mukařovský's modern aesthetic theory from this allegation; for him, pleasure was clearly one of the fundamental features and goals of the aesthetic function.

Although Jauss agrees with some of Mukařovský's descriptions of the aesthetic function, he attacks as a general shortcoming of Mukařovský's definition that it leaves "unexplained how the aesthetic function can be a dialectical negation of the communicative and emotional functions and yet convey something" (p. 116). He alleges that the definition excludes emotions from aesthetic experience, which "makes it impossible for Mukařovský to get a grip on the cathartic achievement of aesthetic experience, though this would be necessary to provide his concept of aesthetic function with the missing anthropological basis" (p. 118).

This harsh criticism indicates several misunderstandings that should be clarified. The problem with Mukařovský's notion of the communicative function, which allegedly contradicts the communicative aspect of the aesthetic function, might be at least partly a terminological problem. Mukařovský, in the Czech original, does not use the term *kommunikační funkce* but the term *sdělovací funkce*—from *sděliti, sdělovati,* to let (a person) know, to transmit (to somebody) information or a message (*sdělení*). The focus—and for Mukařovský it is always the focus or the main goal that discriminates a particular function—is on the transmitted information, the *sdělení.* The signs are used only as means which can be dismissed once the content of the information is communicated. Mukařovský explains this orientation toward the transmitted message by referring to money. Money is also a sign system, matching the short definition of the sign as "something which stands in place of something else and points to that other thing" (p. 71). It is communicative in the wider sense of this notion, insofar as it serves exchange, but its goal is mainly the "facilitation of the flow of goods" rather than the communication of a particular message. It belongs to the "immeasurably broad . . . realm of communicative signs" but not to the class used in the "communicative" or "information-directed" function (as one could probably best translate *sdělovací funkce*).

Language, "the most highly developed and complete system of signs," is always communicative in this wider sense, including its use in aesthetic function (p. 71). But in this particular function—different from that which uses verbal signs only to transmit the content of a message—the signs and their configuration become and remain a constitutive part of the message. The focus shifts toward the construction of the "sign made out of signs," thus modifying the meaning and function of each individual verbal sign and its reference to reality (without canceling the interaction of the whole with reality). "The aesthetic function, by dominating the communicative function has changed the very nature of the communication" (p. 72). Therefore Mukařovský can say that the aesthetic function "dialectically negates" the information-transmitting orientation of the communicative function of the signs without denying their communicative character nor their ability to transmit verbal messages. And Mukařovský does not leave that unexplained, as alleged by Jauss, but discusses and exemplifies it so thoroughly that the meaning should be clear even despite inadequacies in translation.[102]

In the quotation I just cited Mukařovský described the aesthetic function as *"dominating* the communicative function" — a concept which Jauss rejects because for him "the mechanistic idea that the relationship of two functions is clarified by the assertion that one 'dominates' over the other must also be revised" (p. 118). But Mukařovský does not content himself with a mere assertion, nor is his notion of dominating a "mechanistic idea." Instead, he applies here the very dynamic concept of the dominant which had been elaborated and analytically tested by the Russian Formalists. Boris Eikhenbaum, for example, had written in 1922: "A work of art is always the product of a complex conflict between different formative elements, always a kind of compromise. The elements do not simply coexist and do not simply 'correspond' to each other. Depending on the general character of the style some element or other operates as an organizing *dominant,* prevailing over the others."[103] In his analyses of Russian poetry he demonstrated how different "dominants" formed different individual styles or different types of lyrical poems. Only five years later, Yury Tynyanov—who in his book *The Problem of Verse Language* had systematically investigated how rhythm as a dominant principle molds all strata of poetry, from sound and metrical organization to imagery, semantics, and thematics—could call "the dominant" a "factor" and "name" which "has already become established in Russian scholarly works."[104]

The link between the original formulation of this concept within Russian Formalism and the further elaboration of it within Czech Structuralism was—in this case as in so many others—Roman Jakobson, who after his emigration to Czechoslovakia delivered a special lecture on "The Dominant."[105] He called it a "particularly fruitful" concept of matured Russian Formalism and exemplified it synchronically as well as diachronically, in the historical evolution of Czech versification. He described its function in artistic production as well as in aesthetic reception, as a change of focus in the perception by later generations. He pointed out that the dominating factor or function does not eliminate but transforms other factors or functions, such as the emotive and the expressive functions. He concluded by stressing that this concept successfully avoids the two opposed approaches of "the straight monistic point of view" (over-emphasizing harmonious unity) and the "mechanistic standpoint," which conceives of a poetic work as merely "a mechanical agglomeration of functions."

This lecture was delivered in 1935. Mukařovský had already borrowed and applied the concept several years earlier, stating in 1932 that "The dominant gives a poetic work its unity. However, this is a special kind of unity which has been characterized in aesthetics as 'unity in diversity,' a dynamic unity in which one can sense at the same time both harmony and lack of harmony, rather like convergence and divergence. Convergence is determined by a striving toward the dominant, divergence by a resistance to the striving which can be seen in the static background of non-actualized components."[106] It is this (certainly not mechanistic) idea of the dominant which he applied four years later in his book to explain how the aesthetic function dominates other functions by integrating them into a dynamic, controversial relationship.

In Jauss's criticism of Mukařovský's concept of the aesthetic function, however, the notion of the dominant plays only a secondary role. The main point is the allegation that, for Mukařovský, the dominating aesthetic function excludes the emotional function and thus bars the emotions from the aesthetic experience, which therefore loses its cathartic and communicative quality. Referring to Mukařovský's essay "The Place of the Aesthetic Function among other Functions," Jauss states: "In his typology of the functions (1942) which employs 'practical' and 'theoretical,' 'symbolic' and 'aesthetic' as paired opposites, the emotional is consigned to the practical functions and it is asserted that [the aesthetic sign] cannot be the means for expressing emotion" (p. 118).

The essay Jauss cites was originally a lecture which Mukařovský read in the Prague Linguistic Circle in 1942; it was published only much later in his collection *Studies in Aesthetics* (1966).[107] Mukařovský introduces it as a "mere draft," meant primarily to promote a "functional view," which at this time had hardly been applied in aesthetics. Such a view, Mukařovský declares, should neither derive the aesthetic from beauty as a "metaphysical principle" (although he does not deny the importance of beauty for artistic production and aesthetic perception), nor conceive of the aesthetic as an "essence" given with the object. Instead it approaches aesthetic experience by observing "motives and goals of human actions and creations." Mukařovský proposes two basic discriminations. The human subject can either try to refer directly to given reality—what we do in direct or "immediate" functions; or we can use a particular system of signs as a secondary, mediating reality—what we do in "sign-mediated" functions. These two types are subdivided according to their internal subject-object relations.

Among the immediate functions, "practical" functions focus on the object which the subject tries to use or to modify, whereas the goal of the "theoretical" function is the "projection of reality within (and in accordance with) the consciousness of the subject." Among the sign-mediated functions, some use signs as symbols which are supposed to affect the targeted real object (for instance, when somebody creates an effigy of an enemy and then injures this symbol)—a use which Mukařovský calls "symbolic" function. In opposition to such an attitude the "aesthetic" function is oriented toward the sign itself or the configuration of signs and toward the interaction between this semiotic object and the subject (as its producer or perceiver).

It is in connection with this subjective involvement that Mukařovský turns to the problem of emotions in their relation to the aesthetic function. His emphasis on the subject—in comparing the aesthetic function with object-oriented functions like the symbolic and the practical—could, as Mukařovský admits, create the impression that he would favor a theory of art as the subjective "expression of emotions," although he repeatedly and "with good reasons" has repudiated such theories. The crucial difference is that in nonaesthetic functions a sign is used only as a means, as a mere "instrument that *serves* the expression of emotions" (Mukařovský's italics), as, for example, in "erotic function." Under such conditions "the emotional function belongs to the realm of the practical functions. The aesthetic sign does not serve, it is no instrument but . . . its own aim . . . Therefore, as long as it is perceived as an aesthetic sign, and depending on the degree it is perceived as such, it cannot be the means for expressing emotions."[108]

By isolating the last half sentence from its context Jauss misses its genuine meaning. What Mukařovský means here is neither the exclusion of emotions from aesthetic experience nor a sharp demarcation between the aesthetic function and other (practical) functions. Instead he proposes a functional discrimination between those cases of emotional expression in which signs serve as means to transmit these emotions as immediately as possible (therefore serving rather practical functions), and the production and perception of signs and emotions in aesthetic function in which the display of signs itself becomes an aim and the object of attention. The emotional response of the perceiving subject to this display and to the emotions it represents or evokes is for Mukařovský not excluded from aesthetic experience, but on the contrary a constitutive part of it—including the cathartic transformation of such emotions.

Mukařovský, does not elaborate, however, in the writings to which Jauss refers (the 1936 book and the 1942 essay) or elsewhere (as far as I know), a coherent theoretical concept of aesthetic catharsis—as Jauss does. Jauss is also right to claim that Mukařovský's "typology of functions" as presented in 1942 "must be defined further" because it does not give clear answers to some related crucial questions (pp. 117–119). Mukařovský himself, when delivering his lecture in 1942, admitted and stressed its tentative character; he later dropped some of its proposals, and throughout his life he continuously elaborated and modified his definitions or descriptions of the aesthetic function and its place among other functions, keeping it open for further specifications and additions.

Aesthetic catharsis could indeed be such a meaningful addition. One could object that catharsis is too narrow a notion to be fundamental for all kinds of aesthetic experience. It is significant that Aristotle introduces this notion only in the sixth chapter of the *Poetics,* when he shifts from his discussion of poetry in general to the definition and description of tragedy in particular, defining the goal of this genre as "to bring about the purgation [*katharsis*] of such emotions [*pathemata*]" as pity and fear.[109] Throughout the history of poetics and aesthetics this correlation with tragedy or with tragic affects and effects persisted, although the range of application was continuously broadened far beyond this particular realm. Jauss conceptualizes catharsis in a very broad sense and emphasizes the "nexus between catharsis, identification, and communication" (p. 93). Indeed, the reader's or the spectator's emotional identification with what is read or seen and the simultaneous aesthetic distancing from this involvement are formative for aesthetic catharsis. By exemplifying this process, Jauss can overcome limitations of aesthetic theories which exclusively stress the reflective distancing and the negativity of aesthetic experience.

My only doubt is the use of the historically loaded notion of catharsis to grasp the "communicative efficacy of aesthetic experience." Jauss himself brings into his discussion of aesthetic function another very important component of broad anthropological significance. After claiming that only the notion of the "cathartic achievement" would "provide [Mukařovský's] concept of the aesthetic function with the missing anthropological basis" (p. 118), Jauss mentions the human ability to construct and enjoy fictions. He concludes his critique of Mukařovský with the statement: "Aesthetic experience is more than is taken hold of by Mukařovský's concept of the aesthetic function: its 'transparency' is the condition of its specific capacity to thematize as 'subuniverses' the experience of the realities of life in the horizon of fiction" (p. 119).

This remark might suggest that Mukařovský, in his attempts to define the aesthetic function, ignored the role of fiction and the relation between artistic fictions and "experiences of the realities of life." This is not the case. However, this point raises a complex issue that deserves fuller consideration— not the least because fiction, fictionality, and the interaction between fictional worlds and reality have recently become central issues in theories of literature, art, and perception. Some discussion of fictionality thus is a necessary part of any contemporary understanding of the aesthetic function.

6

Mukařovský had already explored the functions of fiction in his book *Aesthetic Function, Norm, and Value*. In everyday life fiction can be used as an intentional lie or mystification, but also as "pure fiction"—openly admitting its own fictionality, for example for the purpose of confronting the listener with "the possibility of some other reality than the one he is living in, to comfort or alarm him by the difference between the invented reality and the real one" (pp. 72–73). The crucial difference about fiction in art is based on attitude: in art the question whether a statement is factually true or not loses its significance. But the problem "whether, to what degree and in what manner the writer presents the narrated event as real or fictional, will be, on the contrary, an important element of the structure of the literary work" (p. 73). Its handling can be decisive for the discrimination between elements within one work (for example, in a historical novel), or between genres (for example, story versus fairy tale), or between periods (for example, Realism versus Romanticism).

As Mukařovský exemplifies in his discussion of Dostoevsky's novel *Crime and Punishment,* literary fictionality both weakens and strengthens the "actual relationship" to reality. Although the question whether the events around the student Raskolnikov really happened is "outside of the horizon of the reader's interest," the reader nevertheless "feels a strong relationship of the novel to reality"—not so much to the specific reality that the novel "directly depicts" ("events set in Russia in a certain year of the nineteenth century") as to those realities with which "the reader himself is familiar" or which he might have experienced "given the circumstances in which he lives," or to "feelings and unrestricted emotions which might—or actually did—accompany the situations . . . Thus the work of art acquires the ability to refer to realities which are totally different from those which it depicts, and to systems of values other than the one from which it arose and on which it is founded" (p. 75).

The quotation shows that Mukařovský neither excludes emotions and the "experience of the realities of life" from aesthetic experience nor depends on reductive "aesthetics of representations," as Jauss has alleged. To illustrate to what degree the relation of a work of art to reality and its effect on emotions does *not* depend on direct representation, Mukařovský even digresses from his discussion of literary fiction to the "athematic" arts of music and architecture (pp. 75–79). Referring to Oscar Wilde's "The Critic as Artist" and to Paul Valéry's "Eupalinos" he explains that whole series of emotions and experiences can be evoked by a work of art without any "content" or "factual reference" to given reality—merely by the succession and correlation of formal elements as "bearers of meaning." Because thematic as well as athematic arts relate to our experience of reality, Mukařovský explicitly rejects any kind of aesthetics that radically separates art—for art's sake or as mere fiction—from reality (p. 74). Because the realities that art actualizes in the receiver's mind are distanced or independent from direct representation of reality, he also rejects any kind of "aesthetics of representation" that reduces art to a mirror of given reality.

Thus, literary fiction, or " 'fictionality' in literature" (p. 74), both distances the reader from a given reality and actualizes the reader's experience. To initiate and to maintain processes in two such opposed directions, the work of literature has to be sufficiently specific and also to offer enough indeterminate elements or relations to bring the imagination of the reader and his own relation to reality into play. The notion of "indeterminacy" as constitutive for works of literature Mukařovský and other Czech Structuralists had borrowed from Roman Ingarden's *The Work of Literary Art.* I discussed this historical connection in Part III. In the current debate, it is Wolfgang Iser who has taken up and critically modified Ingarden's notion; first in his article "Indeterminacy and the Reader's Response in Prose Fiction" (1971), then in his books *The Implied Reader* (1972) and *The Act of Reading* (1976).[110] But the problem of fictionality has been elaborated most fully by Iser in his works published in the 1980s, particularly in his introduction (with Dieter Henrich) to volume 10 of the proceedings of the group Poetics and Hermeneutics, *Functions of Fiction,*[111] and in his essay "Feigning in Fiction."[112]

Iser and Czech Structuralism both share Ingarden's notion of indeterminacy as a source or, more correctly, as a point of departure. Mukařovský and Vodička were mainly interested in Ingarden's concept of concretization and did not apply systematically his category of "spots of indeterminacy." Iser, on the contrary, emphasizes the constitutive role of such "spots" and explores how intentional indeterminacies can be used by writers as strategies to affect the reader and the act of reading. Iser's approach to fictionality is, like Mukařovský's, functional. Whereas traditional definitions assume a radical "opposition between reality and fiction," Iser, like Mukařovský, starts from the different functions of fiction within reality and with regard to reality. More than Mukařovský he stresses the self-disclosing quality of literary fiction: "It is a commonplace that fiction is not confined to literature: fiction plays a vital role in the activities of cognition and behaviour, as in founding of institutions, societies and world-pictures. The difference between all these and the literary text is that the latter reveals its own fictionality. Because of this, its function must be radically different from that of other activities that mask their fictional nature" ("Feigning in Fiction," p. 215).

The statement suggests that the revelation of fictionality is the identifying criterion, although the fully justified stress on self-disclosure could also be maintained by slightly modifying the formulation and attributing literary fictionality to the general class of self-disclosing fictions, in opposition to those fictions used in "institutions, societies and world-pictures" that "mask" their own fictionality. Mukařovský's description, which explicitly acknowledges the use of "pure" or self-disclosing fictions outside of literature and in nonaesthetic functions, can serve as a clarifying qualification.

To Mukařovský's examples I would like to add one of the oldest pragmatic applications, the use of invented model cases (Latin *fictio*, from *fingere, fictum,* "to form, invent, feign") in the legal practice of ancient Rome. Openly admitting and even emphasizing their fictional character, such constructs related actual cases to the reality of institutionalized laws, norms, and values for the purpose of classifying and legally deciding them.[113] Such a use of fictional constructs can also elucidate functional discriminations within the general class of self-disclosing fictions. In the forensic function (as in many practical functions) the act of self-disclosure is needed to indicate that the construction is a mere invention admissible as a tool to solve practical problems. The construct itself remains a tool and has to be marked as such. In literature and, more generally, wherever the aesthetic function dominates, the act of self-disclosure turns attention toward the fictional construct itself—toward how this *fictio* is "formed, invented, feigned." The Russian Formalists would say "how this work is made," to turn our attention toward its literariness and its own making. The Czech Structuralists would add: and at the same time to integrate and to transform elements and aspects of given reality, thus actualizing and challenging our own relation to reality.

Iser shares with Mukařovský this awareness of the double nature of literary fictionality ("Feigning," p. 218). The slight differences that exist between them are historically conditioned differences in terminology. Mukařovský, who in 1936 had just introduced his innovative semiotic aesthetics, describes the phenomenon in semiotic terms. Iser, fifty years later, transcends this terminology, referring to it as one among many of the usual methodological conceptualizations:

> The concreteness of the represented world appears to denote a given world, but . . . it cannot be identical to any given world as it has arisen out of a prevailing intentionality and a relating process. Consequently, the world represented in the text is neither totally denotative nor totally representative of any given world. This may be one of the reasons why in semiotics these fictional worlds of the text are sometimes termed self-referential. ("Feigning," p. 220)

Far more significant for the difference between the two positions and for the development of the theory of fictionality is Iser's linking of literary fiction with the imaginary. He introduces explicitly a new "triad: the real, the fictional, and . . . the imaginary" (p. 204). Just as Jauss proposed approximately at the same time his triad of poiesis, aisthesis, and katharsis as basic for aesthetic experience, so Iser considers the "triadic relationship between the real, the fictional, and the imaginary" as "basic to the literary text" (p. 205). Because I am myself a veteran of the Poetics and Hermeneutics group and of the University of Konstanz, which are known for their contributions to *Rezeptionsästhetik*, I cannot resist inserting the self-critical observation that to conceptualize in triads is obviously still a fruitful way of proceeding in the country of Hegel. As thinking in terms of dichotomies holds sway in other traditions and in current theories of cognition and communication, triadic approaches might at the very least help do justice to the complexity of aesthetic phenomena—provided that such proposals are made sufficiently specific and operable. Thus, although the correlation of literary fiction with reality on one side and with imagination on the other side is not genuinely new,

Iser's specification of this relationship and his discrimination between the imaginary and fictional constructs in literature clearly surpasses Mukařovský's treatment of fictionality.

What is decisive for Iser for understanding the relation of literary fiction to reality and to the imaginary is not only the selection and combination of elements from both realms but also the respective degree of determinacy. Different from the freewheeling imaginary (in fantasies, daydreams, and so on), fictions are always somehow "fixed." Both the integration of elements from given reality and the process of "fixing" make the fictional world more concrete than the imaginary and relate it to the (thoroughly determined) real. At the same time the fictionalizing act indicates the fictionality of its own product, thus "bracketing" it from given reality. But the "as-if" of this self-disclosure is not yet sufficient. Because the fictional world has to be always fixed to a certain degree, it is always in danger of becoming closed in upon itself. Therefore, it has continuously to "transgress" its own structural boundaries so as to transcend its own relation to reality. The "transgression of boundaries" in this double sense and in all procedures of the fictionalizing act becomes crucial for the production and perception of literature as fiction. The combination of representation, self-disclosure, and transgression of boundaries stimulates "affective reactions in the reader" and produces "attitudes . . . through which the represented world will be gone beyond, while at the same time the 'impossible' or 'unreal' will take a particular gestalt" (p. 220).

For Mukařovský, literary works, as fictional constructs, are also perceived as structured wholes (though not as gestalts) which affect the attitude of the reader toward reality. He admits that they can be conceived of as "a sovereign creation of a hitherto nonexisting reality." Suspicious of aesthetic theories which isolate art from social reality, however, he concentrates on the relation between literary fiction and social reality with its changing norms and values rather than on the relation between the fictional and the imaginary. The same can be said of Vodička. His essay on Mácha's Romanticism is a daring defense of literature as a transgression of boundaries set by given reality and by its realistic representation. In his programmatic summary "Literary History, Its Problems, and Its Tasks" he warns us to "always keep in mind that aesthetic perception is not merely determined by traditional conventions but also by the longing for concrete new works which might correspond with uncertain, internally felt rather than clearly articulated ideas or visions of literary beauty not yet realized."[114] His main focus, however, remains on the historically changing conditions in which such "longings" are formulated by authors, concretized by readers, and evaluated by critics. Significantly, Vodička neither elaborates nor takes up Mukařovský's reflections on fictionality in literature. Some of Mukařovský's and Vodička's best students ignore them altogether.

Miroslav Červenka, for example, in his book *The Construction of Meaning by the Work of Literature,* briefly discusses literary fictionality. Although in other respects he refers to Mukařovský's theory as his own theoretical basis, with regard to fiction he mentions only Polish scholars (Roman Ingarden, Jerzy Pelc, and particularly Henryk Markiewicz), without even noting that Mukařovský had treated this topic in the framework of his semiotic aesthetics. Červenka concludes his short remarks with a revealing admission: "As is obvious from the whole concept, I consider the question of the fictional world as only a partial (though significant) problem and clearly not as a realm which is essential for the quality of the literary sign."[115]

Given such a neglect within the Czech school itself, it is not surprising that recent theories of fictionality outside of Czech Structuralism have ignored Mukařovský's early contribution. Nor is it surprising that the current interest in "fictional worlds" is occasionally framed as an attack against the Structuralists for neglecting this problem. Characteristic in this regard is Thomas Pavel's book *Fictional Worlds* (1986).[116] Pavel, who as a scholar and a novelist combines experiences from both fields with a thorough knowledge of related philosophical areas, characterizes the theory of fiction as "a field emerging at the crossroads of literary criticism and philosophy" and interprets the new interest for this topic as a countermove against theoretical and methodological restrictions imposed by Structuralism. He calls his introductory chapter, programmatically and provocatively, "Beyond Structuralism." Whereas he criticizes Structuralism mainly for "literary mythocentrism," for "the perennial influence of linguistics on literary structuralism," and for "the centrality of the text," he finds symptomatic of the new orientation that opposes Structuralism a regard for "reference" and "representation," for "the distance and resemblance between literature and reality," for "the relevance of literature for issues of immediate human concerns," and for "the reader's position in the literary exchange" including the resulting "multiplicity of readings" (pp. 5–10).

These allegations may be justified for some aspects of French Structuralism and those who followed it, particularly the versions promoted by Lévi-Strauss. They are, indeed, the genuine target of Pavel's polemics. But treating this version as *the* Structuralism, without referring to other variants of literary Structuralism, weakens an otherwise valid criticism. None of the three allegations is justified regarding Mukařovský's Structuralist aesthetics and poetics. Although Mukařovský was a leading member of the Prague Linguistic Circle and his theory shares with modern linguistics its semiotic basis, it is otherwise clearly centered on the *aesthetic* function and value of art and literature and their social functions—and thus is different from, for example, the work of Roman Jakobson, who during his activities in Czechoslovakia and in his contributions to poetics and literary study remained first of all a linguist.

Even less are Mukařovský or Vodička "mythocentric"— neither in the sense in which Jakobson's and Lévi-Strauss's famous analysis of Baudelaire's "Les chats" interwines structural linguistics with structural mythology, nor in the more general meaning of concentrating on plots as the narratable *mythos* of literary works. Although Czech Structuralists respect the literary text as basic for analysis and theory, they systematically avoid its "textocentric" isolation from the other constitutive factors of the communicative process. On the contrary, they emphasize precisely those aspects which Pavel claims as prerogatives for the recent turn against or beyond Structuralism: "the reader's position in the literary exchange" (including the ensuing "multiplicity of readings"), the "relevance of literature for issues of immediate human concerns" (in Czech terms the social and anthropological functions of literature and its actual value in concrete contexts), and "the distance and resemblance between literature and reality."

To note such shared tendencies is not to dispute the progress made recently in the theory of fictionality. Mukařovský, in 1936, offered only a short discussion about fictionality in literature and in other functions. Now we have elaborate theories and whole books about the *Functions of Fiction, Fictional Worlds,* and the *Ways of Worldmaking.*[117] These new works have not only elaborated and systematized Mukařovský's theory but also shifted the focus and emphasis. Imagination and the imaginary now play a far more prominent role. The ability to construct and to enjoy fictional worlds is seen as a basic faculty of the human mind, essential for literature as a link between given reality, fictionality, and the imaginary. As I have repeatedly mentioned, the Czech Structuralists also acknowledged the importance of creative, distancing, transgressive, and anticipatory imagination for literary production and perception. But neither in Mukařovský's definition of the aesthetic function nor in Vodička's description of the tasks of literature and literary criticism does imagination receive such a central position as in more recent theories of fictionality and literature. In their analyses of individual works or authors both Czech scholars focus on the ways literature integrates, transforms, and challenges the given, historically changing reality rather than on the ways it makes or feigns fictional worlds of its own. Or, in Iser's terms, how it gives "the 'impossible' or 'unreal' . . . a particular gestalt."

The failure of Czech Structuralists to elaborate Mukařovský's remarks on fictionality into a coherent theory of literary fiction is particularly ironic in light of the literary, cultural, and political context in which they worked; imaginative transgressions of the "given" reality are not at all rare in Czech history. In fact, Czech history and literature feature many examples of a very special mixture of the real and the imaginary, realistic and utopian writing from the period of "national rebirth" and Mácha's rebellious Romanticism, through the short existence of independent Czechoslovakia between the two world wars (after centuries of lost national sovereignty), and on to the Prague Spring movement. The foundation of the Prague

Structuralist School and Mukařovský's own start as an aesthetician and literary theorist coincide with a bloom of utopian and distopian literature in which the Czechs played a pioneering role. It is sufficient to mention the utopian and antiutopian novels and plays of the brothers Čapek, among them *R.U.R.*, which gave us the term "robot."[118] Such genres should be of particular interest for anyone investigating the construction and the function of fictions. Combining literary fiction (the genre novel) with political, social, or technological fiction (utopia), they can double the potential of imaginative fictionality or can play different forms of fiction against each other, as Zamyatin does in his famous antiutopian novel *We*, which opposes the dynamics of the novel to the static closeness of utopias. I mention this Russian novel here because although it was written immediately after the revolution in Soviet Russia, it was banned there and was first published in a Czech translation in Czechoslovakia.[119]

As this novel shows, a problem crucial for modern theories of fictionality in literature, the "transgression of boundaries," is also implied in this distopian genre. How can such a realized fiction, once it is established as a closed political state or formed as a work of literature with a beginning and an ending, be opened up again? Can its own boundaries (as a political or artistic construct) be transgressed for the sake of dynamics and imagination in individual life, politics, and art? I have discussed such problems of "The Double Fiction and Its Self-Suspension" in my own contribution to the symposium on *Functions of Fiction* by the Poetics and Hermeneutics group.[120] I mention this topic to indicate that utopian literature, imaginatively anticipating fictional worlds as already realized, was prominent in Mukařovský's own time and country. But in his aesthetics and his literary theory neither such particular genres nor the imaginative in general play a crucial role. Fiction is explored mainly in its relation to given reality and in its ability to question established norms and values as social facts.

The interaction between fiction and reality is, as we have seen, crucial for recent theories of fictionality. How they differ is not so much in the regard for this relation but rather in Mukařovský's emphasis on its evaluative implications.

Mukařovský does not connect the two notions directly. Instead, he indicates the systematic location and significance of this correlation by placing his discussion of fictionality in the middle of his chapter on value (his third chapter). It is inserted between the first part of the chapter, about aesthetic value, and the second part, about extra-aesthetic values, and it is introduced by a definition of the notion of sign in its purely communicative functions and in its aesthetic function (p. 71).

All these topics are systematically interrelated. Aesthetic value is for Mukařovský first of all *actual* aesthetic value, that is, the ability of a work of art to actualize and challenge the receiver's perception and evaluation of reality through the perception and evaluation of the artifact as an aesthetic object. This effect itself is based on the semiological nature of art and the way the sign when it is functioning aesthetically works in two directions. As a sign, "something which stands in place of something else and points to that other thing" (p. 71), the artifact implies a relation to an "external" reality; but as a sign in aesthetic function it refers at the same time to its own reality as an artistic construct. The tension between these two realities or realizations initiates and informs the actualization and reevaluation. One could say that the receiver evaluates the work of art in terms of his or her perceived reality, but the work of art also serves to evaluate in its turn and on its own terms the receiver's reality. Art is a two-way, not a one-way, street.

This double-directedness, characteristic for all sign systems serving an aesthetic function, is particularly obvious in literary fiction, which constructs a world out of 'real' and fictional elements and relations, openly admitting (self-disclosing) its fictional status without losing its referential potential. Fictionality in literature and its radical difference from other kinds of fiction are therefore particularly apt for showing how art as a sign system functions and how works of art transform extra-aesthetic values into aesthetic value—or, vice versa, how aesthetic value depends on reference to extra-aesthetic values and their actualization in the mind of the perceiver. The production and perception of literary fiction—as a sign system in aesthetic function—mediates between aesthetic and extra-aesthetic values.

I mentioned previously that Mukařovský illustrates this process with *Crime and Punishment*. He concludes his discussion by generalizing in the following way: "The work of art as a sign acquires an indirect (figurative) tie with realities which are vitally important to the perceiver, and through them to the *entire universe* of the perceiver as a *collection of values*. Thus the work of art acquires the ability to refer to a reality which is totally different from the one which it depicts, and to *systems of value* other than the one from which it *arose* and on which it is *founded*" (p. 75; my italics).[121] One can add here—though it should be evident from Mukařovský's general concept of aesthetic value—that *all* elements and relations within an artifact contribute to the process of internal and external evaluation. "The work of art, even if it does not overtly or indirectly contain evaluations, is saturated with values. Everything in it, from the material, and the most concrete material (e.g., stone or bronze in sculpture), to the most complicated thematic formations, is a bearer of values" (pp. 83–84).[122] The stress on value and its pervasiveness is obvious in both statements. The former emphasizes in addition the relation to concrete reality and to systems of value which are constitutive for (and transformed in) the perception of the work by the reader. The first statement presupposes a twofold "transgression of boundaries." First, the work as a fictional construct transcends imaginatively the reality from which it arose. Second, the effect of the work reaches beyond the borders of the fictional world it depicts as the responsive and imaginative reader relates this world to his own general view and evaluation of the world—and thus to totally different realities and systems of value.

One can go further and observe a third kind of transcendence—the ascension from having actual aesthetic value in one particular cultural milieu to the accumulation of general or "universal" aesthetic value under changing cultural conditions (as Dostoevsky's novel has done). For this purpose the work has to be transportable (or reproducible) from its original environment to others, which is possible only because the "material artifact" is a fixed configuration of signs as virtual "bearers" of meaning and value; but in order to stimulate the response of readers in different cultural contexts and to actualize their views and values, those signs and their configuration have to be sufficiently complex, undetermined, multivalent and provocative. If a work is "intended to coincide completely with recognized life-values" it will be "perceived as a fact which is neither aesthetic nor artistic, but simply pretty [*Kitsch*]" (pp. 92–93). If, on the contrary, a work transgresses too radically all dominant norms and values of the cultural environment in which it appears, it will probably be rejected or simply ignored, thus not generating actual aesthetic value. That is why works with very high evolutionary aesthetic value, that is, works whose structure deviates radically from the structure of the surrounding literary system, are often not acknowledged as valid in the milieu from which they arose (for example, Mácha's work during his lifetime). For the same reason one could say that the notion of evolutionary aesthetic value itself presupposes not only deviation and negation but also an imaginative anticipation of possibilities not yet existing in reality. This makes the innovative work comparable with transgressive and anticipatory fiction, although the ontological status of the new work with evolutionary value and those works which it leaves behind (as artistic fiction) is identical, rather than essentially different as between fiction and reality.

More important for Mukařovský's theory of aesthetic value is another kind of transgression: the transgression of the boundaries of his own theoretical construct of three basic categories of aesthetic value—the actual, the evolutionary, and the general. He himself transcends this framework by asking whether one has to assume an "independent" and "objective" aesthetic value beyond historical changeability, attributed to the work itself as an artifact. I have referred to this problem (and to Jauss's critical reaction) at the beginning of this part. Now I return to it in connection with fictionality, because Mukařovský's whole discussion about fictions, their functions, and their value is framed by his asking and answering "the basic question: is objective aesthetic value a reality or a false illusion?" (p. 70). This question leads directly to the related question about "the nature of the sign in general" (p. 71). Is a sign, defined as "something which stands for something else," a reality or mere illusion? Is this illusion necessarily "false" and "deceiving," or can it admit its own inventiveness without losing its ability to function meaningfully within reality? What is the relation of signs to reality—and to the evaluation of reality—in aesthetic and nonaesthetic functions? Can signs in aesthetic function stand not only for something else but also for themselves; can they have their own reality and value? All these questions can also be asked (and are immediately asked by Mukařovský) with regard to fiction. After having discussed them, Mukařovský concludes: "Now we can finally return to the question from which we started: Is it possible, in some manner or other, to demonstrate the objective validity of aesthetic value?" (p. 90).

Mukařovský's answer is, as we know, to insist on the "irreducible changeability" of aesthetic evaluation (p. 94), on the indispensable interaction between the work of art and its reader or viewer (p. 93), and on the impossibility of escaping "the grasp of the social character of art" (p. 70). Hence, "an independent aesthetic value inherent in a material artistic artifact, if we assume that it exists, has only a potential character" (pp. 90–91). Qualified by "if" and "assume," it has only a "potential character."[123] One can derive from it at best some general qualities which a perfect work of art should have, but certainly not "any detailed rules" (p. 93). For such a work to be readable as well as challenging, differences are as significant as similarities, and "multiplicity, variety, and complexity of the material artifact are potential aesthetic assets" (pp. 92–93). These are traditional truisms; Mukařovský is anxious to indicate what is different for him. The "harmony" of diverse qualities within the artifact is "usually suggested as the highest form of perfection and the highest perfection of form in art," but for Mukařovský it is the "tension" among them that is decisive. To "overcome" this tension is "the task for the receiver" (p. 93).

The emphasis on the receiver indeed distinguishes Mukařovský's concept of aesthetic value from most other related theories of his time and connects him with more recent developments. At the same time, one is reminded of Bakhtin's postulate of response as responsibility, the more so because Mukařovský also connects his stress on response with the requirement that art and life interact. He concludes his argument with the statement that "the most fundamental task of art . . . is the control and renewal of the ties between man and reality as an element of human behavior" (p. 94).

For such activity the postulate of a perfect work of art with independent, objective value is indispensable. As a mere assumption, such value is radically different (systematically and ontologically) from actual aesthetic value, which can be continuously realized. Independent aesthetic value, on the contrary, is neither real nor realizable. As a mere construct of human imagination transcending reality, however, it nevertheless has crucial consequences for reality and for the functioning of art in reality—as fiction does. And "any theory of aesthetic value, even when this theory is based on the irreducible changeability of the actual evaluation of works of art," has to confront this problem:

> Only the assumption of an objective aesthetic value, constantly being perceived anew and realized anew in the most varied modifications, gives any meaning to the historical development of art. Only through this assumption can we explain the pathos[124] of the consistently repeated attempts to create the perfect work of art, as well as the recurring of previously established values (e.g., the development of modern drama was governed by constantly renewed incursions of several enduring values such as the works of Shakespeare, Molière, etc.). (p. 94)

The quotation is taken from the last paragraph of the chapter on value and is actually the conclusion of the book's argument (because the remaining chapter is merely a summary in two pages). The statement shows that for Mukařovský aesthetic value depends on both artistic production and aesthetic perception. Artifacts have to be realized before they can be perceived. The author, with his "attempts to create the perfect work" and with his "pathos"; the work, as his product and as a semiotic configuration with potential meaning and value; and the reader, who has to concretize and to evaluate the work as an aesthetic object—all three are constitutive for the process of aesthetic communication, evaluation and "historical development." Indirectly included are critics, historians and theorists of literature, insofar as they evaluate and try to explain this process as a meaningful development. In all respects the emphasis is on process and renewal. Works of art have to be produced and perceived anew; works from older periods can prove to have enduring values only when they are newly actualized by contemporary authors and audiences; and the whole process has to form a development. This "irreducible changeability" is oriented toward the goal of producing the perfect work with independent value, a fictional construct which nevertheless continuously stimulates the production of new, valuable fictional works with which to challenge reality. Fiction is identified as one of the crucial means for achieving "the most fundamental task of art, which is the control and renewal of the ties between man and reality as an element of human activity" (p. 94).

This sentence, which closes Mukařovský's chapter on value, would be an appropriate ending for my discussion of his comments on fiction, if a self-critical caveat were not in order. Have I not overemphasized the significance of Mukařovský's concept of fictionality for his aesthetics and for the ongoing debate about fictionality? It was probably not accidental that this part of his theory remained unnoticed by later aestheticians who otherwise referred to his writings and was not even developed by his own Czech followers. His relatively brief remarks on fictionality may deserve to be underscored all the more, however, precisely because they have been ignored both by partisans and critics of Mukařovský's aesthetics and poetics. His semiotic aesthetics, including the conceptualization of aesthetic value, would probably not lose its validity if the remarks on fiction were left out. Yet the relation between fiction and reality as well as the problem of fictionality in literature are central for his theory. They can both stimulate and challenge the ongoing debate about the construction of fictional worlds and the functions of fiction.

7

We still have to place Mukařovský's theory of aesthetic value within the framework of the general theory of value in its present stage. An appropriate starting point for this purpose is a German publication containing the proceedings of an inter-disciplinary conference on *Values in Communicative Processes*.[125] This volume has the advantage of combining the general theory of value and general theory of communication with special problems of aesthetic value and with concrete analysis of "value information," "value mediation," and "value manipulation" in art, in verbal and visual media, and in "everyday aesthetic processes."[126] In addition, one of its main contributions refers directly to Mukařovský's theory of aesthetic value.

In this essay, entitled "The Connotative Process and Value Communication,"[127] Götz Grossklaus praises Mukařovský as "one of the first who scrutinized the problem of how extra-aesthetic values can be present within the 'internal space' of the aesthetic message" (p. 93). Grossklaus enumerates as particularly important insights—for Mukařovský's approach and "for our own putting of the question" the following: (1) that all elements of "form/content" are bearers of extra-aesthetic values; (2) that the aesthetic value is nothing but the "dynamic whole" of the relations into which the extra-aesthetic values enter within the work of art; (3) that for the contemporaries of the author the "field of values" refers to their collectively shared value system; and (4) that the later "historical recipient" confronts this value system with his own, that is, the value system "of his time" (p. 93). Grossklaus gives Mukařovský only limited praise. He criticizes him for treating the problem only with regard to "the theoretical general example of the work of art and virtually only within the triangle of message–receiver–context; the sender and his value intention are hardly addressed" (p. 94). He also finds that Mukařovský's notion of the bearer refers only "vaguely" to "a semiotic mechanism which Barthes, Greimas, and Eco have identified as characteristic for connotative processes." Therefore Mukařovský has little to say about how "notifications of values" appear within a work and how "textual patterns which guide the attention" make the recipient aware of "positive-negative profiles." Nonetheless, Grossklaus adds, even in this respect Mukařovský points out two facts decisive for the ensuing development of semiotics: that such notifications of values are "semiotically located on a secondary or tertiary level" and that they are arranged in "a series of oppositions along the axis of the culturally specific field" (pp. 93–94).

The praise and criticism are well deserved; but to consider briefly how Grossklaus's criticism might need qualification will open up some related issues. Grossklaus refers only to Mukařovský's book *Aesthetic Function, Norm, and Value* (and directly only to its third chapter). It does contain the core of Mukařovský's value theory, but it represents only the early period of his semiotics, only his theoretical work, and, as the title indicates, it is dedicated to aesthetics, that is, to a theory mainly concerned with art and its functions. That explains why "the theoretical general example of the work of art" prevails and "messages of mass media" are not so thoroughly investigated (Grossklaus, p. 94). Even in this book, however, Mukařovský discussed nonartistic objects in both aesthetic and nonaesthetic functions, such as popular genres, urban songs, and so on.[128] Throughout his writings as scholar and critic—on literature, theater, film, and visual arts—he combined analyses of great artists and their masterpieces with careful studies of aesthetically inferior products. In general one can say that Czech Structuralism—together with Russian Formalism in its last stage of development—were among the very few schools of literary study that were interested in popular authors, works, and genres, decades before special studies of *Trivialliteratur* and mass culture became popular in academia during the late 1960s and the 1970s. This is not to dispute the great progress which the theory and analysis of mass literature and other related media has made since the 1930s. Grossklaus's own article, with its elaborate analysis of a cigarette commercial, is a good example, as is—for the theory of evaluation—Schulte-Sasse's book *Literary Evaluation,* which Grossklaus mentions as a model of this kind, and which itself praises Mukařovský and Czech Structuralism as pioneers in the study of aesthetic evaluation.

Grossklaus is also right in stating that Mukařovský concentrates on the relations among "message–receiver–context" while the "sender" and his evaluative intentions are hardly addressed, but again, this is true only for *Aesthetic Function, Norm, and Value.* In other writings, beginning with the early book on Mácha's *May*, Mukařovský thoroughly investigated the role of the author, his evaluative attitude toward society and the world, his artistic dealing with values, and his successful or unsuccessful attempts to communicate them as a crucial aspect of his message. But although in his specific analyses Mukařovský does show how "semiotic mechanisms" notify values and form textual patterns that guide the attention of readers, he does not systematically elaborate a method that identifies such techniques as characteristic for connotative processes—as later semioticians have done and as Grossklaus exemplifies in his article on "The Connotative Process and Value Communication."

With regard to Grossklaus's topics, the progress recently made in locating "value notifications" on secondary or tertiary levels and in arranging them in series of oppositions that tie in to "culture-specific" hierarchies of values, I should add that in addition to the scholars mentioned by Grossklaus, these issues have been strongly pursued by Russian semiotic Structuralists. Yury Lotman, with his concept of literature as a secondary modeling system, and his Tartu school and the Moscow school of V. V. Ivanov, V. N. Toporov, and others (whose typologies of culture compare different types of relations between textual and cultural structures including their value hierarchies) have made these fields of study their main concern. They have developed their methodology far beyond the indications of Mukařovský.[129]

From the point of view of general value theory, the question on which level values or value notifications are located reactualizes the old question of whether value is a quality of the object itself—that is, objective value—or something attributed to the object by subjects, or a result of interaction among all the components of the communicative situation. Nicholas Rescher's concise *Introduction to Value Theory* shows how fundamental this problem still is when he starts his chapter on "The Metatheory of Valuation" with just this question: "Is value a *property* of objects (like color) or is it a *relationship* (like ownership) that arises out of circumstances linking the value object with the valuing subject in some special way, in which case the further question of objectivity vs. subjectivity arises: is valuation personal and relative; does value reside strictly 'in the mind of the beholder,' or does it have an objective grounding?"[130]

Mukařovský's answer to the first part is unambiguous: value, including aesthetic value, *is* relational. (Relational concepts of value, including Mukařovský's, are often attacked for being relativistic. One has, therefore, to repeat that the two notions are not identical. Something has value *for* somebody. To be a father means to be the father to somebody. A statement about fathership is clearly relational without being relativistic.) The complications and problems begin with the further question about the "objective grounding." I have already said that Mukařovský accepts independent "objective" aesthetic value only as a construct and a postulate. That does not, however, sufficiently answer the question whether valuations are strictly personal, or in what way they are relative, or what kind of objective grounding relational and historically relative evaluations could have.[131]

General theories of value often discriminate between different levels in the evaluative process or in the "genesis of value."[132] The first or "primitive" level—primitive in genetic and in hierarchical sense—is emotional responses of preference or rejection. Such emotional reactions and attitudes, which can be innate or acquired by habit, training, or indoctrination, are important for most evaluative acts, including aesthetic evaluations. Theorists usually acknowledge their pragmatic importance but consider such reactions to be merely preliminary forms of genuine evaluation—an "inarticulate feeling of value"—whereas genuine value and valuation are established only at the level of conscious reflection, as something rationalized and usually (though not necessarily) verbalized and communicated. Hence, evaluations have to be objectified in a double sense: attributable to validated objects as well as articulated beyond purely subjective and emotional reactions so that they can be intersubjectively communicated and argued about. Although emotional preferences and aversions may have particularly strong effects on personal reactions and tastes, emotional factors are not restricted to personal evaluations; and purely personal evaluative judgments can be fully rationalized and argumentatively communicated. But evaluations that are both purely emotional and personal would not qualify for serious considerations in theories and analyses of value.

That is also true for Mukařovský's theory of aesthetic value and for analyses by Czech Structuralists based on his theory. As I have explained in connection with Jauss's criticism, Mukařovský does not deny the role of emotions in aesthetic experience and evaluation, although it is not emphasized and systematically elaborated. *Personal* evaluations are crucial insofar as the act of concretization and aesthetic evaluation is defined and described as a personal, individual act. To be significant for the theorist, the historian, the critic, and other readers or beholders, however, this act has to be articulated in an intersubjective, communicable way. For this purpose the seemingly purely personal evaluation has to refer to words, notions, norms, and values as social facts. In this sense Mukařovský and other Czech Structuralists do not theoretize and investigate purely personal evaluations but focus instead on the relation between the individual act of evaluation and collectively shared socially and historically variable conditions. This is not an objective grounding in a strict sense; but it responds to the "question of objectivity vs. subjectivity" by grounding subjective evaluations in a transsubjective, objectifiable context.

Objective grounding refers in a more direct sense to the object of evaluation itself. Mukařovský, despite his emphasis on the receiver, also stresses the evaluated object, that is, the work of art. His discrimination between the two ontological statuses of the work of art—as material artifact and as concretized aesthetic object—and the identification of the latter as the genuine object of aesthetic evaluation are clarifying and helpful. One could say that for him aesthetic value is grounded objectively in the aesthetic object; but one has then to add that this object is itself a product of an interaction between the work, the reader, and the context—or, to use Grossklaus's formulation, it is produced within the communicative triangle of "message–receiver –context."

The focus on this triangle should not be construed as a neglect of the "sender," the author. If one considers Mukařovský's theory as a whole, the triangle has to be replaced by a quadrangle with the coordinates of sender–message–receiver–context, or, in Mukařovský's less abstract terms, the artist–the work of art–the reader or viewer–and the norms and values of the surrounding society. The growing concern for the author and his "semantic gesture"[133] can also be understood as a response to the "question of objectivity vs. subjectivity," only this time in an intersubjective sense. The author as the creative subject structures his product, the artifact, in accordance with his own value system, thus trying to communicate his values to the receiving subject, the reader, by using devices or strategies which stimulate and to a certain degree control the process of perception and evaluation. Such an exploration of the author's evaluative intentions does not relapse into the "intentional fallacy" as long as it remains focused on the artifact as a semiotic potential for the actualization of meaning and value and investigates how this potential has been actualized by readers, critics, and other authors under historically changing conditions. Grossklaus observes correctly that Mukařovský was groundbreaking in this respect, although the specific semiotic mechanisms used in verbal and visual messages to indicate, to communicate, and to manipulate values have been systematically investigated only by later semioticians. I think Grossklaus is also right when he concludes his critical praise of Mukařovský's theory of value with the remark that those who, after such achievements, "continue to condemn socio-structural investigations of this kind as 'formalistic' or 'pseudoscientific' relinquish the field to those central agencies that have for a long time been trying to get these structures under their control for the purpose of expanding their social impact in the form of 'value management' " (p. 94).

In the general theory or metatheory of value the question of objective value is often connected not only with the problem of subjectivity but also with the debate about so-called intrinsic values.[134] Intrinsic in this case does not indicate value as an intrinsic property of an object, but rather value which is independent from objects or from external goals, existing as an intrinsic end in itself. The same or similar concepts of values are, therefore, also called "end values" and "goal values," or "terminal values," or "orientational values"; and they are used in pairs of opposites like intrinsic versus instrumental values or end values versus means values.[135] The fervent debate about the notion of intrinsic value has also had a strong effect on the development of modern American value theory—particularly with John Dewey's "assault against the distinction of means value and ends value as such" (Rescher, p. 53) and with the critical modification of this position by Monroe Beardsley in his decisive article "Intrinsic Value."[136]

Beardsley accepted Dewey's thesis that evaluation is always a judgment in a "problematic situation" (in which values are questioned or asked for), but added that if everything were in question nothing could be decided, and that therefore "only in terms of certain tentatively held values can we decide, or even ask, whether other things are valuable or not" (p. 7). As a result he—and most current theories of value including those which strictly reject any kind of intrinsic value—tends to discriminate two kinds or levels of values, one functioning as ends or goals of valuation, the others as means or as instrumental possibilities to reach these goals. As a functional classification this distinction allows a shift from one level to the other. What on one level or in one stage of the evaluative process functions as a goal value can, from a higher point of view, be conceived as a means value. For instance, harmony has been considered both as a goal for the perfect work of art and merely as a means to achieve beauty as a terminal goal. But beauty itself can also be questioned and revealed as a means for even higher goals or as only a "tentatively held" end value.

It should go without saying that what might be attacked from the vantage point of some aesthetics appears as a valid end in itself from other positions—for example, the ability of art to let human beings forget their entanglement in everyday life and in conflicting social reality. Shifts from one level to the other occur particularly when one moves from one system or one scholarly discipline to another. To quote the Dutch literary scholar D. W. Fokkema's essay "The Problem of Generalization and the Procedure of Literary Evaluation": "What is considered a terminal value in one literary theory can be an instrumental value in another. Moreover, the terminal value of a literary theory . . . can be an instrumental value in a social theory."[137] We could add "and vice versa," because (as not only Mukařovský has shown) literature is able to transform elements, relations, functions, norms, and values of social reality into actual and even into persevering aesthetic value.

Among the terms indicating the higher level of values, the notion of orientational values deserves special attention. Ernst Oldemeyer and other participants of the conference on "Values in Communicative Processes" discriminated four levels constitutive for valuation: (1) "inarticulate 'feelings' of value"; (2) "articulate evaluation," objectifying value by attributing it to objects as "object values" (also called "good values," "exchange values," and so on); (3) "orientational values," to which articulate evaluations (explicitly or implicitly) refer and which "serve as standards for the attribution of object values (e.g., 'Truth,' 'Beauty,' 'Freedom,' 'Health,' etc.)"; and (4) an optional, still higher level of reflection on "axioms" which might regulate valuation (such as Kant's categorical imperative).[138] The levels correspond approximately with those which were proposed in previous theories (including Dewey's and Beardsley's) and which are generally accepted today. To privilege the term "orientational values" is, nevertheless, more than mere terminological hairsplitting. Compared with the term "goal values" it reduces the teleological emphasis which is unavoidably associated with the notion of a goal; and unlike the label "end values" it has no implication of finality. Instead it directs attention toward the question of which values *orient* the process of valuation, value communication, and the institutionalization and function of whole value systems. There is, of course, a teleological tendency in every kind of valuation insofar as it measures whether and to what degree something is valid for achieving a goal. And on the other side all kinds of values are orientational in the sense that valuation serves to orient our view of the world and our behavior within it. It nevertheless remains meaningful and methodologically useful to distinguish a specific kind or level of values which function as basic orientational standards for the whole process of valuation in a particular realm. At the same time we must keep in mind that they are not intrinsic values that are unquestionable ends in themselves. More important than a rigorous unified terminology is the discrimination between functional levels: (1) the privileged set of orientational or goal values, (2) operational or means values which indicate and validate procedures for reaching the goals, and (3) the objectivation of both by attributing them to objects as object values or goods values.

We can now reconsider a problem that I have mentioned as a still unsolved ambiguity in Mukařovský's theory of aesthetic value and aesthetic function. I refer to the way he defines the relation between function and value in general and how he describes the aesthetic function in particular. As I noted at the beginning of this part, Mukařovský's definitions of the function-value relation vary. Sometimes value is defined as the utility of the object for a particular function that is its aim; on other occasions the function, for example, "the poetic function," is defined as directed toward a particular value. Different kinds or levels of value are evidently implicated. In the first instance value is conceived as instrumental or as means value, serving a particular goal—the respective function. In the second case the value itself is the goal that orients the function. If we consider both statements together and remember in addition Mukařovský's various attempts to define the aesthetic function, it becomes obvious that he often treats the aesthetic function as a goal and as a kind of orientational value which orients the whole realm of aesthetic evaluation.

Neither such transitions from function to value (and vice versa) nor shifts from one level of values to another are—as general value theory shows—theoretically inconsistent or practically unusual. The problems arise rather because Mukařovský, allowing himself such transitions and shifts, approaches aesthetic value and aesthetic function in two methodologically different, in fact almost opposed ways. Dealing with aesthetic value he stresses social variability and historical change; discussing the aesthetic function he tries to define it in general terms as something unchangeable, almost an "anthropological constant." (Remember Grygar's point that I previously quoted, that for Mukařovský the only genuine anthropological constant is the aesthetic function itself.) As far as Mukařovský goes in describing the "place of the aesthetic function among other human functions,"[139] his attempts are fully justified methodologically because typologies of functions are meant to specify different functions as constant human activities or abilities. The danger is conceiving of such definitions as definite and value-neutral, instead of acknowledging and systematically reflecting on their own evaluative presuppositions and implications, which (as evaluations) are variable. This is particularly true for definitions of the aesthetic function, which often explicitly claim to be value-neutral. Actually, the mere declaration that there exists something called "the aesthetic" which is a particular function and deserving of theoretical scrutiny as well as pragmatic support is already an act of validation. It is also an act that, as far as we can learn from history, does not occur under all kinds of "anthropological" conditions but only in particular situations and in stages of relatively advanced cultural development. It is even more obviously evaluative to select qualities that are considered constitutive for the aesthetic function and which, because of this privilege, can then be applied as standards for aesthetic evaluation.

The evaluative implications are not problematic but the degree of their acknowledgment is. One can tie this problem to Beardsley's statements about intrinsic values. First, one has to acknowledge that self-sufficient, intrinsic values either do not exist or at least are not methodologically operable. To quote Fokkema in his reference to Beardsley, "Related to this issue is the problem of intrinsic value, which apparently for the time being has been settled by denying the possibility of justifying intrinsic value" (p. 264). The next step is to acknowledge that despite or within such agreement, one has to *assume* temporarily some values as unquestioned ends in themselves that can orient the process of the concrete evaluation. The crucial difference between the rejected concept of intrinsic values and such orientational values is that the latter are only "tentatively held" as ends and that this hypothetical status has to be theoretically reflected upon and methodologically taken into account. As we have seen, Mukařovský treats the problem of independent objective aesthetic value exactly this way; that is, he acknowledges that such a value does not exist or cannot be proved, but has nevertheless to be assumed and then to be marked as a theoretical construct and postulate indispensable for the pragmatic functioning of aesthetic evaluation. But when Mukařovský defines the aesthetic function and treats it as a goal and an orientational value, these critical requirements are set aside.

To be fair, one has to admit that Mukařovský was well aware of the tentative character of his definitions. Throughout his career he continuously revised his conceptualization of the aesthetic function. When I met him shortly after the suppression of the Prague Spring, in a residence for Czech writers and scholars, and asked him about his current projects, he—at this time almost eighty years old—replied: "If I could start once again, what I would do would be to reconsider and modify my definition of the aesthetic function." As admirable as this statement was with regard to the personal "dynamics" and the personal "pathos" of an eminent scholar, it indicated his willingness to modify his general definition (by adding or omitting particular factors), not an acknowledgement that those general definitions, including prospective reformulations, were tentative because they presupposed and implied acts of validation that were themselves variable responses to changing historical conditions. It is therefore not sufficient simply to replace some elements of the definition by others without scrutinizing in addition the relation between what is described as the variability of aesthetic values and what is implied as orientational value in the putatively unchangeable general definition of the aesthetic function.

In this respect Mukařovský's own modifications remain as insufficient as most revisions proposed by later critics. Such critics usually attack his description of the aesthetic function as too negative or "empty" and then propose new or different essentials that should complement or replace those mentioned by Mukařovský. I have already discussed such proposed amendments as the inclusion of pleasure and of fictionality. The problem now under discussion is not to what degree Mukařovský himself included or omitted these aspects, but rather how far such possible and sometimes helpful reformulations also help to solve—or at least to articulate—the problem of their own implied validation. On closer examination one discovers that most of the essential items put forth in the history of arts and aesthetics as constitutive of the aesthetic function or aesthetic value form a relatively stable (or at least recurrent) core of components. Even decisive modifications are often less genuine additions or omissions of fundamentals than redefinitions and reorganizations of their hierarchy. The process is comparable to the Russian Formalist model for the evolution of literature as a functional system. The changes consist mainly in the different use of traditional elements, in the reorganization of their relations, and in the continuous ascent and descent within the value hierarchy in which some components lose their position on the "mountaincrest" while others are climbing up from the base. That does not exclude the addition of genuinely new elements from other subsystems within reality as a "system of systems" and the continuous interaction between the subsystems, as the Formalists learned during the development of their own method.

Instead of merely deciding whether pleasure, fictionality, the imaginary, or beauty are included in Mukařovský's concept of the aesthetic function, it is more informative to locate them in the hierarchy of his system. As I have tried to show, fictionality not only is included but also has a privileged position, although its connection with the imaginative is not systematically elaborated. Pleasure also has a relatively high hierarchical position. The ideal of beauty is repeatedly mentioned and seems to be acceptable as a tentatively held orientational value, although it is explicitly called into question as a reliable basis for the theory of aesthetic value because it "may have the *semblance* of validity only as long as it is derived from an entire system of metaphysics. Otherwise it seems to be a forced solution with *doubtful* value" (p. 69, my italics). Most characteristic for Mukařovský's own hierarchy is the fact that all these categories, acceptable as orientational values for concrete aesthetic evaluations, are themselves oriented toward a still higher value, which is, as he repeats at the conclusion of his presentation of the issue, to intensify "the ties between man and reality as an element of human activity."

This selection and hierarchical ordering of particular qualities or goals as orientational values for his aesthetics relates Mukařovský to a particular historical situation or context—with its characteristic traditions, limitations, and tasks, but also with the possibility of choosing among them, combining them, and even transgressing established boundaries. As I have mentioned, the situation in Czech aesthetics at the time when Mukařovský started has been described as influenced by two dominant traditions: the Hegelian approach, which emphasizes historical development and the relation between the evolution of art, the evolution of ideas, and the course of general history; and the "Herbartian" tradition, which focuses on form and its aesthetic significance. Mukařovský took over some of the most innovative findings or proposals of Russian Formalism and combined them with elements of his native formalistic tradition, but went far beyond both, particularly in stressing and systematically elaborating the interaction between art and society and between aesthetic and social functions, norms, and values. The introduction of his groundbreaking concept of semiotic Structuralism in aesthetics and in the theory of literature allowed him to emphasize the interaction between art as a semiotic system and the society which establishes this system and uses it for communication, while at the same time insisting on the specificity of this realm as a basic human activity with its own functions, norms, and values. On this basis neither the representational, the referential, nor the self-referential aspects of literature become dominant; but the *tension* among them all acts as a dynamic suspension that stimulates in the reader both aesthetic distance as well as pragmatic commitment and thus makes art able to generate actual aesthetic value under changing conditions.

In accordance with this state of tension and suspension, aesthetic value is conceptualized as indissolubly connected and interacting with nonaesthetic values as social facts. The investigation can go both ways: proceeding from the theoretical reflection on values in general and aesthetic values in particular to the selection of some qualities or goals as orientational values on the top of the hierarchy and going down to appropriate operational or instrumental values and finally to the analysis of individual objects of evaluation—literary works in their evaluative potential and their concrete perceptions and evaluations in different contexts. Or it can proceed in the opposite direction, starting from such concrete analyses of works and exploring how they operate with values and moving to the identification of operational values and then to orientational values characteristic for authors, literary genres, schools, periods and whole literary or cultural systems, and finally to the theoretical generalization of such evaluative procedures. What is important is not the chosen direction but the inclusion of all these levels and the theoretical and methodological awareness that *all* these explicitly announced or merely implied values are from the scholarly point of view only temporarily held ends, which are all socially variable and historically changing, though to different degrees and at different rates.

In this last part I have focused mainly on Mukařovský's theoretical writings about aesthetic value and aesthetic function, along with later writings by others directly referring to them or indirectly related to them. This might have created the impression that Mukařovský and the Czech Structuralists were far more interested in theoretical concepts than in concrete analyses of aesthetic value and processes of aesthetic evaluation. Such an impression would be wrong. If one takes into account Mukařovský's whole oeuvre and the writings of other Czech Structuralists of the second and third generation, one finds an abundance of applications. In historical studies of literary production and reception, in careful analyses of texts and authors, and in actual art criticism (on literature, journalism, theater, film, visual art, and so on), Czech Structuralists intensively tested their own theoretical and methodological proposals. They showed how authors construct artifacts as potential bearers of values, how readers and critics respond—or do not respond—to such attempts by actualizing these values or other values of their own, and how contemporary literature as well as literary works from remote periods and cultures challenge established value systems by confronting readers with their own fictional reality and their own constructive principles, thus calling upon the readers to actualize anew aesthetic and extra-aesthetic values.

Despite this rich variety of application and testing of their theories, Czech literary Structuralists did not systematically develop methods to test literary value empirically or to rank literary works by using quantifiable techniques. Those who are professionally involved with such procedures or are interested mainly in such applications might regret that this school, with its keen understanding of the social functions of literature and of the "social range of the aesthetic function," did not advance in this empirical direction. Recently published attempts like the "Experimental Investigation(s) into Evaluation of Literature" refer to Mukařovský and demonstrate that his concept could serve as a theoretical point of departure for such investigations.[140] But that was hardly the main intention and the main achievement of his theory or of this school of literary scholarship. Other literary scholars who have acknowledged the importance of Mukařovský's aesthetics as a pioneering approach, and who have helped to make this theory and Czech Structuralism internationally known, tend to neglect (or even to deny) the centrality of the value problem. The relatively few recent works that—against the "exile of evaluation"—are dedicated to the theory of literary evaluation either ignore this important predecessor, or mention him merely in a laudatory reference, or at best report some of his theoretical proposals from the early book *Aesthetic Function, Norm, and Value.*

As a result, the pioneering contribution of Czech Structuralism to the theory and investigation of aesthetic value and literary evaluation has still not found the wide acknowledgment it certainly deserves. Previously, during the international boom of Structuralism, the scarcity of available translations was the main obstacle to an appreciation of the Czech school. There was also, to be sure, a widespread lack of interest in problems of aesthetic value and evaluation. Today, in a time supposedly beyond Structuralism and even beyond Poststructuralism, the fact that this theory of aesthetic value was developed by Structuralists has become something of an additional handicap. Why should those who have already left the whole movement behind return to its earliest version in the hope of finding sources of inspiration for their own theories and investigations? Thomas Pavel, in his book *Fictional Worlds*, articulates this experience in a very graphic and direct way. In his chapter called "Beyond Structuralism" he starts the section entitled "Toward a Referential Theory of Fiction" with this statement:

> Structuralist poetics started as a rejuvenation project, confi-
> dent that the right amount of linguistic ideas and methodol-
> ogy would infuse new life into literary studies. Some of the
> doctrines it gradually adopted . . . led nevertheless to a pre-
> mature arrest of the theoretical advances and convinced those
> scholars who, in spite of their disenchantment with structur-
> alism, were not yet prepared to abandon the ideas of rational
> inquiry and methodological awareness, that they had to turn
> elsewhere for new sources of theoretical insight. (p. 9)

The feelings are understandable and justified. But the well-
founded polemics against the once dominant French version of
Structuralism also results, as we have seen, in the neglect of
other "rejuvenating project(s)" at the start of the movement
and ignores the fact that the earliest, Czech version of Structuralism produced some of the most innovative and still very
timely "theoretical insights" regarding the development of "a
referential theory of fiction."

If this happens with a scholar such as Pavel, who actively
participated in the development of Structuralism, it is even
more understandable that those who started their careers or
academic training already "beyond Structuralism" will also ignore these basic achievements. I am not arguing against moving
beyond the limits of this school or any other school. Czech
Structuralism itself moved beyond Formalism. Both schools
continuously revised and even edited out altogether their own
previous positions and proposals for the sake of the advancement of scholarship; both were dynamic and self-critical
enough to welcome justified, constructive criticism. They disappeared not because of such justified criticism or due to some
premature death but because of the interference of external
forces. Personal and scholarly fairness should provide reason
enough not to neglect, once again, their contributions to the
advancement of literary scholarship, which were put forth under extremely difficult circumstances. The idea that we are
somehow beyond Structuralism is not a valid excuse for continuing to neglect the insights of the Czech Structuralists. The
analogy between succeeding schools of literature (and literary
criticism) and the generations of a family, suggested by the
Formalists, comes to mind. Sons and daughters who want to

grow up and free themselves from the influence of dominant parents are well advised to rediscover achievements of their grandparents, because such discoveries can inspire and orient their own innovative attempts, linking them with innovative tradition. Czech Structuralism did not engender French Structuralism (as Russian Formalism did not engender Czech Structuralism), but it is related—like an uncle or aunt. To reconsider what these once groundbreaking schools have tried or achieved in the study of literary structure, evolution, and value might— even in an era beyond Formalism and beyond Structuralism— be a worthwhile task for anyone who wishes to understand the function and value of literature.

Notes

Introduction

1. Victor Erlich, *Russian Formalism: History—Doctrine* (The Hague, 1955; 3rd ed. New Haven, 1981).

2. Boris Eikhenbaum, "Kak sdelana 'Šinel' ' Gogolja" (1918); English trans. in R. A. Maguire, ed., *Gogol from the Twentieth Century* (Princeton, 1974), pp. 269–291.

3. Viktor Shklovsky, "Iskusstvo, kak priem" (1916); English trans. in L. T. Lemon and M. J. Reis, eds., *Russian Formalist Criticism: Four Essays* (Lincoln, Nebr., 1965), pp. 5–24.

4. Yury Tynyanov, Roman Jakobson, "Problemy izučenija literatury i jazyka," *Novyj Lef*, 12 (1928): 36–37; English trans. in L. Matejka and K. Pomorska, eds., *Reading in Russian Poetics: Formalist and Structuralist Views* (Cambridge, Mass., 1971), pp. 79–81.

5. P. N. Medvedev, *Formal'nyj metod v literaturovedenii* (Leningrad, 1928); English trans. Baltimore, 1978; paperback rpt, with M. M. Bakhtin and P. N. Medvedev as authors (Cambridge, Mass., 1985). For the writings of the Bakhtin group and the problem of their authorship see Part IV.

6. The first colloquium was held in Giessen, Germany, in June 1963, with the contributions published as *Nachahmung und Illusion,* ed. Hans Robert Jauss (Munich, 1964). The first published results of my work on Russian Formalism, "Transparenz und Verfremdung" (Transparency and Defamiliarization), appeared in vol. II, *Immanente Ästhetik—Ästhetische Reflexion,* ed. Wolfgang Iser (Munich, 1966), pp. 263–296.

7. *Texte der russischen Formalisten,* vol. 1 (Munich, 1969); vol. 2 (Munich, 1972). Vol. 1 was reissued, without the Russian versions, as *Russischer Formalismus: Texte zur allgemeinen Literaturtheorie und zur Theorie der Prosa* (Munich, 1977).

8. Walter Benjamin, "Der Erzähler: Betrachtungen zum Werk Nikolai Lesskows," in *Orient und Okzident* (1936); English trans. in W. Benjamin, *Illuminations,* ed. Hannah Arendt (New York, 1968), pp. 83–109.

9. This first English translation was published in two parts, as "The Russian

Formalist Theory of Prose" and "The Russian Formalist Theory of Literary Evolution," in *PTL: A Journal for Descriptive Poetics and Theory of Literature*, 3 (Amsterdam, 1977): 429–470; 3 (1978): 1–24. I am grateful to the editors of this journal for giving me an opportunity to address non-German readers in Israel and Europe on topics of Russian Formalism. I have, however, restored the omitted part; and all parts are newly translated for this book.

10. Felix Vodička, *Die Struktur der literarischen Entwicklung* (Munich, 1976).

I. The Formalist Theory of Prose and Literary Evolution

1. Victor Erlich, *Russian Formalism: History—Doctrine* (The Hague, 1955); 3rd ed. (New Haven, Conn., 1981).

2. See Roman Jakobson's preface to Tzvetan Todorov, ed., *Théorie de la littérature: Textes des formalistes russes* (Paris, 1965).

3. For example, Claude Lévi-Strauss, "La Structure et la forme: Réflexions sur un ouvrage de Vladimir Propp," *Cahiers de l'Institut de science économique appliquée* (Paris), 99 (1960): 1–36.

4. Boris Eikhenbaum, "Teorija formal'nogo metoda," *Michigan Slavic Materials* 2, *Readings in Russian Poetics*, rev. ed. (Ann Arbor, Mich., 1971), pp. 45–77.

5. Erlich, *Russian Formalism*, p. 53 (quoting Eikhenbaum).

6. Todorov, *Théorie*, p. 19.

7. Historically the Russian Formalists were not taking off from a nomological conception of how to construct theories and sciences, for such a conception was only developed later on; more probably their point of reference was phenomenology. (On the influence of phenomenology on the Formalists, see Erlich, *Russian Formalism*, pp. 69ff.) Concerning the problem of Formalism and nomological versus nomothetical science, see R. Jakobson's phrase in his introduction to the French anthology of Formalist writings: "L'histoire de la littérature se trouvait dotée d'un fil conducteur et promettait de rejoindre les sciences nomothétiques" in Todorov, *Théorie*, p. 10. See also the essays in Hans Albert, ed., *Theorie und Realität, Ausgewählte Aufsätze zur Wissenschaftslehre der Sozialwissenschaften* (Tübingen, 1964).

8. K. R. Popper, *The Logic of Scientific Discovery* (London, 1959).

9. Jürgen Habermas, *Zur Logik der Sozialwissenschaften*, Sonderheft der Philosophischen Rundschau, 5 (Tübingen, 1967), p. 3.

10. Eikhenbaum, "Teorija," p. 48: "The Formal method and Futurism were historically related."

11. See Jakobson's preface to Todorov, *Théorie*.

12. Erlich, *Russian Formalism*, p. 60: "Viewed from this vantage point, the Formalist school is apt to appear for better or for worse as a legitimate, if somewhat eccentric, child of the revolutionary period, as part and parcel of its peculiar intellectual atmosphere."

13. For comparisons we need go no further than Shklovsky's *O teorii prozy* (On the Theory of Prose; Moscow, 1925) and Tynyanov's *Arkhaisty i novatory* (Archaists and Innovators; Leningrad, 1929; rpt. Munich, 1967). In both the fundamental essays on theory are placed at the beginning. But whereas Shklovsky's opening essay, "Art as Device," is in fact historically the earliest in the collection (1916), Tynyanov's two opening pieces, "The Literary Fact" and "On Literary Evolution," are of a relatively late date (1924 and 1927), his earlier investigations being entirely within the scope of literary history, and most often in the form of a comparison of two poets ("Dostoevsky and Gogol," "Tyutchev and Heine," "Pushkin and Tyutchev," etc.). In turning his interests in new directions and adopting new methods, neither was renouncing his earlier position but rather was expanding his scope.

14. Eikhenbaum, "Teorija," p. 76.

15. For a discussion of the quarrel between early Formalism and Russian Symbolism, see Erlich, *Russian Formalism*, pp. 16–32 (chap. 2, "Approaches to Formalism: From the 'Forest of Symbols' to the 'Self-Valuable Word' "). On Shklovsky's theory of defamiliarization, see Striedter, "Transparenz und Verfremdung. Zur Theorie des poetischen Bildes in der russischen Moderne," in W. Iser, ed., *Poetik und Hermeneutik, 2, Immanente Ästhetik—Ästhetische Reflexion: Lyrik als Paradigma der Moderne* (Munich, 1966), pp. 263–296.

16. Jakobson, *Novejšaja russkaja poezija: Nabrosok pervyj: Viktor Chlebnikov* (Prague, 1921), p. 11.

17. See Erlich, *Russian Formalism*, pp. 40–44, 241.

18. Eikhenbaum, "Kak sdelana 'Šinel' Gogolja" (1918), in J. Striedter, ed., *Texte der russischen Formalisten* (Munich, 1969), I, 122–158.

19. See even the earliest volumes of collected essays by Opojaz, *Sborniki po teorii poetičeskogo jazyka*, I (Prague, 1916) and II (Prague, 1917), and also *Poetika: Sborniki po teorii poetičeskogo jazyka* (Prague, 1919).

20. Eikhenbaum, in "Teorija" (p. 55), had called Shklovsky's article a "kind of manifesto of the formal method."

21. See R. Grimm, "Verfremdung: Beiträge zu Ursprung und Wesen eines Begriffs," *Revue de Littérature Comparée*, 35 (1961): 207–236. Critical studies of "estrangement" in Brecht's work include J. Willett, *The Theater of Bertolt Brecht* (New York, 1959); R. Grimm, *Bertolt Brecht: Die Struktur seiner Dichtung* (Nuremberg, 1960); R. Grimm, "Vom Novum Organum zum Kleinen Organon: Gedanken zur Verfremdung," in *Das Ärgernis Brechts* (Basel and Stuttgart, 1961), pp. 45–70; P. Böckmann, "Provokation und Dialektik in der Dramaturgie Brechts," *Kölner Universitätsreden*, vol. 26 (1961); H. E. Holthusen, "Dramaturgie der Verfremdung: Eine Studie zur Dramentechnik Bertolt Brechts," *Merkur*, 15 (1961): 520–542; and J. M. Fradkin, *Bertolt Brecht* (Moscow, 1965). For general studies on the technique of estrangement in the theory and practice of modern drama, see P. Szondi, *Theorie des modernen Dramas* (Frankfurt, 1956), and M. Kesting, *Das epische Theater: Zur Struktur des modernen Dramas* (Stuttgart, 1959).

22. Preface to Todorov, *Théorie*, p. 11. In his review of this anthology in

Strumenti critici (Turin), 1 (1967): 98–100, V. Strada already undertook a qualifying critique of these complaints against Shklovsky. The most recent systematic investigation of Russian Formalism in German, Aage A. Hansen-Löve's *Der russische Formalismus: Methodologische Rekonstruktion seiner Entwicklung aus dem Prinzip der Verfremdung* (Vienna, 1978), treats the whole school as a "Development out of the Principle of Defamiliarization."

23. The phrase quoted follows P. Brang, "Der russische Formalismus," in the *Neue Zürcher Zeitung,* February 12, 1966, sec. 21: "So präsentierte sich den russischen Formalisten die Geschichte der Literatur vor allem als die Tradition des Traditionsbruchs."

24. For a discussion of these problems in the later phase of Formalism, see Erlich, *Russian Formalism,* pp. 164–181 (chap. 11, "Literature and 'Life' ").

25. Shklovsky, "Kak sdelan 'Don Kikhot' " (1925), in *O teorii prozy,* pp. 91–124.

26. For example, B. Tomashevsky, "O dramatičeskoj literatury," *Žizn' i iskusstvo,* 13, 16 (1924): 5, 5–6; and Tynyanov's study of Küchelbecker's tragedy "Argivjane" in *Arkhaisty i novatory,* pp. 292–329.

27. S. D. Balukhaty, "Problemy dramatičeskogo analiza. Čechov," *Voprosy poetiki,* IX (Leningrad, 1927). Balukhaty's later work on Chekhov, Gorky, and others cannot, strictly speaking, be termed formalistic.

28. A new edition of Shklovsky's work on film appears in Shklovsky, *Za sorok let* (Moscow, 1965). Of the Formalists Osip Brik was the most active in filmmaking. He wrote several screen plays, including one for *The Descendant of Genghis Khan (Potomok Čingis-khana),* directed by V. Pudovkin (1928).

29. See A. Tairov, *Zapiski režissera* (Moscow, 1921); English trans. by William Kuhlke, *Notes of a Director* (Coral Gables, Fla., 1969); German trans. *Das entfesselte Theater* (Potsdam, 1927). On the dramatic and theatrical concepts of the Russian revolutionary theater and its great directors, see J. Rühle, *Das gefesselte Theater* (Cologne and Berlin, 1957), pp. 79–131, and his bibliography, pp. 444ff.

30. Shklovsky, "Svjaz' priemov sjužetosloženija s obščimi priemami stilja" (1916), in *Texte,* I, 36–120.

31. Here, as in his polemic against Potebnya, Shklovsky associates a particular scholar with an entire school, thus obscuring (at least for a less knowledgeable reader) the degree to which the scholar's conceptions transcend those of the "school" that claims to follow him. In his polemic against the "ethnographic school" Shklovsky makes reference chiefly to A. N. Veselovsky, probably the most important of Russian comparatists, whose relevant folkloristic studies on the *Poetics of Plot* (1897–1906) formed only one part of the full concept of a "historical poetic." For the Russian literature on Veselovsky, see *Kratkaja literaturnaja ènciklopedija,* I (Moscow, 1962), pp. 940ff.

32. Shklovsky, "Svjaz' priemov," p. 42.

33. V. Propp, *Morfologija skazki* (Leningrad, 1928); English trans. "Morphology of the Folktale," *International Journal of American Linguistics,* 14 (1958): 1–134.

34. Erlich, *Russian Formalism,* p. 217.

35. For a bibliography of Propp's folklore studies (and reviews of them), see M. J. Mel'c, "Spisok pečatnych rabot V. Ja. Proppa v oblasti fol'klora," *Specifika fol'klornych žanrov: Russkij fol'klor*, (Moscow and Leningrad, 1966), X, 337–343.

36. See V. N. Putilov, "Vladimir Jakovlevič Propp (K 70-letiju so dnja roždenija)," in *Specifika fol'klornych žanrov*.

37. A. Jolles, *Einfache Formen: Legende, Sage, Mythe, Rätsel, Spruch, Kasus, Memorabile, Märchen, Witz* (Halle, 1930), pp. 218–246 (chapter on fairy tales [*Märchen*]). Jolles' book is available in French under the title *Formes Simples* in the Poétique series.

38. Shklovsky, "Svjaz' priemov," p. 50.

39. As is evident from Shklovsky's footnote, he refers directly to the aesthetics of Broder Christiansen, whose writings (*Philosophie der Kunst* [Hanau, 1909], and others) became very important for the Russian Formalists, especially in connection with the concept of the "differential quality."

40. Shklovsky, "Stroenie rasskaza i romana," in *O teorii prozy*, pp. 68–90, appeared first in this collection (1925).

41. Ibid., p. 84, with special reference to *The Decameron*.

42. Shklovsky refers to I. Turgenev's 1860 essay "Gamlet i Don-Kikhot," in *Sobranie sočinenij* (Moscow, 1964), VIII, 169–192.

43. Shklovsky, *O teorii prozy*, pp. 100–101.

44. Ibid., p. 222.

45. See H. J. Neuschäfer, *Der Sinn der Parodie im "Don Quijote"* (Heidelberg, 1963), chap. 4: "Die kompositorische Verbindung von Haupthandlung und eingeschobenen Geschichten."

46. Shklovsky, "Ornamental'naja proza: Andrej Belyj," in *O teorii prozy*, pp. 205–225.

47. Bely's personal acquaintance with Rudolf Steiner began in 1912, and led, during his stay abroad (1912–1916), to a close relationship. *Kotik Letaev* was written during this time and appeared in 1916. See A. Bely, *Kotik Letaev*, Slavische Propyläen, 3 (Munich, 1964); English trans. by Gerald Janecek (Ann Arbor, Mich., 1971).

48. Shklovsky's "učenie o mnogoplannosti javlenija" in "Ornamental'naja proza," p. 206.

49. The Russian terms used by Bely and cited by Shklovsky are *roj* (for swarm) and *stroj* (for order).

50. Shklovsky, "Ornamental'naja proza," p. 207.

51. Ibid., p. 205.

52. Ibid., p. 211: "One must not be led astray by the artist's biography; he writes and only looks for motivation afterward. But above all, one must not be led astray by psychoanalysis." What Shklovsky goes on to say against psychoanalysis is not very sound or very informed, but it does show the general tendency of his polemic against any form of extra-artistic interpretation.

53. Ibid., p. 214.

54. The Anglo-American developments in this area become clear if we compare the state of the debate as described, for example, in R. Wellek and A. Warren's *Theory of Literature* (New York, 1956) with what is found in

J. Margolis, *The Language of Art and Art Criticism: Analytic Questions in Aesthetics* (Detroit, 1965), in which the essence and effect of a work of art are seen as dependent on the recipient's or reproducer's identification with it. The status of recent debate in Germany on how the aesthetics of reception and literary history are interrelated is discussed later in this chapter.

55. Shklovsky, "Novella tajn" and "Roman tajn," in *O teorii prozy*, pp. 125–142, 143–176. Whereas the first article deals with the detective story, the second is not devoted specifically to the crime novel, but to the type of novel that works with mystification more generally (from Ann Radcliffe to Charles Dickens and Boris Pilnyak).

56. Shklovsky, "Novella tajn," p. 136.

57. Ibid., p. 135.

58. See Iser, ed., *Poetik und Hermeneutik*, 2, in which several contributions (of W. D. Stempel, M. Fuhrmann, K. H. Stierle, and others) and discussions are directed specifically to the problem of hermetic lyrics and how to interpret them.

59. Shklovsky, "Parodijnyj roman 'Tristram Šendi' Sterna," in *Texte*, I, 244–299. Translated as "Sterne's *Tristram Shandy:* Stylistic Commentary" in L. J. Lemon and M. J. Reis, eds., *Russian Formalist Criticism* (Lincoln, Neb., 1965).

60. As a reference to this fashion and the polemic against it, see the end of Vinogradov's article "Problema skaza v stilistike" (1925), in *Texte*, I, 207: "when the current era of literary 'Shandyism' passes."

61. K. E. Harter, "A Russian Critic and *Tristram Shandy*," *Modern Philology*, 52 (1954): 97ff.

62. Erlich, *Russian Formalism*, p. 166.

63. Shklovsky, "Literatura vne 'sjužeta'," in *O teorii prozy*, pp. 226–245.

64. Tynyanov, "Dostoevskij i Gogol' (K teorii parodii)," in *Texte*, I, 300–370.

65. Ibid., p. 300.

66. For example, some 83 titles deal with Lermontov (see bibliography in B. Eikhenbaum, *Stat'i o Lermontove* [Moscow and Leningrad, 1961], pp. 367–371) and 61 with Tolstoy (see bibliography in B. Eikhenbaum, *Lev Tolstoj: Semidesjatye gody* [Leningrad, 1960], pp. 287–292).

67. Eikhenbaum, "Kak sdelana, 'Šinel'," p. 130.

68. The controversy already set in with socially aware criticism of *The Inspector General* (1836) and Gogol's own response to such criticism. It reached its climax in the impassioned quarrel between the author and V. Belinsky, first in connection with *Dead Souls* and then, most of all, over *Selections from My Correspondence with Friends*.

69. Eikhenbaum's designation of *The Overcoat* as a grotesque is reiterated and emphasized in his short self-portrait in "Teorija," p. 32. On the history and modern designation of the grotesque see W. Kayser, *Das Groteske: Seine Gestaltung in Malerei und Dichtung* (Oldenburg and Hamburg, 1957), and W. Van O'Connor, *The Grotesque* (Carbondale, Ill., 1962).

70. See V. Setschkareff, *N. V. Gogol': Leben und Schaffen* (Berlin, 1953).

71. Sievers' method received attention particularly in the Formalists' early theory of prosody, notably in Eikhenbaum's "Melodika stikha" (1921),

V. Zhirmunsky's "Melodika stikha" (1922), and R. Jakobson's "O češskom stikhe" (1923).

72. V. Vinogradov, "Problema skaza v stilistike," in *Texte*, I, 168–206.

73. Note the titles of the books by E. Auerbach, *Mimesis: The Representation of Reality in Western Literature* (Princeton, N.J., 1953) and by R. Brinkmann, *Wirklichkeit und Illusion: Studien über Gehalt und Grenzen des Begriffs Realismus für die erzählende Dichtung des 19. Jahrhunderts* (Tübingen, 1957).

74. Even before the Formalists, I. Mandel'shtam made an interesting attempt to characterize Gogol's stylistic system as a whole, and his *O charaktere Gogolevskogo stilja* (Helsinki, 1902) was the subject of critical discussion by them. The following works were written during the same period as the Formalists' own Gogol studies: A. Slonimsky, "Tekhnika komičeskogo u Gogolja," *Voprosy poetiki*, I (Petrograd, 1923), and V. Vinogradov, "Etjudy o stile Gogolja," *Voprosy poetiki*, VII (Leningrad, 1926). On later literature, see W. Kasack, *Die Technik der Personendarstellung bei Nikolaj Vasil'evič Gogol'* (Wiesbaden, 1957).

75. Eikhenbaum, "Leskov i sovremennaja proza," in *Texte*, I, 208–242.

76. Eikhenbaum, "Teorija," parts 4 and 5.

77. Tynyanov, *Problema stikhotvornogo jazyka* (1924; reissued, Moscow, 1965).

78. Eikhenbaum, "Leskov," p. 208.

79. Published by the Department of Verbal Art of the Leningrad Art History Institute as a kind of sequel to the anthology *Poetika* of 1919, the anthologies *Poetika* I–V (1926–1929) convey an impression of this collaboration between distinctly "formalist" scholars and others (of different ages and very diverse interests) who were more loosely associated with Formalism. Because during this period the official polemic against Formalism was rapidly gaining ground and indeed led to the dissolution of the Formalist school, much that was then undertaken and, in part, accomplished in seminars or discussion groups has unfortunately never been published.

80. Eikhenbaum and Tynyanov, eds., *Russkaja proza: Sbornik statej*, Voprosy poetiki, VIII (Leningrad, 1926).

81. See, for example, W. Kayser, *Das sprachliche Kunstwerk: Eine Einführung in die Literaturwissenschaft* (Berlin, 1971), chap. 10: "Das Gefüge der Gattung," and the literature cited, pp. 241ff. For its critical distinctions, see also E. Lämmert, *Bauformen des Erzählens* (Stuttgart, 1955), Introduction, "Gattungsbegriff und Typusbegriff in der Epik."

82. As in V. Zhirmunsky's introduction, "K voprosu o formal'nom metode," in *Problema formy v poezii* (Prague, 1923), the Russian translation of O. Walzel's *Die künstlerische Form des Dichtwerks*. However, Zhirmunsky emphasizes the differences between Walzel's conception of form and that of the Russian Formalists, setting himself apart from the latter.

83. Walzel, *Die künstlerische Form des Dichtwerks* (Berlin, 1916).

84. Walzel, *Gehalt und Gestalt im Kunstwerk des Dichters* (Berlin and Potsdam, 1923).

85. Walzel, *Wechselseitige Erhellung der Künste* (Berlin, 1917).

86. An overview of Formalism that is both critical and informed is offered

by Zhirmunsky in "Formprobleme in der russischen Literaturwissenschaft," *Zeitschrift für slavische Philologie*, 1 (1925): 117–152. On Zhirmunsky's position regarding Formalism and how it developed, see also Erlich, *Russian Formalism*, pp. 75–77.

87. Jolles, *Einfache Formen*, p. 10.

88. Ibid., p. 262.

89. See Lämmert, *Bauformen*, p. 17.

90. First published in *Orient und Okzident* (1936); quoted passages follow W. Benjamin, *Schriften*, II, ed. T. W. and G. Adorno (Frankfurt, 1955), pp. 229–258. In *Illuminations*, ed. Hannah Arendt (New York, 1968), pp. 83–109.

91. See Benjamin's letters to Hugo von Hofmannsthal (February 8, 1928) and to K. Marx-Steinschneider (April 15, 1936), in Benjamin, *Briefe*, II, ed. G. Scholem and T. W. Adorno (Frankfurt, 1966). For a discussion of his relations to the Soviet Union, see the "Biographical Note" by F. Podszus in Benjamin, *Illuminationen: Ausgewählte Schriften* (Frankfurt, 1961), p. 442.

92. Quoted by Benjamin in "Storyteller," *Schriften*, II, 246.

93. Ibid., p. 245.

94. Ibid., chap. IX.

95. Ibid., chap. XII.

96. Leskov's best-known work, which in a subtitle he called a chronicle, is *Soborjane* (Cathedral Folk). It represents a part (and the end product) of several projected and partially executed chronicles.

97. See, for example, Theodor W. Adorno's replies to Benjamin, especially his letter of August 2, 1935, in Benjamin, *Briefe*, II, 671–683.

98. Tynyanov, "O literaturnoj evoljucii," in *Texte*, I, 438.

99. In a discussion following the publication of *Texte der Russischen Formalisten*, Jakobson confirmed that he had introduced *ustanovka* as an equivalent to Husserl's *Einstellung*. In English, Jakobson uses the translation *set*, sometimes adding *Einstellung* parenthetically, as, for example, in his "Closing Statement: Linguistics and Poetics" (in *Style and Language* [New York, 1960], p. 356). On the topic of Jakobson's use of *ustanovka/Einstellung* and its relation to Husserl, see E. Holenstein, *Roman Jakobsons phänomenologischer Strukturalismus* (Frankfurt, 1975), pp. 59ff.

100. Jakobson, *Die neueste russische Poesie*, in *Texte*, II, 31.

101. Tynyanov, "On Literary Evolution" (1927); English trans. in Ladislav Matejka and Krystyna Pomorska, eds., *Readings in Russian Poetics: Formalist and Structuralist Views* (Cambridge, Mass., 1971), pp. 66–78.

102. See also Tynyanov and Jakobson's program "Problemy izučenija literatury i jazyka" (Problems of Research in Literature and Language), in *Texte*, II, 386–390; English trans. in Roman Jakobson, *Verbal Art, Verbal Sign, Verbal Time* (Minneapolis, 1985).

103. Tynyanov presented his concept of the function and evolution of literary genres partly in literary-historical investigations of specific genres (see below on his study of the ode), and partly in general definitions (see his article "The Literary Fact"). The chapter "The Literary Genres" in B. Tomashevsky's *Teorija literatury* (Leningrad, 1925) gives a general characterization of the

Formalist concept of genre. (See the translation of this chapter and of the entire "Thematics" section in the French anthology of Formalist writings, Todorov, *Théorie*, pp. 302–307.)

104. Tynyanov, "Oda kak oratorskij žanr," in *Texte*, II, 272–336.

105. In B. Tomashevsky's chapter on literary genres in *Teorija literatury* (Leningrad, 1925).

106. E. M. Forster, *Aspects of the Novel* (London, 1927; Harmondsworth, 1962), p. 13.

107. Lämmert, *Bauformen*, p. 15.

108. K. Skipina, "O čuvstvitel'noj povesti," in Eikhenbaum and Tynyanov, eds., *Russkaja proza*, pp. 13–41. For a critical response to Skipina's thesis, see P. Brang, *Studien zur Theorie und Praxis der russischen Erzählung, 1770–1811* (Wiesbaden, 1960), pp. 66–69.

109. As examples I cite the work of two non-Formalists of the time who were influenced by the Formalists—V. Vinogradov's studies of the natural school: *Gogol' i natural'naja škola* (Leningrad, 1925) and *Èvoljucija russkogo naturalizma* (Leningrad, 1929); and V. Zhirmunsky's book on the Byronic poem in Russia: *Bajron i Puškin, Iz istorii romantičeskoj poemy* (Leningrad, 1923).

110. Terminology based on S. Kracauer, "The General History and the Aesthetic Approach," *Poetik und Hermeneutik*, (3 Munich, 1968), p. 569.

111. Eikhenbaum, "Teorija," pp. 73–74 (quoted from Shklovsky's 1921 book on Rozanov).

112. Both Tynyanov's study of parody and his article "The Literary Fact" (as well as his essay "On Literary Evolution") set out from a definition of literary succession, not as a continuous development but rather as a battle and a break with one's immediate predecessors, which at the same time is associated with a return to something older.

113. Similar points have already been made in *Rozanov* (1921) and in the essay on Rozanov, "Literatura vne 'sjužeta,' " in *O teorii prozy*, p. 227: "The succession as one literary school gives way to another leads not from father to son but from uncle to nephew."

114. Tynyanov, "Literaturnyj fakt," in *Texte*, I, 392–430.

115. Jakobson, "O chudožestvennom realizme," in *Texte*, I, 372–390.

116. On the history of the concept and the state of the debate, see René Wellek, "The Concept of Realism in Literary Scholarship" (*Neophilologus* [Groningen], 45 [1961]: 1–20); and also "A Symposium on Realism," initiated and edited by Harry Levin (in *Comparative Literature*, 3 [1951]: 193–285).

117. Tomashevsky, chapter on "Thematics" in *Teorija literatury*.

118. Jakobson, "Randbemerkungen zur Prosa des Dichters Pasternak," *Slavische Rundschau*, 7 (1935): 357–374. Reprinted in R. Jakobson, *Selected Writings*, V (The Hague, Paris, New York, 1979), pp. 416–432.

119. A. Flaker, " 'Formalna metoda' i njezina sudbina," in Flaker and Z. Škreb, *Stilovi i razdoblja* (Zagreb, 1964), pp. 75–93.

120. Dmitri Czizhevsky, *Russische Literaturgeschichte des 19. Jahrhunderts*, II, *Der Realismus* (Munich, 1967), pp. 11, 13; translated as *The History of Nineteenth-Century Russian Literature* (Nashville, Tenn., 1974).

121. See Eikhenbaum's theses on the "rapprochement of science and criticism" in "Teorija," p. 75.

122. R. Wellek, "The Theory of Literary History," in *Études dediées au quatrième Congrès de linguistes,* Travaux du Cercle Linguistique de Prague, IX (Prague, 1936), pp. 173–191. See also R. Wellek and A. Warren, *Theory of Literature,* rev. ed. (New York, 1956).

123. Erlich, *Russian Formalism,* pp. 220–221.

124. H. R. Jauss, *Literaturgeschichte als Provokation der Literaturwissenschaft* (Konstanz, 1967); English trans., "Literary History as a Challenge to Literary Theory," in H. R. Jauss, *Toward an Aesthetic of Reception* (Minneapolis, 1982).

125. Ibid., p. 32. See also H. G. Gadamer, *Wahrheit und Methode: Grundzüge einer philosophischen Hermeneutik,* 2nd. ed. (Tubingen, 1965); English trans., *Truth and Method* (New York, 1975).

126. Ibid., pp. 25ff.

127. As one of several examples see the distinction between *evolution* and *genesis* in Tynyanov's "On Literary Evolution."

128. The term *ryad* selected by the Formalists designates both series and ordering.

129. Erlich, *Russian Formalism,* pp. 78–95, chap. 6, "Marxism versus Formalism."

130. See, for example, Eikhenbaum, "Literaturnyj byt," in *Texte,* I, 462–480; English trans., "Literary Environment," in Matejka and Pomorska, *Readings,* pp. 56–65.

131. Title of chap. 11 in Erlich, *Russian Formalism,* p. 164.

132. Ibid., pp. 78–95.

133. Erlich discusses attempts by A. Tseitlin and others to synthesize and combine (ibid., pp. 88–95).

134. I. Stalin, *Marksizm i voprosy jazykoznanija* (Moscow, 1950).

135. K. Kosík, *Die Dialektik des Konkreten: Eine Studie zur Problematik des Menschen und der Welt* (Frankfurt, 1967). The chapter "Die Metaphysik der Kultur" first appeared in *alternative: Zeitschrift für Literatur und Diskussion* (Berlin), (April 1966): 56–73.

136. Ibid., p. 69.

137. The essay "Moderner Roman und russische formale Schule: Ein Beitrag zur Poetik" by the Prague literary scholar R. Grebeníčkova (published in Ibid.) is a good example of such a view: its arguments are close to Kosík's, it refers back to the Formalists, and it polemizes against the aesthetics of Lukács.

138. Kosík, "Die Metaphysik," pp. 66ff.

139. For a Polish account of the dispute between Marxism and Structuralism, see M. Janion, "Marksizm wobec genetyzmu i strukturalizmu w badaniakh literackikh" in *Problemy teorii literatury* (Wroclaw, Warsaw, Krakow, 1967), pp. 393–426. From the Soviet Union the work of Yury Lotman and his circle at the University of Tartu deserves special mention. See particularly Yury Lotman, *Lekcii po struktural'noj poetike,* I, *Vvedenie, teorija stikha* (Tartu, 1964); published in the series Učenye zapiski Tartuskogo gos. universiteta, 160. *Trudy po znakovym sistemam,* I.

140. See Claude Lévi-Strauss, *Anthropologie structurale* (Paris, 1958). English trans., *Structural Anthropology* (New York, 1963). As an example of the direct application of his methodology to literature (and of his collaboration with ex-Formalists), see " 'Les Chats' de Charles Baudelaire," by R. Jakobson and C. Lévi-Strauss, in *L'Homme*, 2 (1962): 5–21. The piece is discussed by Michael Riffaterre in *Structuralism*, Yale French Studies 36–37 (New Haven, Conn., 1966), pp. 200–242, a volume that affords a good view of the status of Structuralism of the most varied sorts and areas of application.

141. This is already evident in Goldmann's book on Jansenism, *Le dieu caché. Étude sur la vision tragique dans les "Pensées" de Pascal et dans le théâtre de Racine* (Paris, 1955) and again in *Pour une sociologie du roman* (Paris, 1964).

142. Roland Barthes, *Essais critiques* (Paris, 1964); English trans. *Critical Essays* (Evanston, Ill., 1972).

143. L. Sebag, *Marxisme et structuralisme* (Paris, 1964).

144. Tynyanov and Jakobson, "Problemy izučenija," *Texte*, II, 386–390; English trans. quoted from Matejka and Pomorska, *Readings*, pp. 79–81.

145. Matejka and Pomorska, *Readings*, Theses 1, 4.

146. Ibid., Thesis 3.

147. Ibid., Thesis 4.

148. Ibid., Thesis 1.

149. Ibid., Thesis 8.

150. Ibid., Theses 7, 8.

151. Ibid., Thesis 8, and final sentence.

II. From Russian Formalism to Czech Structuralism

1. O. Sus, "Typologie tzv. slovanského formalismu a problémy přechodu od formálních škol ke strukturalismu" (The Typology of So-Called Slavic Formalism and the Problems of the Transition from the Formal School to Structuralism), in *Československé přednášky pro VI Mezinárodní sjezd slavistů v Praze* (Czech Papers for the Sixth International Congress of Slavists) (Prague, 1968), pp. 293ff., includes a discussion of the relevant literature. See also H. Günther, "Form and Structure," in *Serta Slavica: In Memory of Alois Schmaus* (Munich, 1971), pp. 218ff., later included in H. Günther, ed. *Struktur als Prozess* (Munich, 1973), pp. 37ff. On the evolutionary theories of the two schools see M. Grygar, "Pojetí literárního vývoje v ruské formální metodě a v českém strukturalismu" (The Concept of Literary Development in the Russian Formal Method and in Czech Structuralism), *Česká Literatura* (Czech Literature), 16 (1968); 266ff.; and H. Günther, "Die Konzeption der Literarischen Evolution im tschechischen Strukturalismus," *alternative*, 80 (1971): 183ff. (later included in Günther, *Struktur als Prozess*, pp. 68ff.). For an indirect comparison, see also A. Flaker, "Der russische Formalismus: Theorie und Wirkung," and M. Červenka, "Die Grundkategorien des Prager literaturwissenschaftl. Strukturalismus," both in V. Žmegač and Z. Škreb, eds., *Zur Kritik literaturwissenschaftlicher Methodologie* (Frankfurt, 1973), pp. 115ff., 137ff.

2. Yury Tynyanov and R. Jakobson, "Problemy izučenija literatury i jazyka," in W. D. Stempel, ed., *Texte der russischen Formalisten* (Munich, 1972), II, 386–390. English trans., without the last, ninth thesis, in Ladislav Matejka and Krystyna Pomorska, *Readings in Russian Poetics: Formalist and Structuralist Views* (Cambridge, Mass., 1971), pp. 79–81.

3. See V. Mathesius, "Deset let pražského linguistického kroužku" (Ten Years of the Prague Linguistic Circle), *Slovo a slovesnost*, 2 (1936): 137ff.; English trans. in J. Vachek, *The Linguistic School of Prague: An Introduction to its Theory and Practice* (Bloomington, Ind., 1966), pp. 141ff. See also R. Wellek, "Die Literaturtheorie und Ästhetik der Prager Schule," in *Grenzziehungen: Beiträge zur Literaturkritik* (Stuttgart, 1972), pp. 125ff.; English trans. in Michigan Slavic Contributions (Ann Arbor, 1969). The "Theses for the First Congress of Slavic Philologists in Prague, 1929" are reprinted in Vachek, *Linguistic School of Prague* and in Peter Steiner, ed., *The Prague School: Selected Writings, 1929–1946* (Austin, Tex., 1982), pp. 5–31. I am indebted to R. Wellek for clarifying these interrelations and for further references for the early phase of this development.

4. See R. Jakobson, *Selected Writings* (The Hague, 1962), and, as a recent presentation of this specific connection, W. Raible, "Roman Jakobson, oder Auf der Wasserscheide zwischen Linguistik und Poetik," introduction to R. Jakobson, *Aufsätze zur Linguistik und Poetik* (Munich, 1974), pp. 7ff.

5. R. Wellek, "Literaturtheorie," p. 126. If what Wellek means here by "obvious reasons" is a stress on national self-reliance, it is true that such a stress may have entered the picture, but it is not a sufficient counterargument. Conversely there is no reason to accuse Wellek, Erlich (see note 6 below), and other Western authors of "downplaying differences between Russian Formalism and Czech Structuralism . . . *in accordance with their ideological position*" (H. Günther, *Struktur*, p. 48). In Erlich's case, the theme of his book *Russian Formalism* dictates a stress on the connection with Formalism.

6. V. Erlich, *Russian Formalism: History—Doctrine* (The Hague, 1955), chap. 9, "Formalism Redefined," pp. 128–141. An extensive critique highlighting the Czech tradition appears in Sus, "Typologie."

7. For example, L. Stoll's book, *O tvar a strukturu v slovesném umění* (On Form and Structure in Verbal Art) (Prague, 1966). For a contrasting view, compare Sus, "Typologie."

8. Especially in the writings of Sus: "Typologie," "Geneze sémantiky umění v české tvarové estetice: Otokar Zich a teorie významové představy" (The Genesis of the Semantics of Art in Czech Aesthetics of Form: Otokar Zich and the Theory of the Concept of Meaning), *Litteraria* (Bratislava), 9 (1966): 196ff.; and "Český formalismus a česky predstrukturalismus: Pokus o typologii" (Czech Formalism and Czech Prestructuralism: An Attempt at a Typology), *Orientace*, 3 (1968): 21ff. On the aesthetics of Hostinsky, see J. Zumr's articles: "Teorické základy Hostinského estetiky: Hostinský a Herbart" (The Theoretical Foundations of Hostinsky's Aesthetics. Hostinský and Herbart), *Filosofsky casopis*, 8 (1958): 311ff.; and "Některé otázky českého herbartismu"

(Several Problems of Czech Herbartism), *Filosofie v dějinách českého národa* (Prague, 1958), pp. 166ff.

9. Sus, "Typologie," p. 296.

10. Ibid. The entire second part of this article is a characterization of Zich's aesthetics and a discussion of its significance for the Czech Structuralist aesthetics.

11. The best-known example is B. Eikhenbaum's "Kak sdelana 'Šinel'' Gogolja" (1918), the very title of which takes up this line of inquiry (How Gogol's *Overcoat* Is Made).

12. In retrospective accounts, members of the Prague Linguistic Circle emphasize these influences and personal encounters. See, for example, Wellek, "Die Ästhetik," p. 127, and Jakobson, "Die Linguistik und ihr Verhältnis zu anderen Wissenschaften," in *Aufsätze,* which discusses Husserl's influence on the Prague Linguistic Circle, "in which Husserl's ideas and his memorable personal address of November 11, 1935—Phenomenology of Language— met with a jubilant response" (p. 154).

13. On the subject of this discussion, see *alternative,* 80 (October 1971), "Tschechischer Strukturalismus: Ergebnisse und Einwände," which includes translations of works by Mukařovský and Kurt Konrad (1934); an introductory article by H. Günther, "Die Konzeption der Literarischen Evolution im tschechischen Strukturalismus" (The Concept of Literary Evolution in Czech Structuralism), pp. 183ff., which emphasizes the contribution of Czech Marxist critics; and "Alternative Editorial Collective" (pp. 201ff.), which poses critical questions from the Marxist point of view. Günther's article is reprinted in his book *Struktur als Prozess.*

14. All three terms occur in the title of Mukařovský's most important work of the period, *Aesthetic Function, Norm, and Value as Social Facts* (1936), Michigan Slavic Contributions, 3 (Ann Arbor, 1970).

15. O. Sus rejects this "genetic formula" of Russian Formalism leading to Czech Structuralism as simplistic in both its positive and negative varieties ("Typologie"). As a working schema to describe the genesis of Czech Structuralism he proposes instead the impact of the so-called Aesthetic School of Prague (Czech Formalism, Durdík, and Hostinský) on Otokar Zich with his formal theory of psychology, and Zich's influence on Czech Structuralism merging with the impact of Russian Formalism (via Jakobson and others).

16. As a recent example, see Červenka, "Die Grundkategorien." This article is especially informative because it fully acknowledges the significance of Russian Formalism for Czech Structuralism, but then, for the purpose of differentiating, posits a "classical Formalism" and remarks: "We pass over the later developments of the school on Russian soil, which already point to the transition to Structuralism and are associated especially with the name of Yury Tynyanov" (p. 144 and n. 23).

17. V. Shklovsky, "Iskusstvo kak priem," in *Texte,* I, 2–34.

18. On this specific aspect, see R. Lachmann, "Die 'Verfremdung' und das 'neue Sehen' bei Viktor Šklovskij," in *Poetica,* 3 (1970): 226ff.

19. See W. Stempel's introduction to vol. II of *Texte:* "Zur formalistischen Theorie der poetischen Sprache," pp. ix–liii.

20. Jakobson, "Novejšaja russkaja poezija," in *Texte,* II, 30.

21. Ibid. On Jakobson's own modification of this thesis, compare his and Tynyanov's "Theses" of 1928, and particularly Thesis 8, which calls for integrating literature into a "system of systems," but continues to insist on attention to "immanent laws of any system," and thus on an orientation to the specifics of literature. That the Formalists themselves soon came to recognize the danger of defining tasks too narrowly (without, however, giving up their attention to the specifics of literature) is proven, for instance, by V. Zhirmunsky's "Zadači poetiki" (Tasks of Poetics), *Načala,* 1921, no. 1. (Also in *Žirmunsky's Voprosy teorii literatury* [Problems of Literary Theory], [Leningrad, 1925].) See also B. Engelgardt, *Formal'nyj metod v istorii literatury* (The Formal Method in Literary History), *Voprosy poetiki* (Questions in Poetics), XI (Leningrad, 1927).

22. Stempel, "Zur formalistischen Theorie," p. xxix.

23. Shklovsky, "Svjaz' priemov."

24. Osip Brik, "Ritm i sintaksis: Materialy k izučeniju stixotvornoj reči," in *Texte,* II, 162–220.

25. Y. Tynyanov, "Problema stixotvornogo jazyka" (1924, 1965); English trans., *The Problem of Verse Language* (Ann Arbor, Mich., 1981).

26. See Tynyanov's "O literaturnoj evoljucii," in *Texte,* I, 438.

27. Roman Jakobson developed and systematized this idea in many essays. He states that selection occurs on the basis of "equivalence, similarity and difference, synonymie and antonymy," whereas combination, as the "construction of every chain," depends on contiguity. And the property of poetic language use is that "the poetic function projects the principle of equivalence from the axis of selection onto the axis of combination. Equivalence becomes one of the principles of constructing the text." Quoted and commented on by the author in "Die Sprache in ihrem Verhältnis zu anderen Kommunikationssystemen," in R. Jakobson, *Form und Sinn: Sprachwissenschaftliche Betrachtungen* (Munich, 1974), pp. 162ff.

28. Jan Mukařovský, "Art as Semiological Fact." This article, first presented as a lecture to the VIII Congress of Philosophy in Prague (1934), was published under the title "L'art comme fait sémiologique," in *Actes du huitième Congrès international de philosophie à Prague, 2–7 septembre 1934,* pp. 1065–1073. Brief and systematic, it is the best statement of Mukařovský's early formulation of semiotically based Structuralist aesthetics.

29. Ibid., pp. 143, 146–147 (sections C, D, and E).

30. On the problem of "concretization" and reception, see Part III, which is devoted to this topic. If we can and do say that the aesthetic of Czech Structuralism is "most emphatically an aesthetic of reception," we must go on to add that we are *not* speaking of a psychologically oriented aesthetic of perception. Mukařovský does not analyze and theorize on the aesthetic experience as such. Rather, his interest is, on the one hand, in the fundamental "aesthetic attitude" and "aesthetic function" in their relationship to other

attitudes and functions; on the other hand, it is in the special conditions for perceiving the work of art as a "sign in aesthetic function," and in how these conditions are built into the semiotic character of the work itself and are realized by reference to norms and values handed down collectively.

31. See J. Striedter, "Transparenz und Verfremdung: Zur Theorie des poetischen Bildes in der russischen Moderne," in *Immanente Ästhetik—Ästhetische Reflexion, Poetik und Hermeneutik*, 2 (Munich, 1966), pp. 287ff.

32. Stated thus in the self-critical summary of the eighth thesis of Tynyanov and Jakobson in "Problemy izučenija."

33. The transition from a perspective that considers deformation alone to one that includes construction is already evident in Shklovsky's early writings, for example, when he addresses problems of plot construction as early as 1916. But the interplay of both aspects was only later elaborated and systematized, most importantly by Tynyanov. The various conceptions of parody (not to mention the writings directly concerning the phenomenon of evolution) make this point plain. Whereas Shklovsky regards parody wholly as deformation and generalizes on this basis, Tynyanov characterizes it as the deformation of traditional construction principles and forms of organization for the purpose of constructive reorganization, as "the destruction of an old entity and new construction out of old elements" (see Part I).

34. Tynyanov, "O literaturnoj evoljucii," p. 446.

35. Ibid., p. 440.

36. Ibid., p. 446.

37. Tynyanov, "Oda kak oratorskij žanr" (*Texte*, II, 272–336), is a paradigm for the literary-historical application of this theory.

38. The term "crest" from Formalist evolutionary theory—used by Shklovsky and Tynyanov to designate the highest level of literary production in the canon of a given time—has found acceptance in current literary scholarship, and especially in discussions of the lines that separate aesthetically demanding literature from the hackneyed literature for the masses. (See, as an example, H. R. Jauss, *Literaturgeschichte als Provokation der Literaturwissenschaft* [Konstanz, 1967], p. 24.)

39. See, for example, Tynyanov, "Literaturnyj fakt" and "O literaturnoj evoljucii."

40. Thesis 8 in Tynyanov and Jakobson, "Problemy izučenija," p. 390.

41. Ibid.

42. Mukařovský's *Aesthetic Function, Norm, and Value as Social Facts* discusses the meaning and function of aesthetic norms for literary evolution. His contribution to the Ninth International Philosophy Convention, "La norme esthétique," specifically addresses the aesthetic norm, as differentiated from other norms such as moral, legal norms, and so on (in *Travaux du neuvième Congrès international de philosophie, XII* [Paris, 1937], III, 72ff). Subsection viii of this part of the published convention proceedings, beginning on p. 57, is given over entirely to contributions on the topic of "Normes esthétiques."

43. This is the title of Mukařovský's paper of 1932, in which his concept of aesthetic valuation is systematically expounded for the first time. In *Aesthetic*

Function, he takes up the theme again, developing it further and systematically integrating it into the semiotic aesthetic he had since conceived.

44. Mukařovský, *Aesthetic Function,* p. 60.

45. Ibid., p. 41.

46. Ibid., p. 60.

47. Ibid., p. 62.

48. Ibid., p. 77.

49. Ibid., p. 89.

50. Ibid., p. 88. Mukařovský characteristically makes direct reference here to the "Formalism of the Russian school of aesthetics and literary studies," affirming its position that all "elements of the work of art, without distinction, are constituents of the form," but adding that, conversely, "all elements of the work of art, without distinction, are also carriers of meaning and extra-aesthetic values."

51. For a more detailed discussion of the anthropological foundation and function of the intrinsically "empty" aesthetic function and of the "aesthetic value," see H. Schmid, "Zum Begriff der ästhetischen Konkretisation im tschechischen Strukturalismus," *Sprache im technischen Zeitalter,* 36 (1970): 305ff.

52. Felix Vodička, "Die Totalität des literarischen Prozesses: Zur Entwicklung des theoretischen Denken im Werk Jan Mukařovskýs," in Vodička, *Die Struktur der literarischen Entwicklung,* intro. J. Striedter (Munich, 1976), p. 21.

53. Pages xxxvi–xlix of the introduction to Vodička, *Struktur,* are omitted. This issue is treated more extensively in Part IV.

54. On Mukařovský's theory of this functional tension and its meaning for the relationship of the arts among themselves to the social system and to evolution, see *Aesthetic Function,* but also and especially his essay "The Location of the Aesthetic Function Among the Other Functions," in Mukařovský, *Studie z Estetiky* (Prague, 1966), pp. 65–73.

55. See J. Ihwe, *Linguistik in der Literaturwissenschaft: Zur Entwicklung einer modernen Theorie der Literaturwissenschaft* (Munich, 1972), pp. 123, 317.

56. Ibid., p. 317.

57. To stress the importance of aesthetics for Czech Structuralism is not to espouse the widely held view (even of some of the Formalists themselves) that Formalism was deliberately anti-aesthetic. Put so simply, this is not the case. True, Formalism unmistakably took a polemical stance against speculative aesthetics and the dependency of literary studies on such aesthetics—especially in the beginning. But the initial, exaggerated concentration on literariness already constitutes a decidedly aesthetic orientation. Besides, phenomenological aesthetics played an essential part in Formalist circles, particularly via the direct influence of the Russian disciple of Husserl, Gustav Shpet, and his *Aesthetic Fragments* (see note 59).

58. Similarities and differences between the various notions of the functions become especially clear if one compares the discussion of function in Mukařovský (but also, for instance, in Vodička) with the development of the classification of functions by Jakobson. For a recent, systematic summary of the latter, see the section "Die Funktionen der Sprache" in Elmar Holenstein,

Roman Jakobsons phänomenologischer Strukturalismus (Frankfurt, 1975), pp. 157ff.

59. Gustav Shpet, *Estetičeskie fragmenty* (Petrograd, 1922–1923), 1–3. For biographical and further bibliographical information, see *Kratkaja literaturnaja ènciklopèdija* (Moscow, 1975), VIII, 782, where Shpet is described as "one of the initiators [of semiotics] in our country."

60. See Erlich, *Russian Formalism,* pp. 42–43, 139, 147–148, and Holenstein, *Roman Jakobsons phänomenologischer Strukturalismus,* p. 18.

61. On the department's impact on the history and effect of Formalism, see Erlich, *Russian Formalism,* pp. 65–66.

62. Engelgardt, *Formal'nyj metod v istorii literatury.* Because Engelgardt was closely allied to the Formalist circle without being a "genuine" Formalist himself, his book is one of the most informative and best-balanced accounts of the school.

63. For Bakhtin and his group, see Part IV.

64. S. Bernstein, "Estetičeskie predposylki teorii deklamacii," in *Texte,* II, 338–384.

65. Ibid., p. 382.

66. Ibid., p. 342.

67. Roland Barthes, "Structuralist Activity," German text in *Kursbuch* (Frankfurt), 5 (1966): 190ff. The original French version was published in 1963 in *Lettres nouvelles.*

68. Ibid., p. 191.

69. Tynyanov and Jakobson, "Problemy izučenija," p. 388.

70. Mukařovský, "Máchův 'Maj.' Estetická studie" (Mácha's "May": An Aesthetic Study) (Prague, 1928); rpt. in Jan Mukařovský, *Kapitoly z české poetiky* (Prague, 1948), III, 7–202.

71. Ibid., p. 89.

72. Ibid., p. 149.

73. See J. Striedter, "K. H. Mácha als Dichter der europäischen Romantik," *Zeitschrift für slavische Philologie,* 31 (1963): 42ff., which specifically takes up this tendency and its identification as a formal and thematic dominant by Mukařovský, Jakobson, Czizhevsky, and others and relates it to the poetic practice and theory of European Romanticism.

74. In addition to Mácha, V. Hálek (1834–1874) in *Alfred* (1858), and J. Vrchlický (1853–1912) in *Satanela* (1876).

75. Mukařovský, "O současné poetice" (On Contemporary Poetry), in *Plán* (1929), p. 393.

76. See Mukařovský's writings of the early 1930s, for example, "La phonologie et la poétique" (1931), in *Travaux du Cercle linguistique de Prague,* 4 (1934): 278–288; and "Intonation comme facteur du rhythme poétique" (1933), in *Archives neérlandaises de phonetique expérimentale* (Amsterdam), 8–9 (1933): 153–165.

77. Mukařovský, in a published talk from 1932, cited by Felix Vodička in "The Totality of the Literary Process: On the Development of Theoretical Thinking in the Work of Jan Mukařovský"; German text in F. Vodička, *Struktur,* p. 4.

78. The review was published in the journal *Čin*, 6 (1934): 123ff.; rpt. in *Kapitoly z české poetiky*, I, 344ff.; German text in *alternative*, 80 (October 1971): 166ff.

79. Ibid., p. 168.

80. Shklovsky, *O teorii prozy*, p. 5.

81. Mukařovský's review, p. 170.

82. Ibid.

83. In this context it is important to observe that the Russian original of Shklovsky's book appeared nearly ten years before the Czech translation (1925), and that it is a collection that includes among other things early and programmatic, polemical essays that mark the initial position of Formalism. In a note to his review (p. 171, n. 2) Mukařovský himself makes reference to Shklovsky's more recent, sociologically oriented writings.

84. Mukařovský's review, pp. 170–171. For a more thorough definition of the same problem from the same period, see also Vodička's "The Totality" (p. 5), where Mukařovský is quoted.

85. The first piece appeared in *Středisko*, 4, no. 2 (July-August 1934), the second in no. 3 (September 1934); both were included in the volume of selected writings, K. Konrad, *Ztvárněte skutečnost* (Formed Reality) (Prague, 1963), pp. 63–87, 88–92. Excerpts in German translation appeared in *alternative*, 80: 172ff.

86. *alternative*, 80:179.

87. Quoted in Vodička, "The Totality," p. 14.

88. Compare Wellek, "Die Literaturtheorie," p. 134, and Vodička, "The Totality," p. 16. On Wellek's own contribution to this discussion, particularly in reference to Shklovsky's *Theory of Prose*, see his review in *Listy pro umění a kritiku*, 2 (1934): 111–115.

89. See Mukařovský's 1942 lecture, "The Location of the Aesthetic Function," pp. 113ff.

90. J. Mukařovský, *Studie z estetiky* (Studies in Aesthetics) (Prague, 1966), pp. 232–233.

91. Ibid., pp. 228–229.

92. Compare M. Jankovič, "Perspektiven der semantischen Geste," *Postilla Bohemica*, 4–5 (1973): 69–87, and M. Kačer, "Mukařovský's Terminus 'Semantische Geste' und Barthes 'écriture,' " ibid., pp. 88–94.

93. H. Günther, *Struktur als Prozess*, p. 61.

94. Mukařovský, cited by Günther, ibid., pp. 61–62.

95. Konrad, *Formed Reality*, p. 88. Quoted in Vodička, "The Totality," p. 14.

III.   Felix Vodička's Theory of Reception and Structuralist Literary History

1. René Wellek, "Die Literaturtheorie und Ästhetik der Prager Schule," in *Grenzziehungen: Beiträge zur Literaturkritik* (Stuttgart, 1972), p. 128. Wellek

emphasizes that in the "basic teachings of the linguists of the Prague Circle" one can speak of a collective effort, whereas in the area of aesthetics and literary theory Mukařovský's theory holds a special place (p. 126).

2. See, for example, his presentation of Mukařovský's theory and its development in "The Totality," esp. p. 20, where he concedes that Mukařovský did not begin fully to account for the "subject of artistic activity" until the second half of the 1930s, though even then his solution was determined "entirely from the viewpoint of the recipient of a work." This may be true of the semiotic foundation as such, but the development of a theory of reception and, based on that theory, the development of a Czech Structuralist history of reception is largely Vodička's own contribution. See my discussion of the theory of concretization later in this chapter.

3. Vodička, "Literary History: Its Problems and Tasks," in *Die Struktur der literarischen Entwicklung* (Munich, 1976), p. 31.

4. On the theory of tasks, see M. Červenka's afterword, "O Vodičkově metodologii literárních dějin" (On Vodička's Methodology of Literary History) in Vodička, *Struktura vývoje* (Prague, 1969), pp. 329ff.

5. Even before Structuralism, Czech literary scholars and critics used the term *ohlas* (echo or reverberation) for reception in a broad sense, that is, the effect of a work or author, including his influence on other authors. "Reception in the narrow sense of the word" is used by Vodička and the Czech Structuralists as the "reception that results from the active relation of the literary public to a literary work that is accepted as an aesthetic object" ("Literary History," p. 91). For the prerequisite to reception, the unique act of aesthetic perception, or the conversion of the work as artifact into an aesthetic object, Vodička introduces the term concretization (in Czech, *konkretizace*), discussed below, but the terminological distinction between reception and concretization is not always strictly maintained.

6. Vodička, "Březina a Baudelaire," *Časopis Českého muzea,* 107 (1933): 86ff.; "J. Vrchlický a T. de Banville," *Sborník Společnosti Jaroslava Vrchlického,* 11 (1932–1934): 84ff.; and "Ohlas Bérangerovy poezie v české literatuře" (The Reception of Béranger's Poetry in Czech Literature), *Listy filologické,* 62 (1935): 301–366.

7. Červenka, "On Vodička's Methodology," p. 334.

8. Vodička, "Mácha jako dramatik" (Mácha as Dramatist), in *Karel Hynek Mácha: Osobnost, dílo, ohlas* (Prague, 1937), pp. 133–141. This collection, by several writers, commemorates the hundredth anniversary of the poet's death. Vodička also participated in *Věčný Mácha* (Prague, 1940), to which he contributed the essay "Doba a dílo" (Time and Work), pp. 73–97.

9. Vodička, "Literárněhistorické studium ohlasu literárních děl. Problematika ohlasu Nerudova díla" (The Literary-Historical Study of the Reception of Literary Works: On the Problem of the Reception of Neruda's Works), *Slovo a slovesnost,* 7 (1941): 113–132; English trans. in P. Steiner, ed., *The Prague School,* pp. 105–134.

10. This is the subtitle of the essay "Literary History."

11. Rolf Fieguth, "Rezeption contra falsches und richtiges Lesen oder

Missverständnis mit Ingarden?" *Sprache im technischen Zeitalter,* 38 (Berlin, 1971): 142ff. Fieguth treats Ingarden's relationship to literary history in new and modified form in "Ingarden und Literaturgeschichte," a contribution to the International Ingarden Conference, Warsaw, 1975.

12. Vodička, "On the Problem of the Reception of Neruda's Works." Compare Ingarden, *Das Literarische Kunstwerk* (1931), English trans. by G. Grabowicz, *The Literary Work of Art* (Evanston, Ill., 1973), chap. 13.

13. Vodička, "Concretization," pp. 94–95.

14. Ibid.

15. Questions like this (and more fundamental ones, for example whether formulations such as "a sign that designates itself," are, from the standpoint of strict semiotics, admissible and meaningful) still arise in the context of Mukařovský's theory. But the answers would require a systematic discussion of the entire complex of problems from the standpoint of contemporary semiotics, which in an introductory study such as this would carry us too far afield. Besides, these answers are not indispensable for explaining Vodička's concept of concretization and its assumptions.

16. Vodička, "Concretization," p. 95; italics mine.

17. Fieguth ("Rezeption," pp. 153ff.) points out that Ingarden's formulations are theoretical and assumptive in character, which raises the possibility of misunderstandings. But he concedes that Vodička, who says here only that Ingarden assumes an "ideal possibility" (p. 95), handles Ingarden "with comparative fairness."

18. H. Schmid, "Zum Begriff der ästhetischen Konkretisation im tschechischen Strukturalismus," *Sprache in Technischen Zeitalter,* 36 (1970): 292.

19. Ibid. See also pp. 293, 310–311.

20. Mukařovský, "Art as Semiological Fact," p. 142.

21. Ibid., p. 139: "to which in the collective consciousness a particular meaning (sometimes called 'aesthetic object') corresponds"; p. 142: "from a 'meaning' (aesthetic object) . . . which is located in the collective consciousness."

22. Červenka, "Literární dílo jako znak" (The Literary Work as Sign), *Orientace* (Prague), 4 (1968): 58ff.

23. Cited by Vodička in "Concretization," p. 92.

24. Ibid.; Vodička's rendering of Mukařovský's concept.

25. Ibid., p. 94. This is a formulation of Vodička's own viewpoint, made without direct reference to Mukařovský.

26. Mukařovský, too, distinguishes between collective and subjective elements, but he does not differentiate between the conditions of perception and the act itself, locating both within the "act of perception," whose "central core . . . belongs to the collective consciousness"; "Art as Semiological Fact," p. 139.

27. Subsection title in Vodička, "Literary History," p. 64.

28. Ibid. Because of their immediate link to aesthetic experience, Vodička considers an age's critical verdicts to be a richer source for the literary-historical reconstruction of contemporary norms than poetic treatises, theories, or even the works themselves. For his evaluation of the function and meaning

of literary criticism as a source for the literary historian, see not only the cited section from "Literary History," but also his remarks in "Concretization," pp. 87ff.

29. This may in part have been because Mukařovský, unlike many other leading exponents of Czech Structuralism (and Russian Formalism), was no linguist but very decidedly an aesthetician. He was less interested in the linguistic organization (of the artifact) than in its effect on aesthetic perception. His attention was directed from the start to the structure of the aesthetic object (even, really, in the early, minutely descriptive analyses of linguistic and formal organization, such as his study of "May" from [1928]). And Vodička takes off from Mukařovský's already formulated aesthetic, going as literary historian deeper into the relation between the aesthetic object and the literary-historical context. It was left to younger exponents of the literary Structuralism of Prague (such as, for example, M. Červenka), whose thinking has been shaped in part by modern linguistics and communication theory, to "take the question back a step" and inquire further into the structuredness and structuring function of the artifact, rightly claiming that their findings are to a great extent systematic elaborations of aspects prefigured in Mukařovský's theory and in the practice of literary scholarship within Czech Structuralism, aspects that had not, however, previously been properly systematized and explored.

30. Compare Vodička, "Literary History," p. 94, and Ingarden, *Das literarische Kunstwerk*, chaps. 4, 5.

31. Ingarden conceives his model explicitly as being developed "from the nature of *every* literary work of art generally," not as restricted only to certain genres (*Das literarische Kunstwerk*, p. 26), and he sets it up accordingly. But in his choice of examples one cannot help but notice that even in his treatment of the lower levels, he passes over lyric poetry. True, Ingarden occasionally analyzes lyric elsewhere, but in those cases he does without a systematic investigation of the phonic level, meter, and so on. He classifies poems in which the orchestration of sounds becomes dominant and deforms the higher, thematic levels a priori as "borderline cases." (Ingarden uses this phrase, in Polish, as the title for an article on the lyric poetry of J. Tuwim included in R. Ingarden, *Studia z Estetyki* [Warsaw, 1970], pp. 178ff.)

32. This translates the title of Y. Tynyanov's seminal book, *Problema stichotvornogo jazyka* (Leningrad, 1924); English trans., *The Problem of Verse Language* (Ann Arbor, Mich., 1987). That Tynyanov, whose own literary productions were in the form of novels and short stories, which is to say narrative prose, demonstrates his theory on verse poetry, underscores how well suited methodologically this special area is for such theorems and models. Shklovsky's theory of defamiliarization, on the other hand, was demonstrated primarily on the example of prose and was later incorporated in his book *On the Theory of Prose* (1925).

33. Vodička, *Počátky krásné prózy novočeské* (The Beginnings of the Newer Czech Belletristic Prose) (Prague, 1948); the manuscript had been completed in 1945.

34. Ibid., pp. 196–212. The subsections are: "The Reduction of Verbal and Phonic Material in Context," "The Phonic Actualization of Word Connections," and "Phonic Series, Their Form and Function."

35. Vodička, *Beginnings,* chap. 1, pt. 2, sec. 1: "The Intended Ideas in Chateaubriand's *Atala* and in Jungmann's Translation," pp. 53–61. Part 1 of this chapter, "Jungmann's Theoretical Attitude to the Questions of Narrative Prose," also concerns thematic problems, though indirectly. But here, too, the linguistic organization of prose and its aesthetic function are the chief concern.

36. It is worthwhile to note the transition from valuable motif inventories, which to this day are indispensable for orientation but whose focus is on content, such as A. Aarne's *Verzeichnis der Märchentypen* (Helsinki, 1911)—frequently reprinted, revised, or amended as A. Aarne and S. Thompson—or J. Bolte and G. Polívka, *Anmerkungen zu den Kinder- und Hausmärchen der Brüder Grimm,* 5 vols. (Leipzig, 1913—) also frequently reprinted, with a new edition in 1963—to the *Morphology of the Folk Tale* by the Russian Formalist V. Propp (1928). See Part I of this book.

37. Käte Friedmann's *Die Rolle des Erzählers in der Epik* had appeared in 1910; Percy Lubbock's *The Craft of Fiction,* in 1921. The 1920s also saw the publication of Robert Petsch's studies in this area, and Vodička refers directly to his *Wesen und Formen der Erzählkunst* (1934): "We follow in the footsteps of R. Petsch," *Struktur,* p. 297.

38. Here as elsewhere Vodička uses, besides the term "plane" (*Beginnings* pp. 296 and passim), the designation "context," which in this case refers to something completely different from the technical term "context" explicitly introduced for the historically contingent conditions of a concretization and the description of it. In the absence of an explicit differentiation, and because the double usage can lead to misunderstandings and imprecision, I will use only "plane."

39. Ibid., pp. 296–299. In place of "expressive means," the more general designations "device" and "method" are also used. The Czech words for "plane" and "expressive means" are *plán* and *výrazový prostředek* (see Czech edition, p. 116).

40. Compare sections "Epic Description and Chateaubriand's 'Atala' " and "The Context of the Milieu in 'Atala' "; ibid., pp. 293–296, 299–305.

41. Ibid., p. 296. (Although Vodička claims that he is disregarding these problems only for the moment, he never does systematize and provide a correspondent analysis of the translated *Atala.*)

42. Ibid., p. 299.

43. For all passages cited in this paragraph, see ibid., pp. 297–299.

44. See, for example, M. Červenka, *Der Bedeutungsaufbau des literarischen Werkes* (The Construction of Meaning in a Literary Work; Munich, 1978).

45. See the studies of L. Doležel: "The Prague School and the Statistical Theory of Poetic Language," *The Prague Bulletin of Mathematical Linguistics* (1967): 97ff.; "Zur statistischen Theorie der Dichtersprache," in *Mathematik und Dichtung* (Munich, 1965); "Motif Analysis and the System of Sensitivity in

'L'étranger,' " in *Problèmes de l'analyse textuelle* (Montreal, Paris, Brussels, 1971); "The Typology of the Narrator: Point of View in Fiction," in *To Honor Roman Jakobson* (The Hague, 1967), pp. 541–552; "Toward a Structural Theory of Content in Prose Fiction," in S. Chapman, ed., *Literary Style: A Symposium* (London and New York, 1971), pp. 95–110.

46. See the studies of such Polish Structuralist literary scholars as J. Sławinski and M. Głowinski. Głowinski's essay "Virtualny odbiorca w strukturze utwora poetyckiego" (The Virtual Recipient in the Structure of the Poetic Work), in *Studie z teorii i historii poezji*, series 1 (Wroclaw, 1967), refers directly to Vodička: "It was Felix Vodička who first sociologized the problem of concretization and at the same time regarded it as a problem of poetics." And, in a note referring to Vodička's two studies on the theory of reception of 1941 and 1942: "My article owes a great debt to both these excellent and trailblazing studies."

47. See, for example, Jiři Levý, *Umění překladu* (Prague, 1963); German text, *Die literarische Übersetzung. Theorie einer Kunstgattung* (Frankfurt, 1969).

48. Here Vodička does not use the term semantic gesture—introduced by Mukařovský and in general use among Czech Structuralists—for the principle that stamps the overall construction of a work or an entire oeuvre and carries the construction of its meaning. See M. Jankovič, "K pojetí sémantického gesta" (On the Term "Semantic Gesture"), *Česká literatura*, 13 (1965): 319ff; and, by the same author, "Perspectivy sémantického gesta" (Perspectives on the Semantic Gesture) in M. Jankovič, ed., *K interpretaci uměleckého literárního díla* (On the Interpretation of the Literary Work of Art; 1970), pp. 7ff. Because the semantic gesture is a principle that informs both the lower and the higher, thematic levels, scholars within and outside Czech Structuralism sometimes speak here of "isomorphism." L. Doležel, for example, writes in "Zur statistischen Theorie der Dichtersprache" (see note 45 above) that Mukařovský's concern is with the "*isomorphism* between the formal and semantic planes of the poetic work" (p. 281; italics in original). And Umberto Eco writes—in a section of *A Theory of Semiotics* (Bloomington, Ind., 1976) that refers directly to Russian Formalism and Prague Structuralism—of "global isomorphism" and says that "the same structural pattern rules the various organizational planes." This last formulation is misleading, as is the use of the term isomorphism in this context generally, since while all levels of construction are aligned by intention and function to the same "telos," the desired result can be achieved not only by similar constructive means on the individual levels but also by dissimilar or even contradictory ones; it is insufficient to equate the interplay of their effects with "uniformity." See Doležel, "Zur statistischen Theorie der Dichtersprache"; and, in Part II of this book, the discussion of the difference between Shklovsky's early concept of the uniformity of the plot level and the stylistic level; and Tynyanov's more recent dynamic model of the literary work of art.

49. This is the title of part 1 of chap. 1, before the analysis of *Atala*.

50. Vodička points out that convincing testimony about the reception of the translation of *Atala* is lacking, which allows him to "speculate by means of

reconstruction." In view of the rather brief effectiveness of Jungmann's translation, Vodička observes that Chateaubriand's influence on Romanticism in several literatures rested precisely on his being the "initiator of subjective Romantic tendencies," while Jungmann consciously reduced this aspect of *Atala,* as well as the mysticism that the Romantics found so attractive.

51. Vodička, *Beginnings,* chap. 5, part 2: "The Vertical Organization of Czech Belletristic Prose in the First Three Decades of the Nineteenth Century."

52. See Vodička, "Literary History," pp. 34ff., in which these three "task complexes" are named in the order characteristic of Vodička and Czech Structuralism: "Works," "Poets," "Public."

53. The term teleologic, frequently used in Czech Structuralism and accounts of it, is to be understood as being opposed to "genetic" or "causal." It has reference to an intentional and functional orientation, not to a teleology in the sense of a development toward a given end. This clarification seems indicated since the point is often obscured in accounts and debates.

54. See Vodička, "Concretization," pp. 98ff., where he indicates that his investigation of nonreception is by design "out of the way."

55. Ibid., pp. 98, 100.

56. Ibid., pp. 98–99.

57. Ibid., p. 98.

58. Ibid.

59. On the full range of associated problems, see Vodička's article "Ke sporům o romantismus, zvláště Máchův" (On the Quarrel over Romanticism, Particularly That of Mácha; 1962), in *Structura vývoje,* pp. 123–136; German trans. in *Struktur,* pp. 162–181.

60. In this respect Vodička is remarkably close to the evolutionary theory of Russian Formalism, which also regarded these two motivations as decisive evolutionary factors. See Parts I and II.

61. Vodička, "Concretization," pp. 116ff.

62. Because of the dissimilar rules of stress in the two languages, the accent is on the first syllable in Czech and on the second in Spanish.

63. So begins the title of the final subsection of Vodička, "Concretization," p. 121.

64. Vodička, "Romanticism."

65. See the particulars of the "enquête" as described at the start of the article, p. 162. Similar enquêtes, particularly on the "quarrel over Romanticism" and on the question of whether particular authors are Romantics or Realists, were at that time customary in the East European countries; questionnaires were even sent out to participants in international Slavists conventions.

66. Vodička, "Romanticism," p. 169.

67. Ibid., p. 165. The Marx passage cited is from *Grundrisse der Kritik der politischen Ökonomie.*

68. Vodička, "Romanticism," pp. 176–177.

69. Vodička's criticism is directed against such tendencies not only in Marxist literary theory but also in Formalism, when attempts were made to trace an author's formal particularities directly to his context. See his remark that Grebeníčková in this point links up directly "with the studies of Boris Eikhenbaum" ("Romanticism," p. 170).

70. Vodička, "Romanticism," p. 171. Because this passage occurs in the immediate vicinity of quotations from Marx and various interpretations of them, presumably Vodička was alluding to Marx's famous statement in chap. 1 of "Eighteenth Brumaire": "Men make their own history, but they do not make it freely, not under circumstances they have themselves chosen, but under the immediate circumstances they find, are given, and are handed"; K. Marx, F. Engels, *Werke* (Berlin, 1958), 8, 115.

71. Vodička, "Romanticism," p. 172.

72. Ibid., p. 181. The words Vodička sets off with quotation marks are taken from Marx's characterization of the romantic view.

73. First version in *Konstanzer Universitätsreden*, vol. 3 (Konstanz, 1967). The revision, with the same title, appears in H. R. Jauss, *Literaturgeschichte als Provokation* (Frankfurt, 1970). The reference to Vodička is on p. 183, n. 91. See Part I, note 124 for English translation.

74. Specifically chaps. III–V.

75. Jauss, *Literaturgeschichte* (1967), p. 49: "This productive function of progressive understanding . . . shall serve to establish our outline of literary history based on the aesthetics of reception."

76. Jauss does discuss the problem of value directly in his polemic with Wellek. It is significant, however, that he shifts the accent from the problem of *value* judgment, which is Wellek's concern, to that of "*comprehending* judgment" based on the "*meaning* potential reified in the history of effect" (ibid., pp. 46ff.; italics mine).

77. See the title of chap. 2 of M. Naumann, D. Schlenstedt, et al., *Gesellschaft—Literatur—Lesen: Literaturrezeption in theoretischer Sicht* (Berlin and Weimar, 1973).

78. R. Weimann, *Literaturgeschichte und Mythologie: Methodologische Studien* (Berlin and Weimar, 1971), pp. 29ff.

79. Ibid., p. 31.

80. Phrases quoted from the chapter titles of this opening part; italics mine.

81. See Naumann et al., *Gesellschaft*, chap. 5.

82. W. Iser, *Der implizite Leser* (Munich, 1972); English text, *The Implied Reader* (Baltimore, 1974). See also his *Die Appelstruktur der Texte* (Konstanz, 1970). Thus, Naumann and the authors of the collection (*Gesellschaft*) criticize Iser not on this point but, characteristically, for ignoring the "mirroring function" (p. 126) and the class-defined ideological "value reference" of reception (p. 127).

83. See H. R. Jauss, "Racines und Goethes Iphigenie: Mit einem Nachwort über die Partialität der rezeptionsästhetischen Methode," *Neue Hefte für Philosophie*, 4 (1973): 1ff.

84. At least Weimann indicates his interest in Vodička's concept in a note;

but he only knows it "as taken up and developed by H. R. Jauss" (*Literaturgeschichte*, p. 487).

85. Naumann et al., *Gesellschaft*, pp. 145ff. True, the book mentions Mukařovský briefly, though not in the chapter on Structuralism and not in reference to the Czech Structuralist theory of reception, but for his concept of aesthetic function and of the signifying act of the aesthetic sign, for which he is condemned: "The failure to recognize the representation's special character as a likeness is thus inevitable" (p. 347).

86. See in particular M. Grygar, "Pojetí literárního vývoje v ruské formální metodě a v českém strukturalismu" (The Conception of Literary Evolution in the Russian Formal Method and in Czech Structuralism), *Česká literatura*, 14 (1966): 367–392. Grygar cites the criticism of Structuralism by Sartre and others in order to show that, for the reason just given, it does not apply to Czech Structuralism.

87. See the discussion in *alternative*, 80 (October 1971): "Tschechischer Strukturalismus: Ergebnisse und Einwände," particularly the section "Redaktionskollektiv Alternative: Einwände und Fragen an Hans Günther," pt. 1—"Der Begriff Individuum" (pp. 202–203). It is Günther who (far more forcefully than other Western authors of such overviews) stresses the role of historicity and social praxis in the theory of Prague. But since the textual basis for the ensuing critique is limited to the Czech discussion of *theory*, and theory only from the one year 1934, it is not hard to understand the impression that the Czech Structuralists abstracted from social reality and the active subject to a very great extent.

88. *Dějiny české literatury* (The History of Czech Literature), vol. II (Prague, 1960).

89. M. Červenka's afterword to Vodička's *Struktura vývoje* (1969) includes a critical appreciation of his "theory of tasks" (see esp. pp. 344–345); see also M. Grygar, "Dialektika literárního vývoje" (The Dialectic of Literary Evolution).

90. On Vodička's preoccupation with the time of the rebirth, see not only "Beginnings" but also, among other writings, his article "The Czech Rebirth as a Literary Problem," *Slovo a slovesnost*, 10 (1947–1948): 182ff., his book *Ways and Goals of the Literature of the Rebirth* (Prague, 1958), and his account of the rebirth in the second volume of *The History of Czech Literature* (Prague, 1960).

91. *Svět literatury, Svazek I, Napsal autorský kolektiv za vedení Felixe Vodičky* (Prague, 1967). Although this book was planned and printed as a text for secondary-school students, it was never released for school use or for public sale. I received a copy as a gift from Vodička when I visited him; both of us understood this as a sign that the literary scholar should regard the task of transmitting literary-historical knowledge to school children or young students not as peripheral, but as central.

92. Červenka's afterword, "On Vodička's Methodology," pp. 332–333. *Struktura vývoje* was published in 1969, but this afterword is dated "Fall 1967."

IV. Czech Structuralism and the Present Debate about Aesthetic Value

1. Barbara Herrnstein Smith, "Contingencies of Value," *Critical Inquiry* (September 1983): 1–35.

2. Jan Mukařovský, *Kapitel aus der Poetik,* Edition Suhrkamp no. 230 (Frankfurt, 1967), and *Kapitel aus der Ästhetik,* Edition Suhrkamp no. 428 (Frankfurt, 1970).

3. The anthology *A Prague School Reader on Esthetics, Literary Structure, and Style,* selected and trans. P. L. Garvin (Washington, D.C., 1964) contains only four relatively short contributions by Mukařovský—mainly on language, style, and verse. An important step forward was the publication of Jan Mukařovský, *Aesthetic Function, Norm and Value as Social Facts,* trans. Mark E. Suino (Ann Arbor, Mich., 1970). Because it was published by the Department of Slavic Languages and Literatures in its Michigan Slavic Contributions series, its impact remained (initially) restricted. The situation has improved recently with the second edition of this book (Ann Arbor, 1979) and the publication of Jan Mukařovský, *The Word and Verbal Art,* trans. John Burbank and Peter Steiner, foreword by René Wellek (New Haven, Conn., 1977), and *Structure, Sign and Function: Selected Essays by Jan Mukařovský,* trans. John Burbank and Peter Steiner (New Haven, 1978). Additional writings by Mukařovský in English translation are also available in *Semiotics of Art: Prague School Contributions,* ed. Ladislav Matejka and Irwin R. Titunik (Cambridge, Mass., 1976), and *The Prague School: Selected Writings, 1929–1946,* ed. Peter Steiner (Austin, Tex., 1982).

4. Smith, "Contingencies of Value," p. 1.

5. Nicholas Rescher, *Introduction to Value Theory* (Englewood Cliffs, N.J., 1969).

6. Douwe W. Fokkema, "The Problem of Generalization and the Procedure of Literary Evaluation," *Neophilologus,* 58 (Amsterdam, 1974): 253–272.

7. Ibid., p. 262.

8. Smith, "Contingencies of Value," p. 7.

9. Fokkema, "Generalization," p. 262. Fokkema's statement, "The aesthetic value, according to Mukařovský, is created by the aesthetic function and measured by the aesthetic norm," is misleading; in the passage to which he refers, Mukařovský explicitly criticizes such traditional views as inadequate, because "the area of the aesthetic function is broader than that of the aesthetic value [and] fulfillment of the norm is not a necessary condition of aesthetic value." (Mukařovský, *Aesthetic Function,* p. 59.)

10. "Básnické dílo jako soubor hodnot" originally published in 1932, republished in *Studie z estetiky* (Prague, 1966), pp. 140–143. See also Mukařovský's reference in *Aesthetic Function,* p. 60, n. 49.

11. Mukařovský, *Aesthetic Function.* Future quotations are from the second edition (Ann Arbor, Mich., 1979), with indications where my own translation differs from this text.

12. Mukařovský, "The Poetic Work," p. 142.

13. In his essay "Problémy estetické hodnoty" (Problems of Aesthetic Value), written in 1935–36 but first published in Jan Mukařovský, *Cestami poetiky a estetiky* (Paths of Poetic and Aesthetics) (Prague, 1971), pp. 11–34; quotation, p. 17.

14. René Wellek, "The Theory of Literary History," in *Traveaux du Cercle linguistique de Prague,* vol. 6 (Prague, 1936), p. 190ff.

15. See, for instance, Zdeněk Pešat, "K teorii a metodologii literárního vývoje" (On the Theory and Methodology of Literary Evolution), in *Československé přednášky pro VI. mezinárodní sjezd slavistů v Praze* (Czech Contributions to the Sixth International Congress of Slavists in Prague) (Prague, 1968), pp. 309ff.

16. The German original, *Literaturgeschichte als Provokation der Literaturwissenschaft,* appeared in the series Konstanzer Universitätsreden (Konstanz, 1967). An abbreviated English version appeared in *New Literary History,* 1 (1969), and a complete English translation in Hans Robert Jauss, *Toward an Aesthetic of Reception,* trans. Timothy Bahti. (Minneapolis, 1982). Quotations refer to this translation.

17. *Ästhetische Erfahrung und literarische Hermeneutik* (Munich, 1977; rev. ed., Frankfurt, 1982). The English translation, *Aesthetic Experience and Literary Hermeneutics,* trans. Michael Shaw, (Minneapolis, 1982) is based on the first edition (1977). I quote from this English edition or—if indicated—in own translation.

18. German ed., 1982, p. 198. The English translation (p. 116) omits "independent of the perceiver," which is crucial for Jauss's criticism.

19. I translate from the German ed., 1977, p. 169, which puts both quotations in quotation marks; the English translation omits them in the second case (see p. 117).

20. Jochen Schulte-Sasse, *Literarische Wertung,* 2nd ed. (Stuttgart, 1976).

21. The prominence of the theory of drama as theater in the Prague School is represented in the selection of Matejka's and Titunik's anthology *Semiotics of Art,* in which the whole third part is dedicated to the semiotics of theater (with additional contributions on folk theater in Part 2).

22. *Axia: Davis Symposium on Literary Evaluation,* ed. Karl Menges and Daniel Rancour-Laferriere (Stuttgart, 1981), pp. 35–45.

23. Jan Mukařovský, "Art as Semiotic Fact," trans. in Matejka and Titunik, *Semiotics of Art,* pp. 3–9. Menges quotes from p. 8.

24. In his essay "The Problems of Aesthetic Value" Mukařovský uses this saying as the starting point for his arguments.

25. See in this respect my comments in "Erwartung und Bildung in Čechovs 'Drei Schwestern' " (Expectation and Education in Chekhov's *Three Sisters*), *Jahrbuch 1984/85, Wissenschaftskolleg zu Berlin* (Berlin, 1986), pp. 115–128.

26. Felix Vodička, "Ke sporům o romantismus, zvláště Machův," in *Struktura vývoje* (The Structure of Evolution) (Prague, 1969), pp. 123–136. There is no English translation of this essay or of Vodička's book. German translation in Felix Vodička, *Die Struktur der literarischen Entwicklung,* ed. Jurij Striedter (Munich, 1976), pp. 162–181.

27. "Literárni historie: její problémy a úkoly" (Literary History: Its Problems and Tasks), in *Struktura vývoje*, p. 41.

28. Published in *Neohelicon*, 1–2 (Budapest, The Hague, Paris, 1973): 27–43. A more elaborate later version of Weimann's concept appears in Gerhard R. Kaiser, ed., *Vergleichende Literaturforschung in den sozialistischen Ländern, 1963–1979* (Stuttgart, 1980), pp. 209–221 under the title "Historizität und Wertsetzung: Zur Kritik der Begriffsbildung in der vergleichenden Literaturwissenschaft (1973–1979)."

29. Rita Schober, "Zum Problem der literarischen Wertung," *Weimarer Beiträge*, 7 (1973): 10–53.

30. Fredric Jameson, *The Prison-house of Language: A Critical Account of Structuralism and Russian Formalism* (Princeton, 1972).

31. Terry Eagleton, *Criticism and Ideology: A Study in Marxist Literary Theory* (London, 1976).

32. Peter Widdowson, Paul Stigant, Peter Brooker, "History and Literary 'Value,' " *Literature and History*, 5 (1979): 2–39.

33. English translations: M. M. Bakhtin and P. N. Medvedev, *The Formal Method in Literary Scholarship. A Critical Introduction to Sociological Poetics*, trans. Albert J. Wehrle (Cambridge, Mass., 1985); and V. N. Voloshinov, *Marxism and the Philosophy of Language*, trans. Ladislav Matejka and I. R. Titunik (Cambridge, Mass., 1986). For the question of authorship see the forewords to the English editions, and Katerina Clark and Michael Holquist, *Mikhail Bakhtin* (Cambridge, Mass., 1984); Tzvetan Todorov, *The Dialogic Principle: Mikhail Bakhtin* (Minneapolis, 1984); and H. Glück's long introduction to his German translation, *Die formale Methode in der Literaturwissenschaft*, foreword by Jurij Striedter (Stuttgart, 1976).

34. Besides the foreign term "polyphony," Bakhtin uses the familiar Russian word *raznorechie*, which combines Russian *razno*, "different," with *rech*, "speech," and means the existence of different languages or kinds of speech as well as contradiction or conflict (see *The Oxford Russian-English Dictionary*, Oxford, 1972, p. 671). Michael Holquist translates this term as "heteroglossia," which is accurate but more artificial than the familiar Russian word. See Holquist's comments in *The Dialogic Imagination: Four Essays by M. M. Bakhtin*, ed. Michael Holquist, trans. Caryl Emerson and Michael Holquist (Austin, Tex., 1981), p. 428.

35. In Bakhtin, *The Dialogic Imagination*, pp. 259–422. All quotations are from this edition.

36. Published first in the journal *Zeitschrift für Ästhetik und Allgemeine Kunstwissenschaft*, 1916, then as a book (Berlin, 1920). For Lukács' self-criticism see his preface to the 2nd ed. (Neuwied/Berlin, 1963). English translation (including this preface): Georg Lukács, *The Theory of the Novel: A Historico-Philosophical Essay on the Forms of Great Epic Literature*, trans. Anna Bostock (Cambridge, Mass., 1983).

37. See Clark and Holquist, *Mikhail Bakhtin*, pp. 99, 271.

38. Bakhtin discusses the relationship between the old epic and the novel in the essay "Epic and Novel" (*Dialogic Imagination*, pp. 3–40) and the history of

the novel since its early beginnings in "Discourse in the Novel" (ibid., pp. 259–422).

39. The Russian title of the essay "Discourse in the Novel" is *Slovo v romane*. *Slovo* means primarily "word" and only secondarily "speech," "address," and "tale"; the usual term for "speech" (and "discourse") is *rech*. Although for Bakhtin and his circle the basic units of verbal and literary communication are not isolated words but whole utterances, the choice of the term *slovo* for the title stresses the importance of the verbal substance and texture, which is rather neglected in Lukács' content-oriented concept.

40. For a comparison of the two critics and their theories of the novel, see Michel Aucouturier, "The Theory of the Novel in the 1930s: Lukács and Bakhtin," in *The Russian Novel from Pushkin to Pasternak*, ed. John Garard (New Haven, Conn., 1983), pp. 227–240. For the application of both to the relation between the novel and utopianism, see my essay "Three Postrevolutionary Russian Utopian Novels," in ibid., pp. 177–201.

41. Bakhtin is referring indirectly to Hegel's *Lectures on Aesthetics*, part 3, "Poetry," particularly to section A, which discusses the difference between poetry and prose, and section C (1) on epic literature and the transition from the old epic to the novel.

42. For the relationship between utopianism and the novel in connection with Bakhtin's (and Lukács') theory see my essay mentioned in note 40, and its more elaborate version, "Journeys through Utopia: Introductory Remarks to the Post-Revolutionary Russian Utopian Novel," *Poetics Today*, 3 (Winter 1982): 33–60.

43. Rainer Grübel, "Methode, Wertbegriff, und Wertung in der Kunsttheorie des Leningrader Bachtinkreises: Interpersonalität, Dialogizität, und Ambivalenz des ästhetischen Wertes," in *Beschreiben, Interpretieren, Werten: Das Wertungsproblem in der Literatur aus der Sicht unterschiedlicher Methoden*, ed. B. Lenz and B. Schulte-Middelich (Munich, 1982), pp. 95–133; quotation from p. 119.

44. Ibid., p. 119.

45. Roland Barthes, "The Structuralist Activity," in *European Literary Theory and Practice: From Existential Phenomenology to Structuralism*, ed. V. W. Gras (New York, 1973), pp. 157–163; quotation from p. 158.

46. Bakhtin, *Dialogic Imagination*, p. xxxiii.

47. Mikhail Bakhtin, "The Problem of the Text in Linguistics, Philology, and the Human Sciences: An Experiment in Philosophical Analysis," in *Speech Genres and Other Late Essays*, trans. V. W. McGee, ed. Caryl Emerson and Michael Holquist (Austin, Tex., 1986), pp. 103–131; quotation from p. 123. The Russian original appeared posthumously in 1976 in the Soviet Russian journal *Voprosy literatury* (Problems of Literature), 10 (Moscow, 1976). As the Russian editor V. Kozhinov, a Bakhtin specialist, notes in his introductory remarks, this essay was probably written between approximately 1959 and 1961 but many of its ideas were conceived and elaborated by Bakhtin much earlier. At the same time it "is typical of most works from Bakhtin's last years in that it is not so much an essay as a series of entries from the notebooks in

which Bakhtin jotted down his thoughts," as Caryl Emerson and Michael Holquist state in their introduction to *Speech Genres* (p. xvii).

48. "Iskusstvo i otvetstvennost'," in Mikhail Bakhtin, *Estetika slovesnogo tvorčestva* (Aesthetics of Verbal Creativity) (Moscow, 1979), pp. 5–6. Originally published in the provincial town of Nevel in the journal *Den' iskusstva* (The Day of Art) in 1919, it was reprinted as the first piece in the 1979 collection. Unlike many other pieces in this collection, as an early work it was not included in the most recent collection of English translations of essays, *Speech Genres and Other Late Essays,* and it is therefore unfortunately not yet available in English translation.

49. Clark and Holquist (*Mikhail Bakhtin*, pp. 53–54) translate the title of the article as "Art and Answerability." That renders appropriately in one word (as in Russian) the double meaning of "response" and "responsibility." However, the original Russian *otvetstvennost'*, as the usual word for "responsibility," emphasizes more directly the need for personal responsibility which is crucial for the article.

50. For the notion of orientational value, see section 7 of this essay.

51. One of the earliest European attempts to apply the Bakhtinian approach to a thorough analysis of one of Dostoevsky's novels is Horst-Jürgen Gerigk's *Versuch über Dostoevskijs "Jüngling": Ein Beitrag zur Theorie des Romans* (Munich, 1965). A more recent American example is Robin Feuer Miller, *Dostoevsky and the Idiot: Author, Narrator, and Reader* (Cambridge, Mass., 1981).

52. Grübel, "Methode, Wertbegriff, und Wertung," p. 122, rightly claims that "in the Bakhtin circle aesthetic value is conceived as a nonmeasurable entity [*nichtmessbare Grösse*]."

53. Bakhtin discriminates between "artistic perception" and "aesthetic perception." Both can refer to the artist as well as to an active, imaginative reader or beholder; but "*artistic* perception" indicates mainly the perception by the author as the creative artist.

54. This essay, the manuscript of which is incomplete and untitled, was published posthumously under the title "Avtor i geroj v estetičeskoj dejatel'-nosti" in Bakhtin, *Estetika,* pp. 7–180 (not included in the anthology in English). Written in the early 1920s, it indicates Bakhtin's early emphasis on value—the hero and his world are explicitly identified as the "center of value" (*cennostnyj centr*). The main issue of the essay, the relationship between author and hero, was a few years later integrated into the book on Dostoevsky (*Problems of Dostoevsky's Poetics,* chap. 2, "The Hero, and the Position of the Author with Regard to the Hero, in Dostoevsky's Art," pp. 47–77).

55. Jauss, *Aesthetic Experience;* this phrase is the title of part B, pp. 152–188.

56. A characteristic example of Bakhtin's systematization of types of narrative discourse is "Discourse Typology in Prose," in *Problems of Dostoevsky's Poetics;* an English translation is found in Matejka and Pomorska, *Readings in Russian Poetics,* pp. 176–196.

57. Bakhtin, "Art and Responsibility," pp. 5–6.

58. To mention only two famous examples among Russian Formalists and Czech Structuralists: Viktor Shklovsky, harshly attacked by the anti-Formalist

campaign in the late 1920s, responded with public "self-criticism," recanting his own formalistic "exaggerations"; see his "Pamjatnik naučnoj ošibke" (Memorial of a Scholarly Mistake) in *Literaturnaja gazeta*, 27 (1930). And after the Sovietization of Czechoslovakia in 1948, Mukařovský distanced himself officially from his Structuralist aesthetics, which enabled him to keep his position and even to become the rector of the Charles University at Prague (from 1948 to 1953).

59. A survey of this recent development can be found in *The Left Academy: Marxist Scholarship on American Campuses,* ed. B. Ollman and E. Vernoff (New York, 1982).

60. As an example, see Gayatri Chakravorty Spivak's reading of Marx in "Scattered Speculations on the Question of Value," *Diacritics* (Winter 1985): 73–93.

61. This label is used by John Fekete in his paper (see note 64).

62. A kind of *summa* of his aesthetics is Georg Lukács, *Aesthetik,* 2 vols. (Neuwied/Berlin, 1963).

63. Agnes Heller, "Towards a Marxist Theory of Value," trans. A. Arato, *Kinesis: Graduate Journal in Philosophy* (1972): 3–76. All quotations are from this translation.

64. John Fekete presented this "Agenda" at one of the panels on value, of which I was also a member, during the centennial convention of the MLA in New York, 1983. I quote from his unpublished paper.

65. For the theory and analytical practice of "secondary semiotic systems" and "models" in Soviet Russian semiotic Structuralism, see Karl Eimermacher and Serge Shishkoff, *Subject Bibliography of Soviet Semiotics: The Moscow-Tartu School* (Ann Arbor, Mich., 1977).

66. For Mukařovský's concept of fictionality and its relation to today's debate on fictionality, see section 6 of this essay.

67. Vodička, *Struktura vývoje,* p. 35.

68. See, for example, Spivak, "Scattered Speculations."

69. Smith, "Contingencies of Value"; all quotations are from this publication.

70. The beginning of this programmatic sentence, "All value is radically contingent, being neither an inherent property of objects nor an arbitrary projection of subjects," suggests in this case the understanding of economy as an exchange or interaction between subject and object, which differs from other statements in which Smith speaks about "his or her personal economy" (p. 12).

71. This quotation is discussed in Part II.

72. Theoretical contributions discussing such problems include Tynyanov's essay "Literaturnyj fakt" (The Literary Fact, 1927) and Eikhenbaum's "Literaturnyj byt" (Literary Environment, 1929, English translation in Matejka and Pomorska, *Readings in Russian Poetics,* pp. 56–65). In the late 1920s and early 1930s Shklovsky studied eighteenth-century Russian writers for the "mass readership" like M. Chulkov, V. Levshin, and M. Komarov; see the discussion of these authors in my book on the picaresque novel in Russia, *Der*

Schelmenroman in Russland (Berlin, 1961), particularly chaps. 2 and 4. Younger Formalists or students of the initiators repeatedly investigated social conditions and functions of literature; see Gritz, Trenin, and Nikitin, "Literature and Commerce," 1929, or Aronson and Reiser, "Literary Circles and Salons," 1929. For this interest of late Formalism in sociological problems, see W. M. Todd, "Literature as an Institution: Fragments of a Formalist Theory" in R. L. Jackson and S. Rudy, eds., *Russian Formalism: A Retrospective Glance* (New Haven, Conn., 1985), pp. 15–26.

73. Mukařovský himself discusses "the relationship between art and horticulture," "the beauty of nature (especially landscapes)," and landscape "as a work of art" in his chapter on the aesthetic function (*Aesthetic Function*, pp. 15–17).

74. "Oda kak oratorskij žanr" (The Ode as an Oratorical Genre), written 1922, first published in *Poetika*, 2 (Leningrad, 1927), then also included in Tynyanov's book *Arkhaisty i novatory* (Archaists and Innovators) (Leningrad, 1929). Reprint and German translation in *Texte der Russischen Formalisten*, II, 272–337.

75. Hans Georg Gadamer, *Wahrheit und Methode: Grundzüge einer philosophischen Hermeneutik* (Tübingen, 1960); English translation, *Truth and Method: Fundamentals of a Philosophical Hermeneutics* (New York, 1975).

76. Jauss, *Literary History*, pp. 29–32.

77. Jauss explicitly borrows both notions from Gadamer, integrating them into his own concept.

78. Examples of such interdisciplinary and international symposia or conferences on canon are two organized by Aleida Assman and Jan Assman, about "Kanon und Zensur" (Canon and Censorship) in April 1984 (Reimersstiftung, Bad Homburg) and in January 1985 (Wissenschaftskolleg, Berlin). See Aleida und Jan Assmann, "Der Nexus von Überlieferung und Identität: Ein Gespräch über Potentiale und Probleme des Kanon-Begriffs" (The Nexus of Tradition and Identity: A Discussion of Potentials and Problems of the Notion of Canon), in *Wissenschaftskolleg Jahrbuch 1984–85* (Berlin, 1986), pp. 291–302; and Aleida and Jan Assman, eds., *Kanon und Zensur* (Canon and Censorship) (Munich, 1987).

79. For the relation among history, revolution, and poetic mythicizing in Marx's "Eighteenth Brumaire," see my essay "The 'New Myth' of Revolution: A Study of Mayakovsky's Early Poetry," in *New Perspectives in German Literary Criticism*, ed. R. E. Amacher and V. Lange (Princeton, 1979), pp. 357–385.

80. Henry James, preface to *The Tragic Muse* (New York, 1908), p. x.

81. Most characteristic for such a development within Formalist criticism is Eikhenbaum's career as a leading Tolstoy specialist from his early, strictly formalistic study, *The Young Tolstoy* (1922), to the extensive and thorough investigation in his monumental work on Tolstoy in the 1850s and 1860s (2 vols., 1928 and 1931).

82. *Aesthetic Function*, p. 29. Mukařovský emphasizes that this is only a small sample—"any number can be enumerated." Here he calls these physiologi-

cally motivated constants "anthropological conditions"; later he prefers the term "anthropological constants."

83. Herta Schmid, "Anthropologische Konstanten und literarische Struktur," in *Maurice Merleau-Ponty und das Problem der Struktur in den Sozialwissenschaften*, ed. G. Grathoff and W. Sprondel (Stuttgart, 1976), pp. 36–60.

84. E. D. Hirsch, *Validity in Interpretation* (New Haven, Conn., 1967).

85. This aspect might have been stressed because of the focus of the conference on Merleau-Ponty and phenomenologically oriented Structuralism.

86. Mojmír Grygar, "Die Theorie der Kunst und der Wertung im tschechischen Strukturalismus" (The Theory of Art and Evaluation in Czech Structuralism), in Lenz and Schulte-Middelich, *Beschreiben, Interpretieren, Werten*, pp. 156–181. Quotation from pp. 177–178, n. 32.

87. Robert Kalivoda, "Dialektika strukturalismu a dialektika estetiky," in *Struktura a smysl literárního díla*, ed. M. Jankovič, Z. Pešat, and F. Vodička (Prague, 1966), pp. 13–39. For the relationship of Kalivoda to Mukařovský, see Jauss, *Aesthetic Experience*, p. 116.

88. Victor Turner, *The Forest of Symbols: Aspects of Ndembu Rituals* (Ithaca, N.Y., 1974).

89. Katerina Clark, *The Soviet Novel: History as Ritual* (Chicago, 1981).

90. Yury Tynyanov, *Problema stikhotvornogo jazyka* (Leningrad, 1924; rpt., Moscow, 1965).

91. For Soviet Russian semiotic contributions, see Eimermacher and Shishkoff, *Subject Bibliography of Soviet Semiotics*. For a Western application of such models in concrete analysis—including the relationship between spatial categories and value—see J. J. van Baak, *The Place of Space in Narration* (Amsterdam, 1983), particularly "Value Correlations of Topological Notions," pp. 55–78.

92. Aristotle, *On the Art of Poetry*.

93. The ambiguity of this passage allows (or even suggests) different interpretations, such as that indicated by Manfred Fuhrmann in the commentary to his German translation of the *Poetics* (Munich, 1976), p. 44. Fuhrmann prefers (as I do) to identify Aristotle's "two causes" as "(1) the ability to imitate; (2) the enjoyment of imitations produced by others," whereas Jauss concludes from the same passage that for Aristotle the "twofold root" of mimetic pleasure is "the admiration of a perfect technique of imitation" and the pleasure of "recognizing the model in the imitation" (*Aesthetic Experience*, p. 23).

94. Aage A. Hansen-Löve, *Der russische Formalismus* (Vienna, 1978). Hansen-Löve dedicates a whole part of his introduction to the topic of "Aristotelian 'Formalism' and the Principle of the 'Unfamiliar'" (pp. 24–30).

95. For the dates, see notes 16 and 17 of this part. I quote, unless otherwise indicated, from the English translations (*Toward an Aesthetic of Reception* and *Aesthetic Experience*).

96. See Hans Robert Jauss, "Racines und Goethes Iphigenie, mit einem Nachwort über die Partialität der rezeptionsästhetischen Methode," *Neue Hefte für Philosophie*, 4 (1973): 1ff.

97. See part A (3), "Aesthetic pleasure and the fundamental experiences of poiesis, aesthesis, and catharsis," as well as parts A (5), (6), and (7), each dedicated to one of the three categories.

98. See part A (3). Wlad Godzich in his introduction to the American edition praises this survey as a "masterful discussion of aesthetic pleasure" and adds informative remarks about Lionel Trilling's related essay, "The Fate of Pleasure" (Aesthetic Experience, pp. xx–xxiii). Godzich thus helps link Jauss's topic to its treatment in American literary studies.

99. Godzich, in his introduction (pp. xiv–xvii), accepting part of this criticism, also stresses—in a kind of indirect defense of Adorno—that Adorno's intention was not a general history or theory of aesthetic pleasure but a theory of aesthetics under the specific conditions of modernity. For a discussion of negativity in the context of the Poetik and Hermeneutik group, see vol. 6 of its publications, *Positionen der Negativität* (1975).

100. Jauss, *Aesthetische Erfahrung* (German ed.), p. 170. The text remained unchanged in the revised version (1982). The English translation (p. 118) changed this passage; therefore I am quoting here from the German original. While Mukařovský put "pleasure" in italics, as did the German translation of his book from which Jauss quotes, Jauss omitted the italics—as does the English translation of Mukařovský's *Aesthetic Function, Norm and Value* (p. 22).

101. The English translation (p. 27) does not render appropriately the Czech original (p. 25); therefore I use my own translation.

102. In German, *sdělovací funkce* is usually rendered (including in the translation used by Jauss) as *mitteilende Funktion*, which corresponds with the English "communicative function."

103. Boris Eikhenbaum, "Melodika russkogo liričeskogo stikha" (The Melodics of Russian Lyrical Verse), 1922, p. 9. English quotation from *Russian Poetics in Translation*, vol. 4, *Formalist Theory*, ed. L. M. O'Toole and Ann Shukman (Oxford, England, 1977). The glossary of this booklet contains, under the heading "Dominant," a selection of quotations from different Formalists and from Mukařovský (see pp. 34–35).

104. Tynyanov, "The Ode" (1927); quoted from O'Toole and Shukman, *Russian Poetics*, p. 20.

105. This lecture on Russian Formalism, delivered at the Masaryk University in Brno in the spring of 1935, was published in English in Matejka and Pomorska, *Readings in Russian Poetics*, pp. 82–87. All quotations are from this translation.

106. Mukařovský, "Jazyk spisovny a jazyk basnicky" (Standard Language and Poetic Language), 1932; quoted from O'Toole and Shukman, *Russian Poetics*, p. 35.

107. Mukařovský, *Studie z estetiky* (Studies in Aesthetics) (Prague, 1966), pp. 65–73. English translation in Mukařovský, *Structure, Sign, and Function*. My quotations from this essay are my own translation.

108. Jauss quotes from the German translation, *Kapitel aus der Ästhetik*, p. 115 (in the English translation, p. 42).

109. Aristotle, *Poetics*, chap. 6.

110. The article is in *Aspects of Narrative*, ed. J. Hillis Miller (New York, 1971), pp. 1–45. The German originals of the books are *Der implizierte Leser* (Munich, 1972) and *Der Akt des Lesens* (Munich, 1976); English translations, *The Implied Reader* (Baltimore, 1974) and *The Act of Reading* (Baltimore, 1978). Quotations are from these editions.

111. *Funktionen des Fiktiven*, Poetik und Hermeneutik, X, ed. Dieter Henrich and Wolfgang Iser (Munich, 1983); the introduction, "Entfaltung der Problemlage," pp. 9–14.

112. Wolfgang Iser, "Feigning in Fiction," in *The Identity of the Text*, ed. Mario I. Valdes (Toronto, 1985), pp. 204–228.

113. See Manfred Fuhrmann, "Die Fiktion im römischen Recht" (The Fiction in Roman Law), in Henrich and Iser, eds. *Funktionen des Fiktiven*, pp. 413–415.

114. Vodička, *Struktura vývoje*, p. 35 (my own translation).

115. Červenka's book has been published only in German translation, *Der Bedeutungsaufbau des literarischen Werks*, ed. Frank Boldt and Wolf-Dieter Stempel (Munich, 1978). I quote in my own translation from p. 126.

116. Thomas G. Pavel, *Fictional Worlds* (Cambridge, Mass., 1986).

117. In addition to Iser and Pavel, see Nelson Goodman, *Ways of Worldmaking* (Indianapolis, 1978).

118. Karel Čapek, *R. U. R. (Rossum's Universal Robots)* (Prague, 1920), in English, *R.U.R.: A Fantastic Melodrama*, trans. P. Selver (Garden City, N.Y., 1923). A novel of this kind is Čapek's *Tovarna na Absolutno* (Prague, 1922); in English, *The Absolute at Large* (New York, 1927).

119. Completed in 1920, the novel was not allowed to be published in Soviet Russia; it appeared in 1924 in Czech, English, and French translations. An abbreviated Russian version appeared in *Prague* (in *Volja Rossii*) in 1927. The complete Russian text was not published until 1952, by the Chekhov Publishing House in New York.

120. Jurij Striedter, "Die Doppelfiktion und ihre Selbstaufhebung: Probleme des utopischen Romans, besonders im nachrevolutionären Russland," in *Funktionen des Fiktiven*, pp. 277–330.

121. The English translation renders as "indirect (figurative)" the Czech *nepřímého (obrazného)*, in which the Czech *obrazny*, from *obraz*, "image," does not simply double the preceding "indirect" but rather implies that this indirect mediation is through images or image-like.

122. I have modified the English translation (in *Aesthetic Function*) because it omits some words important for the problem under discussion.

123. The American edition renders the Czech *předpoklad* as "hypothesis." "Hypothesis" means an assumption which can prove to be realizable or unrealizable. In this special case, Mukařovský clearly implies that this construct cannot be realized; it is more appropriately rendered by "assumption" or "supposition."

124. I have intentionally used the English cognate of the Czech *patos* (instead of "spirit," as in the American edition), knowing that the English notion of pathos has a more restricted meaning than the Czech and particularly the

original Greek word. But I assume that Mukařovský, by choosing the foreign word *patos* in connection with the striving for the "perfect work of art," is implying the full semantic potential of the word, which includes "suffering," "affliction," "passion," and their expression (particularly in art).

125. Götz Grossklaus and Ernst Oldemeyer, eds., *Werte in kommunikativen Prozessen,* proceedings of the eighth Karlsruhe Colloquium for Experimental Art and Aesthetics (Stuttgart, 1980).

126. All quotations from titles of contributions; see the table of contents, pp. 5–6.

127. "Konnotativer Vorgang und Wert-Verständigung," pp. 88–125.

128. See, as a characteristic example, the remarks on "popular urban lyrics" in chap. 2, pp. 57–58, and Jauss's criticism of Mukařovský's related argument, *Aesthetic Experience,* pp. 118–119.

129. See Eimermacher and Shishkoff, *Subject Bibliography of Soviet Semiotics.*

130. Rescher, *Introduction to Value Theory,* p. 55.

131. The English translation misleads by rendering Mukařovský's statement as "We cannot at this point *discuss* relativity" (p. 67), as if Mukařovský avoids or postpones the discussion of this topic. Actually, he states "One cannot *speak* here of relativity" (in the sense that one cannot call this position relativistic) "because for the evaluator, situated in a specific time and place, and in a given social milieu, any particular value of some work appears to him as necessary and constant" (*Studie z estetiky,* p. 43).

132. Grossklaus and Oldemeyer, *Werte,* p. 27.

133. For the notion of semantic gesture in Czech Structuralism, see Miroslav Kačer, "Mukařovskýs Terminus 'semantische Geste' und Barthes' 'ecriture,' " *Postilla Bohemica* (Zeitschrift der Konstanzer Hus-Gesellschaft), 4–5 (1973): 88–94.

134. For the definition and use of the term "intrinsic value," see Rescher, *Introduction to Value Theory,* p. 53 and "The Metatheory of Valuation."

135. Rescher uses the terms "instrumental," "ends," and "means" for values; Fokkema ("Generalization," p. 268) speaks of "terminal values"; the post-Lukácsian Budapest school (Heller, Fekete) speak of "goal values"; Grossklaus and Oldemeyer prefer the term "orientational values."

136. Monroe C. Beardsley, "Intrinsic Value," *Philosophy and Phenomenological Research,* 26 (1965–66): 1–18.

137. Fokkema, "Generalization," p. 268.

138. Ernst Oldemeyer, "Wertvermittlung durch ästhetische Heraushebung: Anthropologische Gedankenkette über ihre Grundlagen, Arten, und Folgen" (The Mediation of Value through Aesthetic Foregrounding: Anthropological Reflections About its Conditions, Kinds, and Consequences), in Grossklaus and Oldemeyer, *Werte,* pp. 51–71.

139. See the title of Mukařovský's essay, "The Place of the Aesthetic Function among Other Human Functions."

140. M. T. M. Segers, *The Evaluation of Literary Texts: An Experimental Investigation into the Rationalization of Value Judgements with Reference to Semiotics and Esthetics of Reception* (Leiden, 1978).

Selected Bibliography

Russian Formalism

Bann, Stephen, and John E. Bowlt, eds. *Russian Formalism: A Collection of Articles and Texts in Translation*. Edinburgh, 1973.

Bennett, Tony. *Formalism and Marxism*. London, 1979.

Eikhenbaum, Boris. *Lermontov: A Study in Literary-Historical Evaluation*, trans. Ray Parrot and Harry Webo. Ann Arbor, Mich., 1981; Russian original, 1924.

———— *The Young Tolstoy*, ed. and trans. G. Kern. Ann Arbor, Mich., 1972; Russian original, 1922. The volumes on Tolstoy in the 1860s and 1870s, also translated, belong to the period after the banishment of Formalism.

———— and Yury Tynyanov, eds. *Russian Prose*, trans. and ed. Ray Parrot. Ann Arbor, Mich., 1985.

Erlich, Victor. *Russian Formalism: History—Doctrine*. The Hague, 1955. 3rd. ed., 1969.

Hansen-Löve, Aage A. *Der russische Formalismus: Methodologische Rekonstruktion seiner Entwicklung aus dem Prinzip der Verfremdung*. Vienna, 1978. Extensive bibliography of Russian sources, translations, and criticism in different languages, pp. 587–609.

Jakobson, Roman. *Selected Writings*. The Hague, 1971–. Six volumes now available; most important for his Formalist and early Structuralist writings on poetry are vol. 3, *Poetry of Grammar and Grammar of Poetry*, and vol. 5, *On Verse: Its Masters and Explorers*.

———— *Language in Literature*, ed. Krystyna Pomorska and Stephen Rudy. Cambridge, Mass., 1987.

———— *Verbal Art, Verbal Sign, Verbal Time*, ed. Krystyna Pomorska and Stephen Rudy. Minneapolis, 1985.

Roman Jakobson: A Bibliography of His Writings, foreword by C. H. van Schooneveld. The Hague, 1971. A bibliography is also part of the Festschrift *To Honor Roman Jakobson: Essays on the Occasion of His Seventieth Birthday*, 3 vols. (The Hague, 1967), I, pp. xi–xxxiii.

Jameson, Fredric. *The Prison-House of Language: A Critical Account of Structuralism and Russian Formalism*. Princeton, N.J., 1972.

Lemon, Lee T., and Marion J. Reis, eds. and trans. *Russian Formalist Criticism: Four Essays.* Lincoln, Nebr., 1965.

Matejka, Ladislav, and Krystyna Pomorska, eds. *Readings in Russian Poetics: Formalist and Structuralist Views.* Cambridge, Mass., 1971; repr. Ann Arbor, Mich., 1978. The most comprehensive collection of Formalist writings in English translation.

O'Toole, L. M., and Ann Shukman, eds. *Russian Poetics in Translation.* Oxford, 1975–. Most important for Formalism is vol. 4, *Formalist Theory* (1977), with biographical-bibliographical notes, glossary, and "A Bibliography of Translations and Commentaries" compiled by Ann Shukman, pp. 100–108.

Pike, Christopher, ed. *The Futurists, the Formalists, and the Marxist Critique.* London, 1979.

Pomorska, Krystyna. *Russian Formalist Theory and its Poetic Ambiance.* The Hague, 1968.

Propp, Vladimir. *Morphology of the Folktale.* First ed. trans. and ed. L. Scott, intro. S. Pirkova-Jakobson (Indiana, 1958); 2nd. ed., rev. and ed. L. A. Wagner, intro. A. Dundes (Austin, Tex., 1968).

———— *Theory and History of Folklore,* trans. A. Y. Martin and R. P. Martin; intro. A. Liberman. Minneapolis, 1984.

Shklovsky, Viktor. *A Sentimental Journey: Memoirs, 1917–1922.* Ithaca, N.Y., 1984.

———— *Mayakovsky and His Circle.* New York, 1972.

Viktor Shklovskij: An International Bibliography of Works by and about Him, ed. R. Sheldon. Ann Arbor, Mich., 1977.

Steiner, Peter. *Russian Formalism: A Metapoetics.* Ithaca, N.Y., 1984.

Stempel, Wolf-Dieter, ed. *Texte der russischen Formalisten,* vol. 2, *Texte zur Theorie des Verses und der poetischen Sprache.* Munich, 1972. Formalist texts, in Russian original and German translation, on poetry and poetic language. Bibliography on Russian Formalism, pp. 429–439.

Striedter, Jurij, ed. *Texte der russischen Formalisten,* vol. 1, *Texte zur allgemeinen Literaturtheorie und zur Theorie der Prosa.* Munich, 1969. Formalist texts, in Russian original and German translation, on general literary theory and theory of prose.

Thompson, Ewa M. *Russian Formalism and Anglo-American New Criticism.* The Hague, 1971.

Tynyanov, Yury. *The Problem of Verse Language,* ed. and trans. Michael Sosa and Brent Harvey. Ann Arbor, Mich., 1981.

Czech Structuralism

Boldt, Frank, ed. *Postyla Bohemica,* vol. 4–5, *Literaturwissenschaftliche Arbeiten von Prager Strukturalisten.* Bremen, 1973. Essays by Mukařovský, Vodička, and others in German translation; with bibliography of translations "in Western languages."

Červenka, Miroslav. *Der Bedeutungsaufbau des literarischen Werks*. Munich, 1978. Bibliography of his scholarly publications, pp. 186–189. This work was published only in this German edition.

———— P. Steiner, and R. Vroon, eds. *The Structure of the Literary Process: Studies Dedicated to the Memory of Felix Vodička*. Amsterdam and Philadelphia, 1982. Bibliography of Vodička's writings, compiled by F. W. Galan, pp. 599–607.

Galan, František W. *Historic Structures: The Prague School Project, 1928–1946*. London and Sydney, 1985. Includes a list of lectures given in the Prague Linguistic Circle and a comprehensive bibliography of publications on Czech Structuralism (in English and other languages), pp. 207–227.

Garvin, Paul L., ed. *A Prague School Reader on Esthetics, Literary Structure, and Style*. Washington, D.C., 1964. Annotated bibliography of Czech publications, pp. 153–163.

Matejka, Ladislav, ed. *Sound, Sign, and Meaning: Quinquagenary of the Prague Linguistic Circle*. Ann Arbor, Mich., 1976. Large collection of essays about Czech Structuralism in its different disciplines (linguistics, literature, aesthetics, general semiotics).

———— and I. R. Titunik, eds. *Semiotics of Art: Prague School Contributions*. Cambridge, Mass., 1976. The most comprehensive available collection in English translation.

Mukařovský, Jan. *Aesthetic Function, Norm and Value As Social Facts*, trans. Mark E. Suino. Ann Arbor, Mich., 1970; 2nd ed., 1979.

———— *On Poetic Language*, trans. John Burbank and Peter Steiner. Lisse, 1976.

———— *Structure, Sign, and Function: Selected Essays by Jan Mukařovský*, ed. and trans. John Burbank and Peter Steiner. New Haven, Conn., and London, 1978. Bibliography of Mukařovský's writings, including those available in translation, compiled by F. Galan, pp. 251–266.

———— *The Word and Verbal Art: Selected Essays by Jan Mukařovský*, ed. and trans. John Burbank and Peter Steiner, foreword René Wellek. New Haven, Conn., and London, 1977.

Steiner, Peter, ed. *The Prague School: Selected Writings, 1929–1946*. Austin, Texas, 1982.

Vodička, Felix. *Die Struktur der literarischen Entwicklung*, ed. Frank Boldt, intro. Jurij Striedter. Munich, 1976. This is the only collection of writings by Vodička available in translation. The anthologies *Semiotics of Art* and *The Prague School* each include one contribution by Vodička in English translation.

Wellek, René. *The Literary Theory and Aesthetics of the Prague School*. Ann Arbor, Mich., 1969; repr. in Wellek, *Discriminations* (New Haven, 1970), pp. 275–303.

Acknowledgments

I am grateful for the advice and friendship of some of the members of the literary schools under discussion: Roman Jakobson, René Wellek, Dmitri Czizhevsky. I also want to thank all the students, colleagues, and friends, European and American, who encouraged me in writing this book by keeping the dialogue alive. This book would not exist without the initiative and help of my colleague and friend Donald Fanger. And it would not have been completed without the patient admonition of Lindsay Waters of the Harvard University Press, whose personal advice and support went far beyond the normal tasks of an editor. Jennifer Snodgrass was also helpful in editing, particularly Part IV. Special thanks go to Matthew Gurewitsch, who translated Parts I–III and tried to render my German as accurately as possible while I tried to learn from him how to express myself in English. I am grateful to the Wilhelm Fink Verlag, Munich, for granting the rights to the translation of Parts I–III and to the Department of Slavic Languages and Literatures at Harvard for financing these translations.

Index

Additive principle, 90
Adorno, Theodor, 222
Aesthetic function, 93–94, 106–107, 122, 159–160; and signs, 4, 93–94, 239–240, 242; historical variability of, 86, 105, 138, 161, 172–173, 191–192, 197, 207, 211, 212; and social function, 86, 197, 257–258; and communication function, 94, 224–225; and aesthetic value, 159–160, 172–173, 197, 253–255; as organization principle, 162, 189, 190, 197; hermeneutic conception of, 221–229; and aesthetic pleasure, 222–223, 226–229, 230, 256; immutability of, 253–256; and general values, 257–258. *See also* Aesthetic norms; Aesthetic value
Aesthetic norms, 70, 86, 101–102; historical variability of, 207–208, 211–213; and general values, 159, 191–192. *See also* Aesthetic function; Aesthetic value; Norms, general
Aesthetic object, 124, 158–159, 210, 249; and concretization, 102–103,

108–109, 125–130, 160–161, 206–207, 243. *See also* Artifact; Concretization
Aesthetic perception, 2, 129, 137, 145–146, 181, 209, 218, 220–221, 243–244, 283n29; historical variability of, 4–5, 45–50, 86–87, 127, 145–146, 170, 212–213; and defamiliarization, 23–24, 34; hermeneutic conception of, 145–147; anthropological norms of, 217; and artistic creativity, 218. *See also* Reception
Aesthetic pleasure, 197, 256; and aesthetic function, 222, 226–229, 230; and aesthetic value, 223
Aesthetic value: objective, 102, 163, 164, 185–186, 195, 208, 210, 241–244, 248, 254–255; historical variability of, 102–106, 146, 159–160, 207–208, 253–258; evolutionary, 159–160, 161, 162, 167, 168, 191, 198, 241; social character of, 159–160, 163–169, 172–173, 185–187; and the aesthetic function, 159–160, 172–173, 197, 253–255; general, 160, 161, 162,

HARVARD STUDIES IN COMPARATIVE LITERATURE